The Road to Hell is Paved With... What?

A Tale of Addiction and What It Can Teach Us

GLEN BRADLEY

TRILOGY

Trilogy Christian Publishers
A Wholly Owned Subsidiary of Trinity Broadcasting Network
2442 Michelle Drive
Tustin, CA 92780

Copyright © 2020 by Glen Bradley

All Scripture quotations, unless otherwise noted, taken from THE HOLY BIBLE, NEW INTERNATIONAL VERSION®, NIV® Copyright © 1973, 1978, 1984, 2011 by Biblica, Inc.® Used by permission. All rights reserved worldwide.

Scripture quotations marked (KJV) taken from *The Holy Bible, King James Version.* Cambridge Edition: 1769.

All rights reserved, including the right to reproduce this book or portions thereof in any form whatsoever.

For information, address Trilogy Christian Publishing
Rights Department, 2442 Michelle Drive, Tustin, Ca 92780.
Trilogy Christian Publishing/ TBN and colophon are trademarks of Trinity Broadcasting Network.

For information about special discounts for bulk purchases, please contact Trilogy Christian Publishing.

Manufactured in the United States of America

Trilogy Disclaimer: The views and content expressed in this book are those of the author and may not necessarily reflect the views and doctrine of Trilogy Christian Publishing or the Trinity Broadcasting Network.

10 9 8 7 6 5 4 3 2 1

Library of Congress Cataloging-in-Publication Data is available.

ISBN 978-1-64773-788-7 (Print Book)
ISBN 978-1-64773-789-4 (ebook)

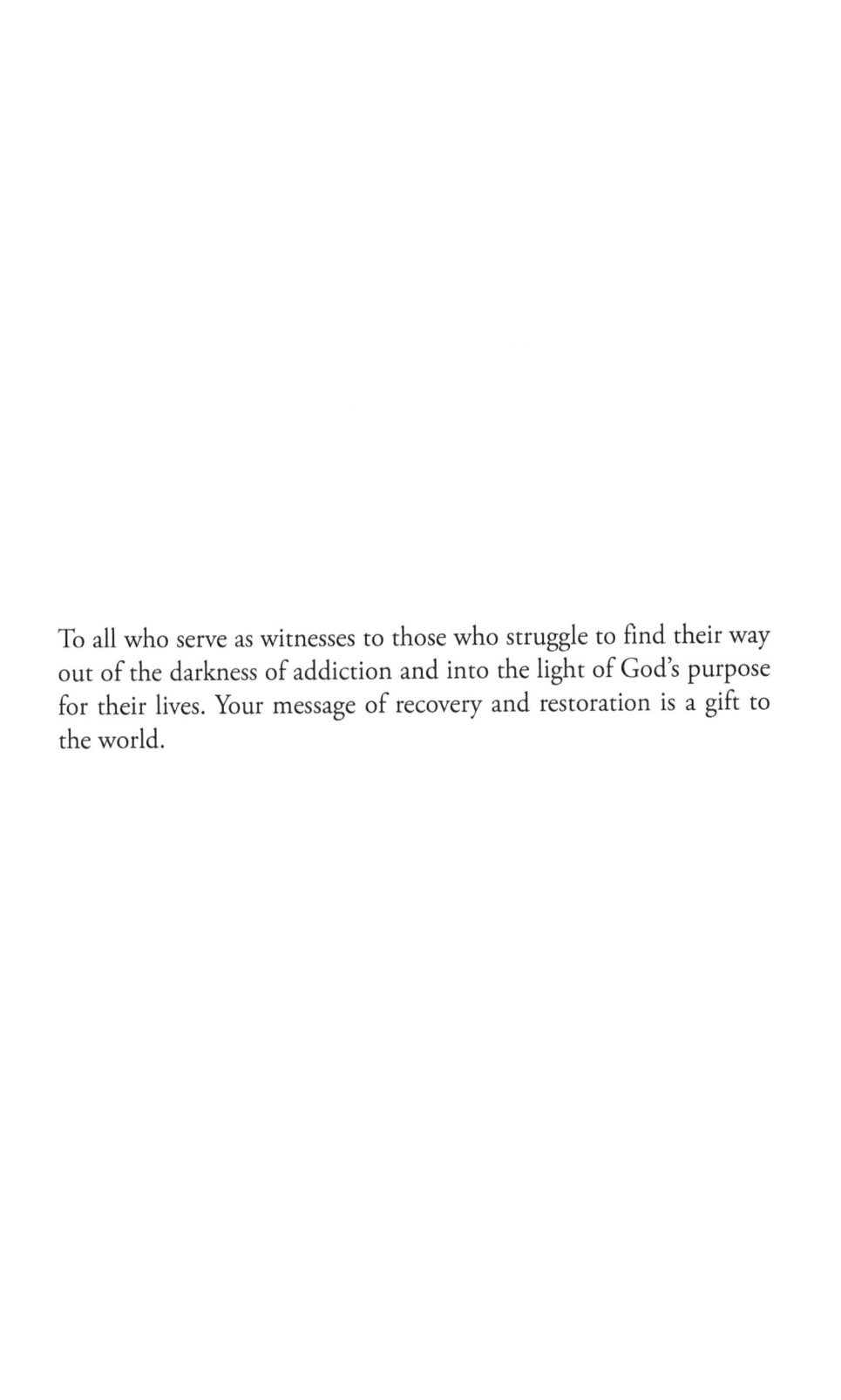

To all who serve as witnesses to those who struggle to find their way out of the darkness of addiction and into the light of God's purpose for their lives. Your message of recovery and restoration is a gift to the world.

Contents

Acknowledgments 7
Introduction 9
Prologue 13

The Lawson Legacy 15
Facing the Old Nemesis 27
The Times Are a-Changing 39
The Dreaded Encounter 47
An Unexpected Encounter 51
The Old Ragged Farm 57
Friends of Grace 69
The Old Farm Holds Secrets 81
The Old Trunk and Its Treasures 93
Aunt Lucy's Ethical Testimony 103
Confrontations in the Graveyard 113
An Unexpected Calling 123
Grace Goes Undercover 133
Deception of the Self 145
An Angel on Assignment 155
Conviction Changes the Direction 163
The Strategy of God 173
A Stunning Revelation 185
Another Curveball 195
A Revelation and a Raid 205
Identifying the Enemy 213
A Dying Confession 223
One Door Closes, Another Opens 233

An Unexpected Turn of Events 243
And I Will Restore unto You 253
A Tragedy and a Gift 263
Blessings Abound 273
Wedding Gifts from Beyond 281
A Hard Reality Check 289
Old Case Closed 293

Afterword 297
Appendix 1: Alcoholics Anonymous 299
Appendix 2: Questions Asked About Alcoholism and Addiction ... 303

Acknowledgments

A group of dedicated and committed twelve-step workers of the early 1980s took me under their wing and guided my miserable life in a very different direction. Without their love, compassion, and understanding, my life might have been destroyed. Over the years, they have taught me the importance of "each one, reach one, and teach one."

Today I humbly thank each one, both past and present, who has walked with me along my journey. In my advancing years, I hope to communicate the message of recovery through the Written Word, relating some of the miraculous stories I have been privileged to hear. I thank Trilogy Christian Publishing for allowing me that opportunity.

Introduction

Over 2,500 hundred years ago, the Greeks engraved two simple phrases on the stone at the Oracle of Delphi:

TO THINE OWN SELF BE TRUE
KNOW THYSELF

There is an old spiritual, re-recorded many times, that says, "People get ready, there's a train a-comin. You don't need a ticket, just get on board." That old song refers to a freedom train that took blacks out of slavery in the South to freedom in the North. That song is remarkably relevant to our time today; it serves as a metaphor for some of us called out of our enslavement to addiction with all its faces back to our spiritual nature and on toward a purpose for which God created us. By the power of Spirit, we are able to choose a path of self-awareness and self-realization; we can get on board the freedom train anytime, anywhere.

Unfortunately, addiction to alcohol, drugs, and behavioral escape habits has imprisoned some of us to the point of self-destruction and trapped us on the road to eventual death. The disease, and the subsequent dysfunction of addiction, tends to repeat itself over the generations, the penalties progressively spread across families and, ultimately, our world. A human being controlled by addiction and operating with a disabled mind and body has lost awareness of the spiritual aspect of its own creation. The power of Spirit lies dormant, unrecognized and unacknowledged, until the addict reaches a point of extreme pain and discomfort with life, sometimes near death, before the call of Spirit can be heard. Powerlessness over the addiction and its destruction brings the addict to despair; the door to Spirit can open.

"The fault, dear Brutus, is not in our stars, but in ourselves" (*Julius Caesar*, act 1, scene 3).

Addiction is a tragedy for so many in our modern world; however, it can be, and often is, our greatest spiritual guide and teacher.

*****

Alcoholics Anonymous was founded in 1935 by two hard-drinking alcoholics whom doctors had long dismissed as hopeless cases. The two men came together and struggled to help each other stop the self-defeating drinking. A short time later, they were joined by others with the same problem. A few short years later, hundreds of people had joined the movement.

Today, nearly eighty-five years later, their program of recovery, a twelve-step systematic account of how the founding members of Alcoholics Anonymous gained their sobriety, has spread over the planet. The twelve steps are restatements of biblical principles, worded in such a simplistic format that even the most deteriorated drunk can grasp the hope they offer. The spiritual practicality of the steps offers hope and healing, not just for alcoholics, but for all who struggle to grow in spiritual strength and maturity as well.

The twelve-step program speaks of a "higher power," or "God, as you understand Him." The Christian has no trouble understanding that this refers to our Lord, Jesus Christ. Countless people have committed themselves to Jesus Christ because of their contact with Alcoholics Anonymous and its related groups. The witness offered by these groups has drawn many a lost soul to freedom.

Alcoholics and other addicts have repeatedly turned to doctors, ministers, and other helping professions and received little, if any, help. Most came away feeling judged. In desperation, they turn to people who have experienced the problem and have some insight.

From the beginning, Alcoholics Anonymous maintained that it functioned as a spiritual "kindergarten" for souls lost in addiction. They have said, "We can't take you to heaven and we can't keep you

THE ROAD TO HELL IS PAVED WITH... WHAT?

out of hell...but we can keep you sober enough to make up your own mind."

*****

In this book, *The Road to Hell is Paved with...What?* the story of an alcoholic's journey unfolds as a talented, gifted academic scholar, respected for her work at the PhD level, loses her footing in life and almost destroys her career. Her addiction started with her genetics, her cultural heritage, and the unfortunate circumstances of her youth. She practiced medicating herself with her beloved alcohol for years before losses in midlife began to pile up and she was forced to seek help, or else. She was desperate.

On the outskirts of the big city where she was employed, where racial diversity and poverty abounded, she found a small church where Alcoholics Anonymous meetings were held. As she listened to this group, their stories and their recovery miracles, her resistance crumbled; her heart opened. She became one of the most dedicated members of the group, never missing a session. She sensed there was something happening in her life; she opened her heart and listened.

*****

Although this is a true story, liberties have been taken with recreating characters and dialogue. This is in keeping with the tradition of anonymity respected by all twelve-step recovery groups. Names and locations have been fictionalized, and dialogue is used to move the story and highlight the principles being taught, as well as reflect the love, compassion, and understanding of the members of the recovery group.

It has been my privilege to hear this story, and many more, over thirty-five years of attending twelve-step meetings of all kinds while working through my own tragic story and struggling to find my own road back to God. It has become my life's work to help those who are seeking relief from their bondage to addiction. At this advancing stage of my life, it is necessary that I travel to fewer meetings and simply relate the miraculous stories I have been privileged to hear through the Written Word.

Read on, dear readers, and as you follow this alcoholic's story, ask yourself some questions. Did your life wind up in a most unexpected place where you are unhappy, if not miserable? Did life take some disappointing turns you didn't see coming? Have you suffered with exasperation and failed expectations more often than you wanted? Despite your best intentions, is the road of life paved with grief?

To find some answers, the twelve-step program, with its fourth step, requiring "a searching and fearless moral inventory," might be a good place to start. Our road may be paved with a genetic predisposition to addiction and the bondage and blindness that deceives us; we have become slaves to our own troubled lives without knowing it.

It is my hope that we can all "get on board" that freedom train, our bondage broken and our lives free to express God's love and power. Our cultural heritage of despair and addiction can be understood, and recovery is possible. We can ride through our human frailties with victory, the generational curses broken. Our children, the next generation, will surely benefit.

"Let us examine our ways and test them; and let us return to the Lord" (Lam. 3:40).

"Only when we find the spring of wisdom in our own life can it flow to future generations" (Thich Nhat Hanh).

As you read, dear reader, just listen with your heart. God's voice can be heard through the hearts of His recovering people, some of the world's most powerful witnesses of God's love, His mercy, and His promised restoration. God has given us a great gift here.

Be grateful and be blessed.

Prologue

Lithe, lean fingers wrapped confidently around the rifle, cheek pressed firmly into the stock, eye sighted down the long barrel, finger on the trigger, waiting patiently for the targets to appear. The shooter lay quiet and still like a rattlesnake waiting on an unsuspecting rat. There in the shadows of the rock cliffs, higher up the rocks than any grown man would attempt to crawl, where the view to the old logging road below was unobstructed and the shooter could take clear aim, there where justice could be exacted and a forgiving God might be offended, the shooter waited…and ruminated.

This business of turning the "other check," "praying for" your enemies, "loving your neighbor as yourself," and living in fear of God while the people you were supposed to love and pray for had clearly gone rabid… well, that had to be a crock. Just look how God Himself had resorted to destroying His own human creation and its offspring. The Old Testament told it over and over. God lost His temper because His humans wouldn't obey His simple rules, and He destroyed them…Himself. And…He didn't warn them too often either. When God had enough, He simply destroyed the sinners.

So…if He made man in the image of Himself, as they say, why not help Him fix some of His wayward, sinning types? Or better yet… just get rid of them, like He'd done…in Bible times. Yeah…that seems right…be less suffering on the earth, that's for sure. Maybe God wants them destroyed. He may get mad, but that'll make two of us. I'm mad… for myself and a few others who can't take up for themselves.

Three of them sinners gonna see hell today.

The Lawson Legacy

Deep in the southern end of the Appalachian Mountains lies a remote little valley much like all the other little valleys buried along the Appalachia Trail. And there's nothing particularly unforgettable about it, unless, of course, you are one of its own. One of its wounded spirits, bred, born, and raised there, and then repeatedly bred, again, right there, more often than not.

Generations have perpetuated that way for as long as the Appalachians are old. And for those whose roots are grounded there, there's a psychic power embedded in their memories that can hold hostage their very souls. Ghosts walk through their minds. The dead refuse to stay buried; secrets won't let them rest. And for some of the living who've been there and remember the secrets, well, hell has been hounding them. The devil himself draws on his fiddle, and demons dance around their wounded souls, or so it may seem.

Come judgment day, however, there might be a few of the devil's hostages missing when he makes his roll call. The backwoods of Appalachia have always been communities of survivors. These people have stood since before the Civil War, through two world wars, the Great Depression, the Korean War of the fifties, Vietnam in the sixties, the ongoing Gulf Wars, and all the harsh, blizzard-like winters in between, not to mention the crushing poverty that Appalachia is known for. Pure backwoods backbone and an unwavering faith in the God of their creation has sustained them.

The personal legacies and stories of human tragedies that have passed from generation to generation are phenomenal. Therein lie the next great volumes of *War and Peace*, culture-specific. Some who inherited the legacies, however, don't have much to say about the peace aspect of their experience. They've been busy with the wars, and some still are, of one type or another, in one place or another.

As the various wars had come and gone, the casualties had been severe, but all in all, life in these mountain communities just marched right on. Those who were fortunate enough to survive the wars come home and take their place in the community, had local battles to confront. After all the dust had settled and the smoke cleared, some won, some lost, and some just died in the ruckus. It had much to do with how much political clout could be mustered, or a willingness to "grease the palms" of the local powers that be. It required whatever the best chance of survival demanded.

Win or lose, most simply picked up their plows, hitched up the mules, and planted their crops, thereby teaching the next generation to "hoe the long rows." Some raised crops that the sheriff frowned on, tended their moonshine stills, transported their products, and tried to stay a step or two ahead of incarceration. Unfortunately, many developed rebellious and reactionary personalities with a leaning toward incarceration, sometimes lasting a lifetime.

Many from the younger generations just ran away, as far away as they could get, as fast as they could get there, wherever "there" happened to be. Somewhere out *there* they might just be discovered, become the next Dolly Pardon, Meryl Haggard, or Elvis. And actually, a few did manage to find some measure of acceptable notoriety. But the notoriety of some others…well, the FBI and others are looking. Remember, run, Eric, run.

A few of the more ambitious left and returned after a while with enough monetary or educational advantage to help those who had been left behind. At least that might have been their intention, and perhaps well aimed, but their targets were sometimes elusive. The legacy of defeat had already beaten some, discouragement and poverty had already burned holes in their souls, and their inherited predispositions toward self-defeat had grown and rooted in. They didn't have the heart, the aptitude, or the spiritual stamina to work toward betterment. The world had battered them, God had seemingly deserted them, and they just didn't bother with hope anymore. They settled for what they already knew, harsh as it was; it was still easier than tackling an outside world that took more social skills than they had.

Many just dug into the hill country's way of life and accepted it as their lot in life. The rest of the world could mind its own business. Shotguns, coon dogs, moonshine, turnip greens, and taters, with corn bread on the table every day. That kind of life was understood, and it worked—at least it was comfortable for them.

Sociologists tried to come up with terminology to explain the peculiarities of these mountain people and their way of life. The term of reference they often used was *cultural retardation*. That misnomer, unfortunately, reflected as much ignorance and lack of insight on the part of the pointy-headed intellectuals around the halls of higher learning as it did the mountain folk. The two groups seem to be more alike than different on that score.

Other labels stuck. *Mountain people, hillbillies,* and *rednecks* all became common references, until finally the politically correct crowd lent a bit of dignity with the term Appalachian Americans. It was a good beginning, but understanding the culture would take a bit more work before the forgotten people of the backwoods Appalachian communities could hope for recognition and be invited to join the rest of the country. And hopefully, they could find a way to tolerate it.

*****

Yes, over the generations, these Appalachian Americans have fought different kinds of wars and survived, with their heads bowed and bloody much of the time. But the most heroic of their battles have been fought on personal turf, deep inside the hearts of souls of the people, at the spiritual level. Some lost, just out and out lost. Tragic, but true.

For the majority, however, the jury is still out. These are hardy souls, the toughest of the tough. They're almost impossible to take down; defeat doesn't sit well with them. It's like demonic forces have been hounding them for centuries, just busting their evil butts. But the game is taking place on the home team's turf, and the scoreboard reads: "Saints, aplenty; Sinners, way behind." One can almost visualize the devil himself stomping around in the basement of hell, looking through his arsenal. He's looking for a way.

What is it gonna take? What else? Alcohol, drugs, guns, sex, and anything else that might bring fast, easy escapism and distract the honorable souls from grace—it has already been dumped on the hill folk. And where any of it catches on, it becomes front and center of focus for those already struggling and nearly broken by the harsh, bitter circumstances of their existence. Anything that brings with it some relief, or "instant gratification," as popular phrase would describe it, provides a resting place, a place where emotional pain can be denied and physical hardship can be forgotten for a while. It's just the grandest, sweetest place some of the tired, bedraggled souls have ever been, and they become addicted to it. Delusional, yes, but does the world care? It works, for some, for a time. Maybe. At least that's the lie that seems so believable, and the deception cuts deep, sometimes generationally.

Where relief is so seductive and escapism is so easily available, where the detour bypassing the misery of soul and circumstance is so conveniently found, right there is where the foundation of the soul is cracked and the termites of destruction take up squatters' rights and begin to chew. Escape habits become habitual, addictive, and often genetic. The trap is set; the devil can throw his head back and laugh. The numbers will pile up on his side of the scoreboard, guaranteed.

*****

If there was ever a poster child for this unfortunate evolution of hell-bent souls, it would have been Grace "Little Girl" Lawson, granddaughter of old preacher Tom Lawson, long-ago functioning pastor of Bethel Baptist Church. Grace was his only grandchild, and she'd fled that old valley when she was barely seventeen, never to return, she said. And it was never her intention to return, but on a clear Sunday morning, somewhere during the early spring, later in her chronological life than she liked to admit, here she came. It had been almost forty years since she had left.

THE ROAD TO HELL IS PAVED WITH... WHAT?

The time had come, but not so much of her own choosing. She was coming back to put some things to rest, secrets held for too long, issues never understood, habits that couldn't be broken, and pain she couldn't put down. Her heritage of pain and misery, most of which had ridden her back for as long as she was old, had to be faced. She was determined to find some peace for herself, find some answers; too many dangerous things continued to happen in and around her life. Win or lose, she had brought herself out early for what might turn out to be her personal Armageddon. The war had started long ago at the old Baptist church.

Grace pulled her newly purchased Lexus along the main road leading into the old Baptist church's parking lot—no need to get jammed in by the local folk. She might need to make a fast escape. She parked along the edge of the main road leading to the church. Glancing toward the church parking lot, Grace could see that nothing much had changed. There was the usual assortment of aging sedans, outdated station wagons, farm vehicles, and hunting trucks, complete with firearms hanging in the gun racks.

Her gaze lingered over the little church itself—not much had changed there either. The church itself was just a bit bigger than a double garage, and maybe twice as long, the bell tower and steeple standing tall, facing east. The old metal roof had rusted over the years. The plank-sided outhouse was missing. What appeared to be a fellowship hall complete with signpost indicating "Restrooms" had been built. Grace laughed, wondering if they had something besides the old Sears catalog for toilet paper these days.

The old church cemetery sprawled up the hill just to the left of the church, running almost to the crest of the ridge. Gravestones were scattered haphazardly all over the hill, all facing east, awaiting the second coming. Grace smiled and smirked. She had known a number of folks buried up there, now with their feet pointed east, and she hoped their God was forgiving; otherwise, the graves would be empty when Jesus returned and called them forth. Some had surely dropped on "down to that other place"; that seemed where they were headed when she was young.

A few of the Sunday regulars standing around the churchyard glanced across the parked vehicles and tried to get a closer look at Grace's car. It must have stood out like a clown at a funeral. She was glad the windows were tinted. Grace watched the gazers as they peered. She thought she knew their thoughts.

Could this be some politician from over in town, come to say a few words and shake a few hands to draw out some votes come next election? Or could it be the mayor's wife, come to prance around, all smiles and good graces, hoping to garner enough votes to keep her husband's checks coming next year? Let's hope Aunt Belle brought her famous Southern pound cake this morning. Looks like we'll need some cake and coffee to offer whoever has come to grace the amen corner.

Grace was quietly watching the curious glances and surveying the old scene when suddenly a noise broke out. *Clang! Clang! Clang!* Grace jumped with alarm. *What on earth?* She almost screamed. She'd forgotten that church bell. The sound pealed out across the valley, bounced off the ridges, and reverberated across the mountains; it was deafening. That church bell had summoned the faithful to worship for more than a century. Before telephones made it to the valley, that bell had served as communication for the valley and for miles around. The local people could read its tempo, its message; it announced fire, death, accident, and illness. If trouble was afoot, the locals came running to the church to hear all about it, see what needed to be done. And sometimes it rang out a celebration; some soldier had made it home. Since many of the soldiers had fallen in the wars, that bell pealed out a welcome for the heroes who made it back alive. The boys got well-deserved hero status in the community, and the locals turned out to pat them on the back and sing a song of praise.

The bell had an unsettling effect on Grace. She felt sick, her stomach boiling with nausea like she'd had way too much booze. But not this time. No, not this time. It simply wasn't the booze.

Her memory took her back to a time when she'd rung that bell herself. Her little bare feet had gone flying across the fields, through the barbed wire, down the gravel road, through the old cemetery, sometimes in the dead of night. She'd pull on that rope to ring that

THE ROAD TO HELL IS PAVED WITH... WHAT?

bell with all her strength, then wait for the first neighbors to come barreling down the roads to help out. Then, likely as not, she'd hop into the back of some pickup truck and ride back toward whatever situation had sent her. Sometimes her little feet were bruised, bleeding, and her clothes torn.

Grace must have been all of six years old whenever she ran the first mission to call for help. It was about two miles from where she'd had to watch her mama die, and maybe twice that far after she came to live with Grandpa Lawson. She'd had to make plenty of runs for that old pastor of the church. She silently said to herself, *Better not go there. Don't even think of it. I have to get this little trip over with as painlessly as possible. No need to start off remembering the old trash... not now.*

She took a deep breath, opened the car door, and stepped out onto the paved road where she remembered there used to be gravel. She looked around. It looked like a nice early-spring day, dogwoods flowering along the tree lines, sun shining all over the valley, birds singing in the bushes. Everything felt familiar, but Grace felt a chill. Maybe it was the dread, maybe some fear, but she suddenly felt weak and in need of a good, stiff drink. Grace set her jaw and ground her teeth; no, not this time. For a brief moment she had a vision of Grandpa Lawson's face snarling and barking at her. She mentally flipped a hand signal in the direction of his grave and walked toward the church. She was determined to get the visit over with; the time had come.

As she walked toward the reception committee waiting on the church's little porch, she tried to recall the words of Shakespeare: "There is nothing either good or bad, but thinking makes it so." She made a mental retort: *Yes, but that's the rub, ain't it, Brother Shakespeare, the thinking? Thought occurs as a direct product of our experiences, our only frame of reference, and some of us have in our reference book a big cauldron of witch's brew, been stirring right down through the generations, and we're wired for craziness. But...so what? I'll give it a go, at least while I'm here in this holier-than-I-am place.*

Grace tugged at her skirt. She was a tall lady, and that miniskirt made her seem to have four feet of bare legs. That had been a mistake, her choice of clothes. She'd dressed herself in a red suit with low-cut camisole blouse, red stiletto heels to match, and for the life of her, she couldn't remember making the choice. A Freudian slip, no doubt, signifying something akin to regressive rebellion. The psychologists could sort it out—no time to be worrying over the proper attire now. The welcome committee waited just a few steps ahead, and they were watching her every move, scratching their heads, murmuring among themselves. *Who on earth...anybody we know?*

Grace smiled as she drew up an old memory. Grandpa Lawson, during his tenure as pastor of the church, would have thrown a spit-slinging, Bible-thumping, hell-and-damnation sermon at her for wearing something like she had on. She'd heard lots of his sermons for her misadventures while she was growing up. This time, she laughed, and the memory helped her keep the much-needed fake smile on her face and hold out her hand to the welcome committee. They were all just waiting to find out who she might turn out to be. There might be someone left who could remember.

Grace held out her hand and said, "Hello, I'm Grace Lawson, granddaughter of Tom Lawson, who used to be pastor here many years ago."

Not a soul seemed to register the significance of her introduction. They shook hands all around, politely standing back, waiting for Grace to enter the church ahead of them. Grace tried to look pleasant and remember proper protocol.

One of the men, who appeared to be the pastor, dressed in a dark gray suit and black-striped tie, indicated with a sweep of his hand that Grace might choose to sit just anywhere she pleased. He said, "It's good to have you with us this morning. We're all glad you came."

Grace had often heard these same words when her grandpa Lawson had greeted the visitors.

Grace chose a seat on the end of the pew, right next to the aisle, in case she had to make a hasty retreat. She breathed a sigh of relief; so far, so good. Not too bad, yet.

She took a slow look around; everything looked much as it did when she was growing up. The little church still had the same old picture of Jesus hanging over the same old upright piano, sitting directly behind the podium. To the left of the piano sat four wooden pews that served as the choir loft. To the right of the piano, there were four matching pews, except, lo and behold, they had been padded for comfort. Grace smiled to herself; the amen corner was certainly "coming on up"—the dignitaries and special visitors had a soft seat, anyway. But something seemed amiss, and Grace couldn't figure it out. Suddenly she remembered. Where was the old potbellied stove?

The old potbellied woodstove, her old archenemy, had stood to the left of the podium, just a few feet off the altar, and a few steps away from the side door of the church. The old contraption was gone! That stove had been the heating system in the days of yore, and Grace had hated that thing with a passion.

Grandpa Lawson, for as long as he was pastor of that church, had given Grace the job of carrying in firewood and firing up that old stove while he prepared his Sunday sermon. He considered that chore to be a much-needed lesson in humility, serving to strengthen her character in "service to God's people." He had enforced her church attendance with an iron hand, and any resistance on her part brought out his belt. Her religious rituals were the enforceable law of God, according to Grandpa, and Grandpa spoke for God—never doubt it.

Grace shivered with cold as she remembered knocking snow and ice off the sticks of stacked firewood some tithing soul had left near the back door of the church. And the old stove had taken its own slow time in getting cranked up. Meantime, Grandpa Lawson sat with his head buried in the pages of his Bible, muttering to himself, looking up just long enough to bark, "Get that thing a-goin', girl. Them folks'll be a-comin' out anytime now."

Often Grace wondered why Grandpa Lawson didn't fire the thing up himself, but as she got older, she caught on. Grandpa Lawson spent almost every Saturday night down in town at "the lodge"—meaning, to Grace's little ears, the Masonic lodge, where secret important community business was discussed. Funny thing, though; sometimes he never made it home until daybreak, and he'd be drunk as an old blind mule. And like as not, his clothes would smell like perfume one or two of the ladies wore to Sunday school. Grace had seen a couple of them wax all shy and silly when Grandpa greeted them on Sunday morning.

And then there was that business of the big sweaty circles around the underarms of his starched Sunday shirts and his balding head glistening and dripping wet with sweat. This was, of course, during the hell-and-damnation sermons he felt called to expound on during the preaching. Grace remembered it all too well. She wondered how on earth he managed to stay on track, strung out like that. Or did he? No doubt Grandpa was certainly "in the spirit" of one sort or another—and just about every Sunday.

Little children were peering over the backs of the pews to take a look at the strange lady. If the adults glanced over their shoulders and happened to make eye contact, they smiled, nodded politely, and shifted their gaze to front and center. Grace mused about what they could be thinking. *Some lady dressed like a high-dollar call girl with legs showing all the way to her waist...well, that could make for some interesting dinner conversation over the mashed taters and fried chicken later. Now, if they could just find out who she might be and where she hailed from...*

But had they known even half the truth of where she'd hailed from and why, the little valley's gossip mavens would be kept busy for months to come. Grace shuddered. *God forbid, even Grandpa would come tearing out of his grave. That old coot was responsible for much of it.* Grace stopped her thoughts and clenched her teeth.

The organ had been softly playing; it softly faded, and the old piano sprang to life, banging out the introduction to an old familiar hymn, "Victory in Jesus, My Savior Forever." Grace didn't need a hymnal to follow the words; she simply brought them out of memory. They were still embedded there.

As the singing came to the end of the last chorus, the pastor rose from his seat, took his place behind the podium, and raised his arm toward the congregation. "Let's all stand and make our visitor welcome. She's come a long way to be with us. She is Grace Lawson. Some of you might remember Tom Lawson, who was pastor here some time ago. Ms. Lawson is his granddaughter, and we all want to make her welcome."

All heads began to swivel in Grace's direction, murmuring all around the pews. Grace felt like crying, or running, or screaming, but she calmed herself down. She was determined to settle her score with the ghosts, win or lose. She tried to smile pleasantly; she'd just have to use that big fake religious front that she'd practiced all her young life. Meanwhile, she'd let them know she was no longer the little church mouse; she would not fetch and tote, would not carry water, would definitely not endure the shameful, abusive insults of the "righteous." And don't start with the finger of blame—no shame either. Grace would get it right this time.

But in many ways, Grace still resembled that little proverbial mouse. Her starvation had its roots deep in her soul, and she hadn't been able to find its source. She had brought herself back to the beginning, back where she thought it started. She wanted to settle it with herself and her God as well. Her prodigal journey had brought her full circle, and she was willing to fight for the truth, although her worst adversary might be her own self.

Facing the Old Nemesis

Grace stood as the members of that little congregation at Bethel Baptist Church circled around to shake her hand and "make her welcome," as the pastor had instructed. Of course, some just wanted to take a closer look at their unusual visitor. Most extended a hand with a timid, gracious, quick smile and a rapid move back toward their seats. A few simply patted her hand and made some welcoming remark, like, "It's good to see you this morning. God be with us, everyone."

Almost everyone had returned to their seats, and Grace was about to sit down when the pastor stepped to the podium again. He said, "Ms. Lawson, would you come to the podium for a big surprise? Please just step right up here for a minute. We're plain informal when the situation calls for it. Come on up here, please."

Grace's thoughts went wild. *Oh, dear Lord, what on earth! Surely, he won't expect me to speak or sing? God forbid, I haven't tried to sing in years.* One of the old slogans of recovery popped in her head: "Fake it till you make it." She said to herself, "Okay…here goes."

The pastor stepped back as Grace made her way toward the front. As she stepped up past the altar to take her place beside the speaker, he gestured toward the piano located right behind the podium. Grace turned to look. She gasped. There, on the piano stool, sat an old frail purple-clad skeleton with her bony fingers hovering over her breast and tears streaming down her old, weather-beaten cheeks—Grace's aunt Lucy. The old dear was obviously blind, with her red cane leaning against the piano. Aunt Lucy held her frail arms out as Grace carefully embraced the fragile old soul. Tears began pouring down

Grace's face. She hadn't seen that old soul since she had left the area many years ago.

Grace said, "It's me, Grace, Aunt Lucy. You remember me, don't you?"

Aunt Lucy cackled with laughter, which brought the whole congregation to applause. The pastor picked up a hymnal and brought the little congregation together with a resounding hymn of praise. Aunt Lucy and Grace had their tearful reunion between the old upright piano and the podium while the little church praised the Lord.

When the song of praise finally ended, the pastor stepped back to the podium. He asked the congregation to bow their heads. In a prayer of sincere gratitude, he talked of the "gifts" of family and friends who travel with us along our spiritual journey and how blessed we are to have them. When the "Amen" was said and echoed all over the church, Grace felt a strange uplifting of emotional energy and a surprising surge of appreciation. She had been seeking peace and gratitude for a very long time. She sat with Aunt Lucy in the amen corner and thanked God for her old blind family member.

*****

Aunt Lucy had lost her sight many years ago, but her ears and her memory were intact and just as acute as ever. Grace spent the Sunday afternoon and evening visiting with her in the little cottage home. It was all just as Grace remembered and might have expected. An accumulation of family pictures standing on all the tables, hanging thick around the walls, and piled on the bottom shelf of the coffee table was an assortment of albums, history just waiting to be viewed. Grace couldn't help but wonder why so many pictures when the dear old lady was obviously blind.

Aunt Lucy didn't miss a beat as she described every one of her children and the grandchildren; she knew them all. She made a hands-on inspection and got a good description of each precious one. She knew their individual voices, and she made sure they knew she loved them, equally and dearly. She could wax downright stern if their prankishness went too far; not many challenged her.

Aunt Lucy had been documenting the history, and Grace hadn't noticed the time flying by. She had been listening as Aunt Lucy recalled with clarity events that had occurred years ago. Aunt Lucy was a virtual library of history for the various families that had spawned around that valley for generations. She had played that old piano through several generations and could bring Grace up-to-date on almost every family within miles. Aunt Lucy was into her late nineties and a treasure trove of history, but time was running out.

There were so many unanswered questions that Grace wanted to bring up, so many things she never had the opportunity to understand, way too many screeching demons that could capture her memory and cause grief. She prayed, *Please, God, let me bring my painful questions gently to this precious old soul. So much truth is hidden. Please don't let me offend this dear old soul.*

"Now, Gracie Girl, you are not leaving for no motel…no, you're not." Aunt Lucy held her bony little index finger in the air, pointing it in the direction of Grace's place on the old sofa. "You gonna stay right here with me for as long as you're with us. I need the company, and we got a lot of catchin' up to do. That motel is eighteen miles away, and they say it's not the cleanest place around, so…just bring your stuff in. I got a guest room. You'll have to find the linens and make the bed for yourself, but you were always good about things like that. I bet you ain't changed."

Grace tried to be gracious. "No, no, I haven't changed there, but I don't want to be a bother to you."

"Bother nothing. An old woman like me needs company. I want to hear all about where you've been and what you've been doing all these years. Lordy, how long has it been, chile? You got to stay and bring me up-to-date. Besides that, we gotta look into that last will and testament of your grandpa's. Something ain't right about that. It didn't come out right, Gracie."

*****

Aunt Lucy was Grandpa Lawson's sister. She had served as pianist for the Bethel Baptist Church during her teenage years and right up until her late seventies. Her eyes had gone out, and she retired from the bench except for the occasions when the younger pianist had to be absent. She could still play from memory, and being the oldest member of the church, she was granted a seat on the padded pews of the amen corner. Her ears were good, however, and she never missed a thing. Her grandkids learned to behave; she could pick them out all the way to the back of the church. They didn't get away with disturbing "God's house"; she'd call them out by name.

Grace could breathe a sigh of relief. She knew Aunt Lucy's kids would never have been doled out the "cough syrup" Grandpa Lawson brought along for the restless young'uns. Grace learned early on how to feign an oncoming cough or sneezing fit just so she could get a swig of that special cough syrup. It took the chill out of the blood and helped with her singing voice; at least that was what she told Grandpa.

That old piano player had been Grace's best friend and ally during all the years Grandpa Lawson stormed the pulpit. Regularly, Aunt Lucy would take that "preacher man" to task. That tiny little woman had the spirit and strength of a mountain lion when it was required of her. Grace knew that strength sometimes came from the many secrets she and Aunt Lucy had kept. They had covered his butt for him many times, and Aunt Lucy taught Grace about arm-twisting, her own special brand of blackmail.

*****

Grandma Lawson, frail little soul that she was, never challenged Grandpa's position as head of the home, or the church. His word was law, his authority unquestioned. If his behavior didn't quite match up with "spiritual leadership" qualities, Grandma Lawson simply said, "It's a matter we need to take before the Lord." After that, she shut her mouth and carried out her duties. Preacher Lawson would have to "answer to his Maker for hisself," according to her.

THE ROAD TO HELL IS PAVED WITH... WHAT?

Grace often wondered why Grandma put up with Grandpa's disrespect and dismissive attitude whenever she tried to offer an opinion. One day, Grace was furious with Grandpa about something she'd overheard that was particularly harsh and disrespectful to Grandma Lawson. She spouted off, "Why do you let him do that, Granny? I'm a young'un, and I have to know my place, but you… you've got a right to speak up. Why don't you?"

Granny sighed and said, "Chile, don't worry your little head. Sometimes it pays to just keep your mouth shut and mind your own business. Let 'em spout off their trash. God knows they will cook their own goose sooner or later. Don't take it serious, honey. Mostly it's the devil's work coming out of that ole poison they drink. That stuff might be good for a few ailments, but too much of it can destroy a man's good works. But that's between a man and his God. We can't do nothing about it."

Grace wiped at her tears but couldn't diminish the pain. She simply didn't understand how a man who believed in God could behave so contrary to what the Bible clearly said. She couldn't hold back her outrage. "Sometimes I just hate to hear him carrying on at you, Granny. It ain't right, and he knows it."

Granny Lawson smiled an old, tired smile, pulled Grace close in her arms, patted her head while Grace cried. Finally, she spoke. "Girl, if he should ever come to any serious harm to us, especially you, I'll put him down. He knows I got my limits. You just tell me about him or anybody else that brings harm to you. I'll take care of them."

As Grace was drying her tears, she looked toward Granny's face for reassurance. What she saw would haunt her later in life. Granny was gazing off into space as though she had lost her thoughts, and she had a steely look in her eyes. There was a strange smirk on her mouth. Grace had never seen her granny look so strange. She shivered. Maybe it was time to shut her little mouth and "get out of God's business" with His people. That was what Granny had just said.

*****

Aunt Lucy and Grace had said their good nights and Grace was stretched out on the little guest bed when, without warning, a stunning image came across her consciousness. The image of her mother's face floated like a vapor right through her mind, her face crinkled up with laughter and her long hair flowing as if she were caught in a breeze. She appeared for a brief instant, and then she was gone. Grace lay perfectly still, waiting for the image to appear again. She wanted to see that sweet face, but the image disappeared and didn't come back.

Grace's mother had died when Grace was six, a traumatic event in Grace's young life. But sometimes her mother appeared in a vapor-like flash through Grace's thoughts at the most unexpected times, and always preceding a turn of events in Grace's life. She somehow served as an omen of good things to come. This time the smiling, laughing, gleeful presence signified happy things were about to happen. Grace whispered, "Don't let me mess up, Mama, okay?"

Out of the jumble of historical details that Aunt Lucy had shared throughout the afternoon and well into the evening, something came to the forefront of Grace's awareness. Aunt Lucy had said, "We gotta look into that last will and testament of your grandpa's. Something ain't right." Grace was feeling exhausted and emotionally drained; she needed a drink so bad.

*****

Grace's trip back through her childhood had been suggested by her psychiatrist numerous times over the past few weeks. Grace's support group, Alcoholics Anonymous, whom she had dubbed the God Squad, had agreed with him.

"Ms. Grace," the doctor had said, "we can't get much further along until you face some of the pain created by your childhood memories. As long as you refuse to re-experience the trauma associated with that period of your life, you'll keep repeating the same behaviors and digging a deeper hole for yourself. You think it's too painful to examine, but I assure you, most of what you feel about that time of your life is just fear. The reality doesn't exist anymore, and your reaction to it is the reaction of that young child. You are now an adult, and long removed from that period of your life. We can take an objective look at your experiences, re-experience the emotions if we need to, and let it go. It's controlling your function now, unfortunately, but it's all in the past, not appropriate for where you are today."

"So, Doctor," Grace asked, "you think I'm being controlled by emotions left over from my childhood and I'm allowing those emotions to dictate my attitude and behavior today, after more than forty years?" Grace couldn't believe how insistent the doctor had become, but he didn't let up.

"Yes, and you know that nothing gets buried and forgotten in our psyche. It all goes underground and comes up again, in some inappropriate way most of the time, even in our physical health. Your physical health is still pretty good, but it's just a matter of time. And that business of your job being in jeopardy, you'll have to face that, make up your mind. How important is it?"

Grace felt nauseous, but she answered, "Yes, I realize I've created some problems for myself, and I don't want to lose my position, not now. I'm almost ready to retire."

The doctor said nothing; he folded his arms and waited.

Grace began to speak. "Yes, I know I am progressively losing control around certain issues. I've talked about some of them, and you're right, they are worse than I've been willing to admit. If something doesn't change, I may wind up dead. I've got a lot to lose, and I know something has to change. My support group agrees with you. I'll take a few days off and take a trip back where those old memories are the most painful. You will have to push me. I don't fancy the idea, but I will give it a shot."

The doctor said, "Grace, you carry my number and don't hesitate to call me any hour. I'm available to you. Things will turn out to be a lot less threatening than you think. You'll see that things have changed, and so have you. You'll be fine. Nothing to be frightened of now, not after all this time."

Somehow Grace couldn't quite tap into the doctor's enthusiasm despite his reassurances. He extended his hand for the usual sign of commitment. Grace shook his hand and headed for the door before he could see the tears; she couldn't get out of it now, and she knew that.

*****

Aunt Lucy's little antique bed wasn't exactly a comfortable fit for Grace's tall, lanky frame. Grace tossed and turned, trying to make herself fit between the tall headboard and footboard. She pulled her knees up toward her chest, scrunching into something of a fetal position, and turned on her side, facing the wall. Suddenly, just before she closed her eyes, there on the wall was her mother's face again. The same happy laughter, the same twinkle in the eye, the same wispy vapor. But this time Mama spoke into Grace's mind. *You gonna be all right now, baby doll. You did really good.* Grace whispered, "Thank you, Mama. You stay with me. Don't let me screw up. I'm scared to death. I just want to drink something."

*****

Grace woke up to a loud pecking at the bedroom door. She heard noises coming from outside and Aunt Lucy's raspy voice coming through the mental fog. "Grace, are you up? We got things to do today. Com'on, chile."

Grace couldn't believe it. Morning already?

The roosters crowed early in that part of the world, and Aunt Lucy had a flock of chickens, replete with a big red-feathered rooster that was now crowing right outside the window. Grace tried to put her best response in her reply, "Yes, Aunt Lucy, I'm up. Be out in a minute."

Grace's body popped and cracked as she tried to unfold her long frame. Apparently, she hadn't moved all night. She was thinking, *Oh lord, I need that coffee I'm smelling. Where did the night go? I don't remember being sleepy, and I never sleep without a drink. But I'm feeling weirdly energetic, like I have to hurry for something. God help me. Here I go.*

She grabbed her clothes. Somewhere deep in her psyche, she had a monitor, something akin to Doppler radar that knew before she did that something was afoot. Her instincts told her to follow, wherever it pointed, just follow, like a leaf following a stream. Flow with it. Grace was reminded of the great philosopher who said, "Follow your heart. It knows the way."

Over breakfast, consisting of oatmeal, whole wheat toast, and a big cup of coffee, Aunt Lucy filled Grace in on a plan she had hatched. Aunt Lucy said, "Sorry if there's nothing on the table that you like, Grace. An old woman like me has to watch it. Troubles enough without eating something my body won't digest. You'll find that out when you get older."

Grace laughed and said, "You might be surprised just how old I've gotten to be, Aunt Lucy. I have to watch it too. As they say, getting old is not for the faint of heart. I get that."

The two of them worked on Aunt Lucy's plan amid their joking, laughter, and the pure entertainment the reunion was providing. When they had settled on the first steps of their adventure, they cleared the table, put the dishes away, and put their plan in motion.

"Now, Gracie Girl," Aunt Lucy said, "you know my old body won't allow me to go traipsing all over the county with you. You'd have to bury me before sunrise. We can get my grandboys, Al and Ronnie, to come help you. They can bring their hunting Jeep and take you right up there to your grandpa's old place. They're scamps sometimes, but I'll warn 'em not to play any of their tricks on you. Just let me talk to their mom about it."

Aunt Lucy picked up her old phone and dialed. "Hello, Helen. Would you ask the boys if they would come over after school and take Grace up to the old place, that is, if you don't need them for something?"

That request was not likely to be ignored. This was a special event for Granny Lucy; she had prayed for years for "Little Gracie" to come home. At every prayer meeting for years, she had ended her prayers with, "Lord, in Your good time, please bring our little girl home."

Grace listened to Aunt Lucy end the conversation with the boys' mother. She said, "We thank you. You know how important it is to me, and the boys will enjoy Grace. She's a fine lady. She'll be a good influence. But, Helen, you tell them boys Granny won't put up with any of their tricks. Grace don't need that right now. I'll skin 'em if they scare her. Bye-bye."

*****

Aunt Lucy sent Grace off to the local courthouse, or "anywhere else" she might have to go, to find the necessary records to explain what had happened to Grandpa Lawson's last will and testament. Why had the old Lawson farm and all that mountain land fallen into ruin because the title to the property couldn't be cleared?

"You run and look up the records, Grace," Aunt Lucy said. "I'll get my housekeeper to bring in the boxes of your grandpa's papers from the shed. You can have a look at all that stuff. We might be able to find some answers. Lordy, chile, I have prayed for this day."

*****

Grace drove slowly, not sure just where to begin. Along the way she tried to spot anything she could remember about the area, any familiar landmarks. Strangely enough, there wasn't much. What she saw instead were modern houses sitting all along the route and paved streets running through what she remembered as cow pastures in the valleys. All along the mountain ridges were houses, affluent homes clustered all along the edges of what were mostly craggy ridges running to the top of the mountains. Grace stared in amazement; her mind couldn't take it all in. Where had all the wealth come from, and the money, the people?

Old memories came flooding through Grace's mind. That old school bus ride she had hated but had to tolerate. Grandpa Lawson said, "Get on that bus, young lady. Don't even think about quitting. Don't ask."

*****

The school was located about eighteen miles from the old Lawson farm. The old bumpy roads where the school bus had clattered along were now paved, but Grace remembered the route very well. The bus picked the Lawson kids up at the old Baptist church, about two miles from the Lawson residence. Way before daylight sometimes, Grace would run to catch the bus through bad weather or not. Grandpa said, "You make sure you get on it, girl."

But oh, happy day, when the weather prohibited the bus from running and Grace got a break. That old battery-powered transistor radio would squawk out the road conditions and the school closing before Grace left the house. She would grab her books and sit by the fireplace and read. She had lots of different books she had borrowed or begged, and those were her escape. She could go far away, become the characters she read about, for a while, at least. What a life she could have somewhere out in the big world, out there where things could be better for her. Someday, someday, somewhere, anywhere; her dreams came to life whenever she got those beloved "snow days" and she didn't have to work outside. She could read and dream.

Grace knew her dreams had sustained her somehow, but she wondered, *How on earth did I do it? I hung in there, God help me, when most girls didn't, or couldn't. I came close...oh my lord, how many times I wanted to run away, just anywhere.*

Most of Grace's girlfriends had fallen into the trap of having babies and family obligations before they finished high school. Grace knew they weren't much better off than they were back then; they were caught in the cycle.

The cycle of poverty and the perpetuation of disadvantage and despair had hounded the people of Appalachia for centuries. Grace knew she herself would have been one of the wounded, despairing souls had she not fled whenever she got the chance. She'd fled with the determination to never look back. She was feeling a surge of pride about herself when her stomach lurched. The nausea was coming on; she needed a stiff drink. With no drinking possible, at least for now, she had to face the pain. She thought, *No, no, no! I'll face the ugly truth. I didn't leave of my own accord. I was exiled, practically shipped out for bringing disgrace on the family and the church, after I was gang-raped and pregnant. Nobody believed me when I told the truth…and my poor baby had to be adopted. That's what happened, Grace. Stop lying. It won't help you find the truth.*

The Times Are a-Changing

Grace could hardly keep her mind on managing the car as she made her way along the old school bus route that would take her into the center of town. All along the way, she found herself staring at the new developments that had gone up everywhere. All the changes of the last forty years were bewildering. There was actually a shopping center on what used to be an old farm on the north side of town. The old schoolhouse had spread itself over all the acreage where the ball fields used to be and had taken up the east side of the town. Fast-food eateries were everywhere; nothing like that existed when she was young. There was one ice cream store, simply called the Parlor, where she and her friends might afford an ice cream once in a blue moon. That was a rare occasion; Grandpa Lawson didn't allow for much indulgence in "wasteful habits," particularly if it had to come from his pocket.

Despite her curious scanning and her bewilderment at all the modernizing that had taken place, Grace made it to the old county courthouse, where she thought records might be found. She pulled the Lexus alongside an antique brick street where she found a parking space marked "Visitors Only." The old town square had taken on a new look. The old courthouse now stood dwarfed by gigantic trees that were towering over the whole lot, and there were park benches scattered all along the area. Tulips were blooming, pansies were everywhere, and pots of spring daffodils were swaying in the breeze.

Grace went through the arched entryway and took the walkway toward the front door, stopping just long enough to stare up at the old building. The antique red brick had yellowed over the years, but it was beautifully arranged, all the way to the top, three stories high, not much bigger than one of the larger churches of Grace's memory. The old courthouse had apparently been restored and now sat in its antique splendor, surrounded by majestic trees and blooming flowers, reflecting the beauty of antiquity. This was not what Grace remembered at all. Through the windows Grace could see antiques and artifacts. The old town square had been turned into a relic, restored and reserved for future generations to gaze upon. It didn't take Grace long to grasp that she wouldn't be finding records in that lovely old museum. It had become a tourist attraction.

*****

As Grace finished her tour around the museum, now known as the Old Courthouse Square, she heard a man's voice asking, "May I help you, ma'am? You look like you might be lost this morning."

The voice was moving in her direction. Grace peered through the low-hanging tree branches toward the sound. An old white-haired gentleman, somewhat stooped and frail, had stepped out in the clearing. Grace walked slowly in his direction. She answered, "I think I am lost, somewhat, anyway. I was looking for the tax office, or the county clerk's office, where the records are kept. Looks like I found the original place, but it's now a museum."

The old man chuckled. "Where you from, young lady? There ain't been no records kept here in twenty years. We got ourselves a new courthouse, called the Justice Center. It's over off the bypass as you come in off the main highway. You probably passed it when you came in."

Grace tried to thank the old fellow, but he was still chuckling. As she turned to walk away, he said, "You know, there's always somebody looking for old records and stuff, somebody from out of town. They wind up here every time. My job is to straighten 'em out. I been here since Noah landed his ark. You remember him, don't you?"

The old man's eyes were sparkling, and Grace caught the joke. She said, "Yes, I do remember him. I'm one of Noah's great-grandchildren, and Grandpa Noah sent me off to replenish the earth, which I have mostly failed at, so I'm here to look up my roots. I bet you could help me out. Do you remember Preacher Lawson from up on Lawson's Creek?"

The old gentleman scratched his head, reflecting for a minute, staring at Grace. "You mean you are one of his'en? Why, you wouldn't be that little scrawny granddaughter…that'un everybody's been asking about for years, would you?"

Grace nodded.

The old gentleman put his palms together, held his arms up in front of his face, closed his eyes, and said, "Thank you, blessed Lord."

Her curiosity got the best of her despite the emotional signals going off in her head. Grace tried to sound pleasant, but deep inside the old feelings of shame and resentment began to roar; she didn't really care what anyone thought anymore. She asked, "What has everyone been asking about me? Why are they asking?"

The old fellow laughed and offered his hand for a handshake as he said, "Why, little lady, everybody around these parts is trying to git their hands on your old grandpa's place. Them lawyers have tried to get a clear title to that place for years. We keep telling them that there's a granddaughter someplace…and she'll come back one day and claim it. Your aunt Lucy tells that to every one of them. And… here you are. I reckon that is why you're here, ain't it? You gonna lay claim to what's yourn?"

Grace waxed completely speechless. She would have expected anything else, something derogatory, or at least gossipy. She took a few steps toward the nearest park bench, motioning for the old fellow to follow. She managed to say, "Would you sit with me, here, for a minute? I'm feeling a bit surprised." She spotted a badge on his uniform that read, "Cloy Ledford, County Historian." "It's Mr. Ledford, isn't it?"

"Yep! I'm the official county historian around the Old Courthouse Square these days. Mostly I just entertain the tourists, tell tall tales and all that. It beats sitting at home, waiting for the grim reaper, and it can get interestin' some days. They can ask some doggone dumb questions sometimes, and I gotta come up with a dignified answer, or joke. It's fun to do."

Grace was pressing her palms firmly together while trying to slow her breathing to deep, slow rhythms. She was prone to unexpected bouts of what her doctor said were the DTs, tremors caused by her withdrawal from alcohol. The doctor assured her that if she could relax, breathe slowly, and press her palms together, it would help to calm her nerves. She was giving it her best. As the tremors began to quieten, she propelled herself back forty years and tried to remember who on earth she had just encountered. Who was Cloy Ledford? Where did he fit? Was he one of Grandpa's old "lodge" buddies, one of the cousins, one of the extended family members? Who would know so much about Grandpa Lawson and remember her being a "scrawny" little girl?

The old man was chattering on. "Now, you go right down to that Justice Center and ask about the records. Then git ahold of Bob Henderson Jr. That is old Lawyer Henderson's boy. His daddy died some years back, but that boy can help you. Tell him you gotta git that property title straightened out. That property of your grandpa's ought to belong to you. Don't let them tell you anything else."

*****

Grace pushed herself through the motions of properly thanking Mr. Ledford for his help. She made it back to the car, where she caught herself thinking, *I need a drink right now.*

Her usual stash of fortifying medicine was no longer under the car seat. She was searching the glove compartment frantically when it occurred to her that in her new car nothing would be found, thanks to her recovery group. The old God Squad had cleaned her out before she had left on this adventure. Not only that, but they had also made her promise she wouldn't touch any alcohol while she worked on her fourth-step inventory, a much-dreaded investigative search through her childhood influences. She'd made them a promise she wanted to keep, at least this week, after which she'd be sure to make no such promises.

She sat for a few minutes, trying to reflect on what to do. She felt terrified. She asked herself, "Okay, what is it I fear the most?"

The answer popped right up. "Lawyer Henderson's boy…he's the last person I want to see. So I guess I'll 'fake it,' like the group says. It's got to be done, and I can't let Aunt Lucy down either. She's waited so long for me. I've got to do this."

*****

On the way to the Justice Center, she was reciting the twelve steps of recovery. "I'm powerless over alcohol. Please, God, restore me to sanity. I'm willing to let go. Please, God."

After finding her way to the appropriate division of the new Justice Center, Grace explained to the clerk's staff what she was looking for. She hardly noticed the inquisitive stares she was getting from some of the ladies who occupied the various desks. They pointed her to a section of the office where the old records were kept. Everything in the last twenty years, they said, had been digitized, upgraded to computer data. She would have to look up the old records of the bygone days. She found herself in the basement, where the old records were kept.

Grace took time to pursue every lead she could find in the old dusty books, going back as far as she could remember. She had copies made of everything she thought could bring some clarity to the problem. The ten-cent-a-page charge didn't faze her; she copied on. Sometime before noon, she gathered the paperwork and stopped to pay for her copies at the front of the office. One of the clerk's staffers, an aging, broad-shouldered, stocky lady with a loud voice, came up smiling. She looked at Grace quizzically and asked, "If we can be of further service, we're always happy to go out of our way. What was your name again?"

"Grace Lawson, and I'm doing research on my grandfather's behalf. His name was Tom Lawson, and there seems to be some confusion about ownership of his old farm. I'm hoping we can clear that up. I appreciate your willingness to help, and your patience. Thank you so much." Grace turned to the exit, but the lady persisted.

"Why, Lord, honey, we can all help you with that. That old Lawson place has been researched over and over, mostly by these high-dollar tourists coming in here to buy up everything in sight to build more of their fancy houses, develop all these old mountain farms, and make a big profit off us poor folk. I hope you ain't planning to sell. I tell you, I hate to see the mountains ruint by that kind of thing."

The lady wasn't bothering to contain her voice, and the rest of the staff had turned their attention to what Grace thought should have been a quiet interchange of information.

Grace answered quietly, "Oh, I assure you, if it is up to me, there won't be an inch of that old property sold to 'that kind of thing.' But at this point, I'm not sure it's up to me. I'm trying to find out."

The loud lady took a business card from the counter, wrote her phone number across the back, and handed it to Grace. "Here. You just call anytime. There's a bunch of us natives around here who will do whatever we can to help. We're sick of these lowlanders, snowbirds and all, coming in here to ruin the land. They can spend their money any way they like, but we don't want the land destroyed, not to speak of the traffic jams we got now."

As Grace tried to exit the front door, she found the opinionated lady had followed her. Outside the door, the lady quickly scanned the area and bent to whisper in Grace's ear, "It's the lawyers, honey, that have that old place locked up. They're waiting on Lawson's sister to die. Can't fool me. I been around here a while. Wasn't her name Lucy Bradford? She says the place belongs to her niece, and that would be you, I reckon. The lawyers are betting you won't come back, then they can shuffle the paperwork around the relatives, buy that farm out for a ridiculous price, and make a ton of money. Your aunt's kin are not wealthy or educated. Everybody knows that. They would sell in a heartbeat if Aunt Lucy dies. Lawyer Henderson is behind it, lying his tail off about that last will and testament of your grandpa's. That man is a thief. You be careful…and keep this between us, you and me."

The big lady gave Grace a wink and made a hasty retreat back to her office, waving as she left. Grace glanced at the business card she had been handed. Edith Ledford had left her phone number. Grace thought, *Heavens, these Ledford people are everywhere! And thank You,*

Lord, for them. I need help, and it seems everyone so far is on my side, rooting for me to come back and claim the land. Lord, I have to try.

*****

"Now," Grace said, "where is that newspaper office? There are some old stories I want to read for myself. Wonder if it is in the same place. Let's have a look, Grace, ole girl." Some kind of peculiar determination had begun to empower Grace, and she moved right along.

At the newspaper office, located right where she remembered it, Grace asked about the dated issues that she particularly wanted to see. The old archives had been stored in an old warehouse that used to house the printing presses. Grace was accompanied to the warehouse by a purple-haired, seemingly distracted twenty-something girl who showed more interest in her fake nails than anything else. She smacked her gum as she instructed Grace. "Sorry, but we handle all the old records and copier ourselves. We'll copy what you need, but we have to be careful that nothing is lost, or misplaced." Ms. Purple-Hair gave Grace a stare to go with that comment, as if to say further, "And nothing stolen by people like you."

It didn't take Grace long to find the specific dates she needed. She thanked the young girl and made a hasty exit. Her sinuses were tightening up, she had sneezed a few times, and she felt teary eyed. Allergies, of course. The old records were dusty and yellowed with age, not to speak of the condition of the building—it hadn't been swept in years. Grace went to her praying again. *Dear God, not allergies on top of everything else. Please help me. I have to make the last stop, and it's gonna take all I can do. Please help me.*

*****

Before Grace stashed her copies of the old newspaper articles in her car, she scanned the articles she had so wanted to see, the stories about the deaths of the loggers who had raped her years ago way up on the east ridge. She'd have to ask Aunt Lucy if any of it was true or just sensationalism, hyped journalism. Aunt Lucy would tell the truth. Grace put the papers down to look at later. She had a bigger fish to fry before she chickened out.

As she drove toward the last dreaded stop, the old Henderson Law Office, she recalled what a stickler Grandpa could be about his newspaper. He didn't read well, and Granny didn't read at all, so Grace had the job of reading to them as she got older. It was one of the few dignities she was allowed in the grown-up world. She could feel good about herself, and she learned to interpret words from an old dictionary a teacher had given her for "being such a studious little girl." That dictionary was her go-to book. The Bible was Grandpa's thing; he gave her no credit for interpreting a thing there. She left the Big Book alone.

The Dreaded Encounter

Finding the location of the old Henderson Law Office would be easy, or so Grace thought. However, she found herself driving around slowly, puzzled that it didn't appear where she and Grandpa had visited many years ago. In fact, on the lot where Grace remembered it was located, there was a three-story building housing a medical complex, with several doctors listed on the shingle. The parking lot seemed to circle the building, and on a hunch, Grace took a side road that ran along the parking lot and came out behind the building. There on the back of the lot sat the old law office, just like she remembered, except it was secluded from the street by the larger medical complex. Grace smirked. The big profits and higher purposes had taken over even the trusty ole lawyer's front door.

Grace was hoping she could just stop in briefly, ask some pleasant receptionist to make an appointment for later in the week, and then she'd make a fast escape. But no such luck was in the cards for Grace that day. She stared at the old brass plaque that graced the door. It still read, "Law Office of Robert T. Henderson, Esquire." *Are we outdated or what?* Grace thought.

She quietly opened the door and looked around for the pleasant receptionist. None appeared. But to the left of the door, in what appeared to be the waiting room, a large man was sitting with his boots propped up in the windowsill, leaning back, smoking a big cigar. He swiveled his chair around, rose to his feet, and just grinned at Grace. He was a tall fellow, showing off his yellowing teeth as he grinned. His hair was gray and mostly bald on top, except for the wispy comb-over. He looked Grace over, head to toe, before he spoke.

"Well, girl, it took you long enough. I been expecting you since earlier this morning. Old man Ledford told me you would be coming. My secretary took off for the day, and I been sittin' right here, just waiting to see you." The man put the cigar down and extended both hands to Grace. She stared at him in confusion but managed to offer her hand. "You do remember me, don't you, Grace? You come down from that Lawson place and put my young heart in a spasm."

Grace was stuck with a dumbfounded, deer-in-the-headlights stare. She was thinking, *He can't be...oh, my soul, Bobby Henderson.* She felt herself turning red and redder. She was speechless and not at all in Seattle, or anywhere else she wanted to be.

Bobby Henderson, or Lawyer Henderson, as the townspeople called him, chuckled on, chattering away about their teenage pranks, maneuvering their little romance around Preacher Lawson so they could indulge in their little experimentations. He was having so much fun while Grace stood dumfounded. She had the presence of mind to go along with his little foray into their escapades, but her mind was calculating. *How old is he now? Nearly sixty? Oh my gosh.*

Henderson had run his eyes up and down Grace's body several times while Grace was trying to get her thoughts together. And he kept pulling her into a hug under his big arm while slipping his fingers up and down her back and across her shoulders. Grace hated men who behaved like lecherous animals looking for their next prey. She was fighting to keep herself smiling, pretending to go along with his friendly intrusion of her personal space. Grace tried to remember what the recovery people had taught her. "Don't start any fights. Don't go to every fight you're invited to. Let your opponent define themselves before you jump. Then you can turn the situation to your advantage. Don't give away your power by losing your temper."

Grace could feel her tolerance limit fast approaching. She tried to smile sweetly as she asked, "Could you spend some time with me later in the week? I want to go over my grandpa's last will and testament, see if I can understand it correctly. I might need your opinion on a couple of other issues as well." She tried to sound sincere.

Suddenly, Henderson started shaking his head. "There is no last will, Grace. We've looked everywhere. You know, my dad died some years back, and I don't believe he ever prepared a will for your grandpa. At least none was ever found here. Your aunt Lucy insisted that we look for it, but it never turned up. So…let's just get together, and if you want me to, I'll take the day off and we'll go up to that old Lawson place and look around. I been up there a few times, riding and hunting. I had hoped someone could sell me that old ragged thing. You could sign a power of attorney, and I could take that off your hands, pay a fair price for it, too."

Grace hedged, saying, "Oh, I don't know what I'll do just yet. I have to be clear on Grandpa's wishes before I decide, you know. Could be I don't have anything to sell."

Henderson answered, "Well, you gonna have a hard time getting that old farm back in shape. You been gone too long, little lady, and that old place has gone to ruin. It's a mess. Won't be good for much of anything now except hunting. I'd be glad to take it off your hands, pay a fair price for it, anytime."

Henderson was pushing, and Grace hoped her eyes wouldn't betray her. She came up with what she hoped would postpone the situation until the last minute. She asked for a Thursday-afternoon appointment, around three thirty. She had to be back in the city before 8:00 p.m., and that wouldn't leave much time to tolerate him before she could escape. Her trip home would take about three hours, and she had to report to her recovery friends; she had promised, and she didn't have any intention of being hijacked by an aging Romeo who still operated with the principles of a high school jock.

Grace walked away from his insistent hug, shuddering and thinking, *Dear Lord, this man is going to offend me, and I can't control my own actions. He is intolerable.*

As she walked to her car, Grace decided to hand him a smidgen of his own game. She put her long legs in a sexy swing, turned, and gave him a suggestive wink and a wave. As she drove away, she pulled that new Lexus right around in full view of that front window; there he stood, smiling like he had just won the lottery.

Grace was feeling the fury by that time. She was almost yelling, "How dare him! He thinks I'm dumb as dirt, and just as vulnerable as that young high school girl that 'put his heart in a spasm'! Well, here's a thought for you, old boy: it may be your pants we invade this time. I had to leave this town in total disgrace and humiliation, and I never got even a Christmas card from your cowardly butt. Now, here you are, lying through your teeth about my grandpa's will. How else would you know that I can sign a power of attorney and let you have the old farm? I may have to invite your butt to a fight before this is over—I'm not kidding!"

She was so infuriated she forgot which road would take her out of town and back home. In her confusion, she turned back to the Old Courthouse Square. She just wanted to escape, find something to drink, before she lost all control. She was pushing herself too far.

An Unexpected Encounter

That highly polished little Lexus that Grace had dubbed Lexie Lady made its way back to the Old Town Square and parked itself near the west side of that beautifully landscaped old courtyard. Grace couldn't remember making the decision to drive in that direction and couldn't explain why she needed to stop there again. She wearily pulled herself out of the car, swung her legs over the stacked-stone border wall that surrounded the park, and stumbled toward a park bench. The emotional dam broke as soon as she sat down. Feelings began to surface, and she couldn't stop the pain. Tears began to pour, sobbing shook her body, and the pain was almost unbearable. She let it come. Soon the rage began to surface, and Grace had reached her limit; she took it up with God.

I was just a child, and You took my dad and then mom. Then You sent me to live with an abusive old closet drunk, a hypocrite preacher, for my guidance. I was raped on the mountain and then had a child. You took my baby too! I worked by butt off for years trying to regain some sense of self-respect, and now I'm about to lose my job. I stopped the alcohol. Now I've got these stupid DTs! Can't think straight most of the time. Now You want me to settle this mess with my grandpa's estate. And…I have to deal with this lying dog, Henderson. Can You make this any harder? Don't I ever get a break?

Grace was shaking with rage, attempting to stifle her sobs with her scarf. She didn't notice a quiet figure slip in and sit next to her on the bench. As she blew her nose and wiped her face with the scarf, a voice said, "Here, Gracie Girl, this always helps." Mr. Cloy Ledford was holding out a double-dipped ice cream cone and slurping away on one of his own.

She hadn't seen an ice cream cone like that since her high school days. That kind of thing was certainly a rare treat. Grace didn't hesitate to accept that special prize, but she did try to apologize. "I'm sorry if I'm disturbing the serenity around here, Mr. Ledford. I was trying to collect my thoughts, and I just lost control. It's been a long time since I've been here, and it brings back some painful memories. I get overwhelmed with it all."

Mr. Ledford didn't offer any sympathy; he just slurped his ice cream and crunched the pecans. Grace shrugged and followed his lead. The two sat quietly, enjoying their treats without talking. When the ice cream was gone, Mr. Ledford wiped his mouth and stood, saying, "Gotta go, girl. My break is over."

Grace took his hand and again attempted to apologize. "I'm sorry about my emotional condition. There's just so much in my memory that is so painful. Thank you for the ice cream. That ice cream is one of the best things I remember about my childhood, and it brought back some good thoughts. Thank you."

"Well, Gracie, sometimes we all have to have our little spats with God," Mr. Ledford said. "We have to trust that God knows why He brought you back after all this time. You can work on that thought and let the old memories go. They're just so much water under the bridge. Life don't have no reverse gear. We have to go forward. We don't get no redos. We get to look at our mistakes and learn as much as we can. Then, we find some way to make something better of ourselves. It's life. That's how it works."

Mr. Ledford started to walk away, but he turned back to Grace. "It's sort of like this old courthouse here. Do you remember how it looked whenever you were young? Now the old thing has been restored: new paint, new lights, new yard with flowers and trees. Now it's a work of art, and everybody enjoys it. Try to see your life from God's perspective. He might have a plan for you just like that. Kneel in prayer and ask Him. If God can make a masterpiece out of this old raggedy courthouse…well, think what He might do for you. Ask, and he'll show you."

Grace sat for a long time after the old man was gone. She kept staring at the old courthouse. The flowers were dancing in a gentle breeze, their leaves and petals stirring as the trees overhead seemed to sway in a peaceful dance. All was quiet, just peaceful and serene. Reluctant to move herself from such peaceful presence, she began to pray. "God, if You are working a similar restoration in me, please help me to see some evidence of it. I'm weak and overwhelmed and shaking like a leaf. Can't You help me? I've put the alcohol down. I want to do Your will, but…I simply don't have a clue. I can't see it. Please help me."

Grace waited for an answer but got what she had long ago experienced as "silence from heaven." She had often tried to communicate with God and always got the same thing: nothing. It seemed to her that God was saying, "You're on your own, stupid girl." She sighed, gathered herself as best as she could, and turned in the direction of her car. As she slugged along, feeling the awful depression beginning to take over again, she dropped down on the stone boundary to swing her legs over into the street. A voice spoke nearby. "Shine a different light on it, girl. God is the master artist. He has the plan." Grace looked around for Mr. Ledford, but he wasn't there; nor was anyone else. She heard herself say, "Thank You, Lord. I'm listening."

All her life, Grace had been accustomed to hearing her mother's voice speak into her thoughts during stressful times. Her psychiatrist had told her it was a figment of her memory that had been brought to life as a comforting presence during her childhood stresses. But Grace held on to that memory and welcomed its presence, imaginary or not. She had trusted her mother and found great relief from her anxieties whenever that image appeared and spoke to her. Now that voice had appeared to come as Mr. Ledford. A strange, joyful peace was beginning to move through her consciousness. She jumped off the boundary wall and dashed to her car. She grabbed her purse and joyfully skipped up the street to the Old Parlor. Minutes later, she was armed with a half-gallon of that superb ice cream and was headed out to find the Kentucky Fried Chicken she had promised Aunt Lucy for the grandboys. She had the presence of mind to apologize to the Lord. "I'm sorry for my pity party. You know I do that often, and You always listen, allowing my tantrums. Then You reward me with ice cream like I'm still a little child, which I am, in my head, sometimes. Please protect me from myself, Lord. I'll try my best to hold it together. When I'm in charge, I make a mess. Your will, Lord, is what I want. I'm listening, I am."

*****

Making her way up the valley toward Aunt Lucy's little cottage, Grace found herself musing about the difference between the young Bobby Henderson she used to know and the obese, balding, and lecherous old man she had just met in the law office. Not only was he a bit outdated, but the office itself was also hidden behind the new buildings, stuck in the same place where the elder Mr. Henderson had conducted his own law practice. Young Bobby hadn't bothered to take the old shingle down and put his own name on it. Where was the man's self-respect? Did he not have any interest in bringing his building up to par with the rest of the town? Was the practice of law too much for him? Why was he hiding behind the medical complex? What on earth had happened to him?

Muse as she might, Grace had been taught well by her recovery friends that she herself had been emotionally stalled out, stymied, and inhibited by the disadvantages of her youth and the trauma associated with her family. She'd had a tough childhood, no doubt about that; poverty and hardship had left their scars. But that didn't make any sense for Bobby Henderson; his family was different, prosperous and well respected.

Grace was talking to herself, and she said, "Bobby Henderson had it made! His folks were relatively wealthy, had all the trappings of the upper class, and were known to totally spoil their kids. Bobby had all the advantages. What has happened over the years? Apparently, he was able to attend law school, educate himself, and like myself, came out with an extended education. Jeez, I don't get it. Why is the rest of the town just teeming with transplanted wealth running up every ridge and he's stuck in the past? He was so good-looking and so athletic while we were in school. Every girl's dream. He could have moved to a bigger city and built a practice for himself. Where did he drop the ball?"

THE ROAD TO HELL IS PAVED WITH... WHAT?

Grace was beginning to feel some sympathy for Bobby, her old beau, until she caught herself and yanked her thoughts back to reality. "What am I thinking? Aunt Lucy says he is the biggest land thief in the county. He steals property from the poor people by shaking money in their faces, buys up their properties, and sells again for a much higher price to the snowbirds and what Aunt Lucy calls 'Floridiots.' He is known to make a living that way. In addition to that, according to her, he even pays off the liens, mortgages, and debts and takes property as collateral." Grace was almost yelling again.

Aunt Lucy's precise words had been, "That rascal will take property from the poor people who have run up a nursing home bill, pay off the charges, and take the property away from the heirs. He's a crook! He's got your grandpa's last will and testament somewhere, Grace. He's just waiting on me to die and get out of his way. You can handle him. Didn't you say you are a doctor of some kind, Grace? Then, you got enough education to kick the stuffing out of him. He's not gonna get that Lawson property, not while I'm alive, and I've told him that. Our family is not gonna sign it over to a crook."

*****

Aunt Lucy had been rattling on about so many things the previous evening that Grace's attention had drifted. She wasn't focused on the matter of Grandpa's last will and testament or the disposal of the old property. It hadn't occurred to her that she would be required to fight the biggest "land crook" in the county over the title to the old Lawson farm. Had she known how that fight would evolve, and what it would involve, Grace would have disappeared. Sometimes ignorance sustains fools and, in that way, becomes a blessing, indeed.

The Old Ragged Farm

As she drove up the valley, Grace made up her mind. She found herself determined to see that the old Lawson property belonged to the Lawson family. At some point, if they decided to sell, a fair market price would be acceptable, not some "fair price" determined by the biggest land thief in the county. Lawyer Henderson would have to go suck his thumb!

"I will not stop until we get to the bottom of this mess," Grace declared. "Aunt Lucy has waited such a long time, and she can't help herself anymore. Now, first things first. Like the recovery people say, I need to get some idea of the fair market value of the property. I need to take a good look at the whole thing and then find good legal counsel to help establish ownership and settle disputes. That's the plan. In the meantime, I need ice cream and fried chicken to inspire the young boys. Their Granny Lucy says they're always hungry."

*****

Aunt Lucy was waiting, rocking in her old rocker on the porch, when Grace pulled up. Loaded with the ice cream, the chicken box, and a big stack of paperwork, Grace nearly missed the steps. Aunt Lucy cackled. "Oh, I can smell that chicken! Come on in and let's get it ready. My boys will be here in a bit, and they'll be starved."

Grace answered, "I'll need to make a quick pit stop, Aunt Lucy, and I'm starving too."

In the bathroom, Grace got a look at her appearance. *Oh my goodness! No wonder I got some funny stares. I'm not hungover this time, just emotionally wrung out. Well, young boys don't expect much from some 'old girl' like me, anyway. They won't even notice.* She looked as if she had been in a storm—makeup gone, mascara streaked, messy hair, and a pallid look to her skin; she'd seen that look before after a hard-drinking episode.

From the kitchen, Aunt Lucy yelled, "Here they come! Tell 'em to come on in and get ready to eat."

Grace stepped to the screen door to greet the boys, but they were busy flipping out over the new Lexus. "Man, what a ride!" "What a piece of art!" "Cool, man, cool."

Grace listened to their comments and made a mental note to take them for a drive later. She might be brave enough to allow the licensed one to drive. For the present time, though, she must summon them to the kitchen.

The boys trotted up to the porch but ignored the steps; they jumped like playful cats to the porch floor. The taller one said, "I'm Al, and this is my brother, Ronnie. We're your humble escorts for the rest of the day, ma'am." He took his hat off, bowed from the waist, and stepped inside. The younger brother mimicked his brother, giggling.

Grace caught their playful act and responded, "I'm happy to meet you, young knights. Now, let's step to the table of your Granny Lucy and partake of some good nutrition before we set forth on our adventure."

The younger, Ronnie, quickly found his tongue. "Oh, KFC and all the trimmings! Cool!"

Aunt Lucy was barking at them about washing up. "You boys wash your hands. Grace won't appreciate dirty hands and bad manners. And hurry up! There's only so much time left before dark."

As the ice cream was being shoveled, the boys agreed that the Old Parlor still made the best ice cream in town. The older one, Al, offered Grace some practical wisdom. "Ms. Grace, you might want to find some old clothes. That old farm is in rough shape, and you'll ruin your nice clothes. You can't wear shoes like you got on."

Aunt Lucy chimed in, "Just go out there on the back porch, where my housekeeper hangs some old clothes that she wears in the

THE ROAD TO HELL IS PAVED WITH... WHAT?

garden. She won't care if you borrow her stuff. Take whatever you can find and wear some boots. Snakes might be out already."

While the boys had a second helping of the ice cream, Grace borrowed clothes from the gardener's corner of the back screened-in porch. She found herself clad in a pair of coveralls, a flannel shirt, a ball cap, and rubber boots that fit almost comfortably. She dropped several rolls of film in her pocket, strapped her camera across her shoulder, and presented herself for inspection. She thought the boys would laugh, but they took it all in without a snicker. Grace thought, *I was right. No woman of my vintage is worth the notice.*

She was offered the passenger seat in their old Jeep. Grace had never ridden in an open Jeep with a windshield and what looked like a crude, handmade roll bar over the top. There was no back seat at all; Ronnie took a standing position, holding on to the roll bar. That old Jeep had been around a while and showed evidence of some rough going.

Ronnie warned Grace, "You have to duck and hold on when we go under some of the limbs. Just hold on to something. It gets rough. This ride ain't your pretty Lexus."

The road was paved for the first couple of miles as they drove north, but then it suddenly ended near a fork in the road. During the ride, Grace had noticed several homes along the road that were not there when she was young; most of the area had been pastureland, cornfields, and hay. At the fork in the road, the old Jeep took an abrupt sharp turn to the left, following an incline into the woods. The driver slowed the Jeep and geared it to a crawl.

Grace knew the direction they should take, but she was appalled at the condition of the road. The trees had grown over the little narrow road, shading the whole area, and the rainwater had apparently washed all the gravel out of the roadbed. There was bare rock jutting up where gravel should have been, and the ditches along the sides of the road were muddy holes full of trash and limbs. The old round galvanized tiles that were supposed to carry water under the road were crammed with limbs and trash. Grace couldn't believe the neglect. Grandpa Lawson spent many a day of his life keeping the road graveled and the ditches clean so the galvanized tiles could do their job carrying the water under the road to creeks below.

Al was busy keeping the old Jeep as level as he could, picking a way through the jutting rock that might be workable. Ronnie was busy keeping the low-hanging branches from hanging up in the roll bar. Here and there, Al simply took a detour off the rocks and through the woods, deliberately missing some of the worst of the rocks.

Grace was thinking, *Oh my stars, Grandpa Lawson would never have let this happen. He would have worked himself to death before he let it go this far.* She was feeling so appalled and annoyed she didn't see it coming.

Ronnie yelled, "Hang on, Ms. Grace, here we go!"

Al accelerated the Jeep and plunged into the creek that flowed across the road. Grace had always crossed the creek on an old log that spanned the creek and allowed foot traffic. She had never crossed that creek in a vehicle, certainly not an open one. She grabbed for the windshield as the water splashed up the sides of the Jeep. The old Jeep lurched its way across and spun sideways as it climbed the opposite bank. Grace was hanging onto the windshield and screaming, "Oh my lord! Oh my lord!"

The Jeep climbed up the opposite bank and stopped; the boys doubled up in laughter. Of course, Grace didn't see the humor. She sat down, took some long breaths, and tried to calm herself. When she found her voice, she said, "Okay, guys, unless you are interested in having me whine to your Granny Lucy about this little bit of fun, don't scare me again. Is this a deal, or do we have to negotiate further? You know your granny doesn't cut much slack with this kind of thing. Deal, or no deal?"

After they apologized, Al asked, "Will you let us drive the Lexus sometime?" Ronnie was nodding. Their agreement negotiated, they moved on up the ridge to spot the old rusty-roofed barn beginning to show up in the distance.

The road was steep, but it leveled off where Grace remembered the old pastures used to be. Smaller, younger trees, brushy undergrowth, briars, and bushes were everywhere, blocking the view of the flowing creek on the right. Grandpa had kept his range animals along the creek in spots where they could reach the water. Grace remembered looking for the new spring calves around that part of the creek.

She was caught up in her memories when the dilapidated old barn came into view. The rusty old tin roof hung over a two-storied structure covering the hayloft above and the stables below. The barn had aged and looked a bit neglected. The door to the upper loft was missing, and the double doors below were chained together, hanging at a lopsided angle, a lock dangling from the chains. Grandpa Lawson had held the doors together with a horizontal board across both doors, held up by wooden slots built for just that purpose. Grace was busy staring at the barn and was about to ask about the lock, but she found the old Jeep turning to the left toward the back door of the house.

"Where are we going?" she asked. "Why are we going to the back? And where is the grape orchard?"

The boys were quiet. The backyard, which used to be Granny Lawson's busy area, was now a beaten-down, dirty area with horse tracks and manure all around; the whole area between the back door and the barn looked like an overused horse corral with no fence.

Grace asked, "Why aren't we going to the front?"

The boys were quiet again. Grace pushed. "Okay, guys, what's with the silence? What's this all about? I need to know. Let's have some answers. Give me some direction, okay?"

Al spoke up. "We can't go in the front anymore. It's too risky. And the porch has sagged—too many snakes around the old steps, and the boards on the porch have rotted. It's too dangerous."

He was short with his answer, too short. Grace tried another tactic. "Your granny didn't tell me about this, that everything is locked up. I can see there won't be any access to the house. Com'on, guys, what's the deal about this? What's going on?"

Young Ronnie began stuttering with an explanation. "Ms. Grace, somebody rents the old place for riding and hunting, and they keep their things in the house and the barn, you know, and we are not supposed to bother it."

Grace couldn't believe her ears. "It's rented? By whom? Your granny didn't tell me about that. She doesn't know, does she? Why are we keeping that a secret?"

In an attempt to change the focus, Al jumped in. "Hey, we can take you up the creek a ways, and you can take some pictures of the laurels. They're about to bloom. Wanna do that?"

Grace looked from one to the other of the brothers; she could tell something was being withheld. Her experience with young students had trained her well to sense some avoidance going on around the truth.

"Guys," she said, "I need to know why this place is chained up and why Aunt Lucy doesn't know about it being rented. And I need to know who rents it. Which one of you wants to tell the truth?"

Young Ronnie took the lead while his brother glared at him. "Ms. Grace, you can't tell Granny. You have to promise you won't tell."

Grace held up crossed fingers, indicating secrets kept, and she promised, "No blabbing to Granny. You got my word, as long as you tell the truth."

Al took the lead, after he had glared at his brother sufficiently. "Ms. Grace, that lawyer Bob Henderson and his buds rent the place for their weekend riding and hunting clubs, and they stash their beer and things in the house. Sometimes they bunk in there, play cards and gamble. You know how that is…" He trailed off and looked away.

Grace answered, "Granny Lucy would never allow such a thing, and certainly she would never accept money for someone to use the place for drinking and gambling. My goodness, guys, if she knew about this, she would have an old-fashioned conniption."

Ronnie piped up, "What's a *conniption*?"

Grace replied, "Something related to a fatal heart attack…after she tries to murder whoever allowed this to happen. She considers this old place her family heritage, and she would never let it go to something like this. Whom is Henderson paying the money to? It certainly won't be your granny."

THE ROAD TO HELL IS PAVED WITH... WHAT?

Al hung his head for a few seconds, then with a very pained expression, he explained, "Ms. Grace, you don't know this, but our family fell into some real hard times after Dad got hurt, and Henderson offered Mom a hundred and fifty dollars a month if she and Dad would rent the place to him. Mom said the old place was going to ruin, anyway, and it wouldn't hurt anybody. We're not going to tell Granny because we need the money. That's the truth."

Grace was stunned. She was thinking, *One hundred and fifty bucks for the right to house horses, riders, alcohol...and carry out a gambling operation where no sheriff would think to look. I see! No wonder Henderson wants the property. How much is he making? Lord, I will not stop until I strangle him.* But quickly she gathered her wits about her and thanked the boys for their honesty. "You're right, guys, no talking about this to your granny...heavens, no."

Ronnie was elated, and he rattled on, "Yeah, me and Al can come up and sneak a beer or two from their stash. We know how to get in the house."

Al yelled at Ronnie, "Shut up, man! You talk too much!" But Ronnie was already pulling Grace around the corner of the old house to show her where the stash could be found.

The old house was an L-shaped structure with old-fashioned clapboard siding. It sat facing the creek, which was a few hundred yards to the east, with the old east ridge towering over the creek. The gurgling flow of the creek could be clearly heard from the front porch, which spanned the entire length of the house. On the south end of the porch, the old porch roof had collapsed from the outside edge, and it hung from the roof, dangling over the old porch swing.

The old swing was still hanging from its hook near the wall of the house; the outside edge had collapsed with the roof.

Ronnie was showing Grace how he could crawl under the old swing near the wall of the house and open a window to the rear bedroom area. He and Al could crawl in and find beer and other goodies, and they often did, according to him. Grace was listening to Ronnie while Al was giving his brother a grimacing glare.

Grace tried to keep her breathing even, her face straight, emotions in check. Recalling some of the slogans of recovery, she silently recited to herself, *Do not go to every fight you are invited to, and don't start fights of your own. Just listen and let the truth present itself. Don't overreact.* She decided to walk away for a few minutes.

"Guys," Grace said, "why don't you go on up and wash the Jeep in the creek or something? I need to go look at the old springhouse and get a cold drink from the spring. I'll be back in a bit. And no filching beer today, okay? That is breaking and entering where I'm from. We don't need that, not today."

*****

Grace made her way along a horse trail in a northwesterly direction across a small ridge and into a ravine where she knew the old spring would be. That small ridge ran south from the higher mountains above, which bordered the National Forest lands. The water source for the spring poured in a constant stream down through the interior of the ridge and came out in a channel in the cliffs below. The water was clean, clear, and cool.

Granny Lawson had prided herself on that source of clean water, and she used it exclusively for cooking and canning her vegetables. Grandpa Lawson, being something of a rock mason, had constructed a lovely stone facade at the opening where the stream of water came out of the rock and fell into a spring hole below. Granny Lawson and Grace had carried rock for weeks to construct that arched facade, and Grandpa had built some rock benches to match his artwork. The hole where the water fell was expanded and lined with beautiful rock as well. The overflow from the "spring hole" flowed south, through the pastureland below, and served as a water source for the animals.

Grace was walking along the trail, reminiscing about the old days, and she nearly missed the old springhouse where Granny Lawson kept the fresh fruits and vegetables. That springhouse was built under a willow tree just to the side of the spring where the food could be kept cool. The tree had grown much older and had spread itself all over the building. Grace was staring at it when she noticed a chain and lock had the door secured. She also noticed that the tree roots had pushed the little building into a tilted position; it appeared to be ready to collapse.

As Grace moved past the springhouse toward the area where the water flowed from the cliffs into the spring below, she was horrified. The place was full of mud and horse manure; the spring hole had been tromped down, and the water was running down the overflow branch, a dirty stream. She nearly screamed, "Are you kidding me? A water hole for horses? Who would dare ruin this beautiful spot, this stonework?"

She made it to one of the old rock benches before she collapsed. She noticed that Grandpa's rockwork was all covered with what looked like kudzu vines and wild ivy. The tears poured as sobs racked her body; the pain in her heart was unbearable. She began vomiting the chicken and ice cream she had eaten earlier. She began shaking all over. She failed to notice the patch of poison oak that had grown over the bench where she was sitting.

Recovery friends had taught Grace a few things she would need to remember during the tough, emotional times. She tried to bring them to mind. *Feel the feelings. Like clouds, they come and go. The sun comes out again. Acknowledge the pain, accept its message, and then move on. Write a gratitude list. The sun comes up tomorrow. Don't allow emotions to rule your behavior. Pray, pray, pray. God is listening.* Grace decided to try the praying first; she was totally out of control.

Grace put her head down on her knees and hoped God would be listening. "Okay, Lord," she said, "I'm feeling outraged about this mess and the disrespect that I'm seeing. My poor old grandparents worked hard to make more out of the little they had. They taught me to work as well. I'm grateful for that. But what I'm seeing here defiles their life's work, and I'm furious that anyone would do this. Bobby Henderson is paying a few measly dollars to destroy everything Grandpa and Granny worked for. It's a disgrace! I can't stand it, Lord, I just can't stand it. I have to do something."

In a sudden movement, Grace jumped to her feet, held out pleading hands to the sky, and asked a question. "Did You bring me back to clean this up? What can I do about it? What do You want me to do? I am listening, God. I promise, I am listening."

Grace began pacing back and forth across the area, muttering to herself. Soon she noticed a strange quiet beginning to settle in the area. She heard the birds singing, the water splashing from the cliffs as it had for centuries, and the serene gurgling of the overflow branch making its way south. Words from an old Bible came to mind: "Be still and know." She took that to mean "walk in faith." She looked toward the mountains, remembering strength *cometh from the Lord who made heaven and earth.* She lifted her arms in surrender, bowing her head. She began to feel peaceful, and she started walking back to the old house.

*****

The old Jeep horn was blowing, and Grace hurried along. The boys were ready to go, and she would have to be strong enough to handle them, especially if they had snitched any beer.

Ronnie was yelling, "Come on, Ms. Grace, we have to be back before dark!"

Grace answered, "I'm coming! I'm coming!"

As she climbed into the Jeep, the boys were glancing at her from the sides of their eyes. She apologized, "Sorry, guys. I haven't been here in a very long time, and it brought back memories. Had to do some bawling, you know, like most females. I'll get it together."

The boys weren't buying it. Al spoke first. "Why did you stay away so long, Ms. Grace? Why didn't you come back before?"

Grace tried to think of a way to answer that might satisfy young minds. She took a deep breath and simply told the truth. "When I was about your age, I was on my way to school one morning and I stopped to put some out-going mail in the old mailbox for Grandpa. There were some loggers that had contracted with Grandpa to cut pulpwood up on the ridge east of the creek. They spotted me, grabbed me, and had their fun with my body up by their camp. You understand?"

The boys were quiet, but they nodded, looking to Grace for the rest of the story.

She went on, "Soon after that, I found I was pregnant, and Grandpa and his church elders thought it best to send me to a girls' school, where I had a baby boy that I never got to see. After that, I was enrolled in an educational system where I spent the next twelve years. When that was over, I transferred to a university, where I've been teaching all these years. I never really wanted to come back. It's a long tale. I don't really understand it myself, but I think God has called me back for His own reasons. We'll see."

Ronnie, ever the talky one, spoke up. "Well, if God brought you back, it might be to please Granny. She's been praying about you for years."

Al offered his opinion. "Yeah, she has. She says you didn't get treated right by the church or anybody else. Says that's why we need to help you now. Tells us to do everything we can to help make it right."

Grace high-fived the boys with a smile and said, "Thank you, guys. I know you mean it, and I'll need your help, I'm sure. Now, let's get on home before your granny gets mad with us. And no tricks at the old creek this time, okay?"

The boys were mostly quiet on the way home and dropped Grace off in the yard, reminding her of the promise to drive the Lexus. The old Jeep hightailed it south toward home.

*****

Aunt Lucy was waiting with questions. Grace had to be careful with the answers—no lying to her dear old aunt. She described the general neglect and erosion of the old road, the condition of the buildings, and the extreme need for clearing and landscaping.

Aunt Lucy commented, "Well, I thought it might be a good mess. Nobody's been able to keep it up for years. Can we get it cleaned up and fixed up again?"

Grace answered, "Yeah, sure we can. I didn't see much that would be beyond help, Aunt Lucy. Even the old chimney can be reworked. There's a lot of work, but we can do it. We'll have to get the title cleared first before we start." Grace sounded more enthusiastic than she was feeling.

Aunt Lucy nodded with enthusiasm and sounded joyful about the whole thing. She told Grace, "My housekeeper brought in some of your grandpa's boxes from the shed. She says there's an old trunk out there that is stuck to the floor. It got wet somewhere along the line, and it won't budge. The kids looked in and said there is no sign of a last will and testament. Grace, you have my full permission to look anywhere you might find something. I've been blind for a long time, and I miss a lot of things. You've got to look at your grandpa's house again. We've missed something someplace. That man made his last will and testament, I know he did, and there is a witness still alive who says he remembers the same thing."

"Aunt Lucy," Grace asked, "would you mind loaning me your telephone to make some calls? I'm going to talk to some people who might be able to help us out. My cell phone won't work in this area. I'll be sure to pay your next phone bill."

*****

The two ladies chatted away over some ice cream for a while, and then Aunt Lucy clicked her old cane and headed down the hallway toward her bed.

Grace picked up the phone, planted herself under a reading lamp, took pad and pen in hand, and began to consider who she could call for help. Her friends would all be willing to lend their expertise; she just needed to ask. She knew she couldn't go it alone. Her body was revolting with withdrawal syndrome, and she was craving way too much sugar. She also knew the old farm was being coveted by Lawyer Henderson for a reason. She was determined to put his backside in a crack for the disrespect of the land and the paltry sum he was paying for its use. Her instincts told her she would have a fight.

Her instincts would prove to be right on target. The old farm place would be under surveillance before the week was out, and shortly thereafter, Henderson's butt would be in jail.

That man had pushed his arrogance and presumptuousness way too far. Grace was ready to fight.

Friends of Grace

Grace sat in her aunt Lucy's old chair, phone in hand, talking to herself quietly. "Okay, which of my friends could help here? I'm simply not able to go it alone at this point. Which of these good, supportive friends do I need to speak to? You lead, Lord, and I'll follow."

*****

Grace's friends, her support group, were an alcoholics anonymous group where she had been attending for weeks. The court had mandated that she attend ninety meetings in ninety days, a common occurrence for offenders who wished to avoid jail time or yet another rehabilitation experience. Grace had gone through a rehab clinic just a few months prior to being arrested for DUI while driving on campus. Needless to say, she had to use all her persuasive power to convince the regulatory board that she was simply drinking with friends at a party and didn't realize. Blah, blah, blah. The board didn't buy her excuses because she had been, in their words, "a recurring problem." They lauded her ability to teach, her rapport with most of her students, and her dedication to her job; however, they would not tolerate another offense. They couldn't have made it clearer: Grace would lose her position, and where would she go from there? They couldn't recommend her to another college, under the circumstances. That scared Grace into whatever-it-takes. She took herself to every twelve-step meeting she could find in the area, except those close to campus, of course.

*****

Alcoholics Anonymous, and most all recovery groups, use the twelve-step program to share their "experience, strength, and hope," in an effort to support and encourage one another to deal with life and its challenges without the use and abuse of alcohol, drugs, substances, or habitual behaviors that are distracting and destructive. Members share their own personal stories of recovery, their struggles and their progress in the program. With an attitude of "each one, reach one, and teach one," they sponsor (support) one another and work to "pass it on" to others who are struggling with the same thing.

Some attendees remain with their respective twelve-step programs for years and are known to be the go-to people for their experience, knowledge, and spiritual understanding. The spiritual strength they embody can have a phenomenal impact on the rest of the attendees. They instill hope, lives are changed, nonbelievers come to believe, and miracles happen. Desperate people hear some good news; a higher power is available and, with cooperation of a willing spirit, can take the most tragic of circumstances and turn them around for good. One must be "willing" to put faith into practice and walk away from the self-destructive habits that have developed. It can be done with the unconditional understanding and love of those who have suffered and recovered, who have been restored to a better life than they ever imagined. They stand as a witness to the lost.

*****

Grace had been lost, for sure, as she made her way around the big metropolis trying to find yet another group to attend; ninety meetings in ninety days had begun to wear a bit thin. The city was big enough, and Grace thought she might try the low-rent districts, where she wouldn't be known. She left one Thursday evening to find a small church in a remote part of town.

The little church, located in an older part of the city, apparently in a densely populated area, was teeming with people on the streets and kids riding bicycles in their midst. Grace sat in her car for a long time before she decided to go in. She was greeted by an older lady who came walking up the sidewalk on a cane. The lady smiled at

Grace and summoned her to come on out and speak with her. She asked Grace, "Are you looking for the AA meeting? We got the best one around. Com'on in and meet some of us."

Grace tagged along with the nice lady, hoping she could just sit quietly and count off another of her "assigned" chores, but it didn't go exactly as she had hoped. The group called her out; with love and understanding, they explained, "That old trick won't fly in this group." Despite herself, Grace opened right up and found herself talking away about things she never intended to say. She felt completely understood and accepted. That group became her "home group," even though she had to drive quite a distance to attend. She couldn't bring herself to miss a meeting; something compelled her to pay attention. Something she couldn't explain.

Shortly after that first meeting, the origins of the twelve-step movement became a fascination for Grace. Being the academic person that she was, she began researching the various groups that had come out of the original concept of the AA movement and the worldwide ministry that had followed. She became an apostle, so to speak, of the twelve-step philosophy and its power to change lives.

Comparing the twelve-step approach to her experience in Grandpa's time, Grace understood a little about why Grandpa Lawson had preached an ole-time religion that he believed, but he couldn't seem to find the power to manifest it in his own life, or to stay on track with his own teachings. Grace said, "Neither could I, Grandpa, neither could I."

While doing research on the genetics involved with addictive personalities, Grace considered her family tree. The various old stories she could recall about some of the ancestors spoke about their "moonshining" habits and customs of using corn liquor and honey for their medicines. Grace remembered being administered plenty of that concoction most of her young years. Honestly, she had enjoyed most of it; pain went away, and she could sleep or sing better. It had its advantages for sure.

Unfortunately, somewhere along the line, the use became a dependency, and it never occurred to Grace that any harm was being done. Her research in alcoholism brought out the truth; Grace was a self-destructive addict, hooked on alcohol from the very beginning, and the result would be disastrous. Her professional life was in peril, her financial life would collapse, and the physical body wouldn't sustain itself under the onslaught of the poison: liver failure, heart disease, and dementia would be her fate. Grace was scared to death; she made up her mind with conviction. She told her group, "Whatever it takes, I'm not going to wind up in the same place where I started years ago. I've been in humiliation and poverty already. I won't let this happen to me again." She developed an urgent need to dig into the twelve steps and see if she could make some progress toward healing.

*****

Step 1 of the program spoke of "powerlessness" over alcohol, and Grace didn't exactly care for the word, but she soon came to realize that her habits were ingrained to a stubbornly resistant degree. She couldn't just ignore her need for a drink, especially when she went home at night. Generally, she made it home with her favorite "night toddy" already half-consumed, and she had the rest before bedtime. Grace had to look at the volume she was consuming, and her bank statements revealed that a big percentage of her budget was going to the liquor stores.

Step 2 didn't faze Grace. She already knew she would need to believe in a higher power greater than herself, but she thought she hadn't gone completely "insane," as step 2 suggested. She was convinced she could catch on before that happened, of course.

Step 3 spoke of "turning our will and our lives over to the care of God, as we understand Him." Grace had a problem with that. The God of her understanding had never heard a thing she had prayed for, never seemed to notice her existence or taken any interest in her plight. Grace might have to believe in the group's faith and hope they were right. Maybe God would reveal His identity somewhere along the line. She had her doubts.

The fourth step, involving the "personal inventory," didn't make any sense to Grace. The group assured her that she'd find some answers for her self-destructive habits and the emotional turmoil in her heart if she'd have a look at her life's experiences objectively and think about her formative years without "shaming, blaming, complaining, explaining, proclaiming, and throwing fault at others." The past would have to be accepted as "It is what it is," and Grace would need to be responsible for her attitude toward it. The group advised, "Be grateful that you can start over, take responsibility for yourself, and allow the higher power to guide you. Accept your experiences, look for the good in all of it, don't take the hard stuff so seriously. We all have our heartbreak and hard times. Be grateful and walk in faith. God will restore your life to good purpose. Be willing to trust Him."

When it came to examining her past, Grace could only manage a willingness to be willing to do that. The group kept pushing her, and she thought a psychiatrist might suffice; at least then she could get that crazy fourth step off the plate. Unknown to her, the psychiatrist that the group recommended had been a member of the same group. He nailed her with, "Grace, are you still living in an early stage of your life where so much damage occurred that you have stalled out in your emotional growth and development? Wouldn't you like to give up the victim role? How does that serve your life now? You're trying to cope with old damage with a dependency on alcohol to soothe your emotions, and that leads to destruction, if not death. In the meantime, you will manage to destroy your own life's work. Is that going to be acceptable to you?"

Grace made a promise to herself and her recovery group that she would make every effort to leave the alcohol alone and walk through her old, painful memories in an effort to work the fourth step "personal inventory" as required. She had several voluntary sponsors who helped make a list of places to revisit and experiences to reconsider. The old Bethel Baptist Church quickly rose to the top of the list of places to begin the process. Grace had started there with a vengeance.

*****

Now, just one day after that rebellious and haughty appearance at the old Baptist church, Grace sat in her aunt Lucy's living room, phone in hand, looking at the list of numbers she could call for support.

Before she lost her nerve, she dialed the number of one of the oldest and more professional members of the group, a man who identified himself as Spotter. This man was a retired police lieutenant, having retired after many years of admitted "closet alcoholism" and the loss of his family as a result of his habit. He now worked part-time doing investigative work for the Drug Enforcement Agency. He chose the moniker Spotter because, he said, it explained his job.

Grace quickly explained to her friend what she had seen at the old farm place, her concerns about the stash of alcohol, the illegal locks on the doors, and how the young boys were snitching the alcohol. Spotter got the lowdown on the status of ownership of the property. He began to ask questions and was obviously jotting down names, addresses, and personal information about Lawyer Henderson. He asked Grace questions about herself, as to her full name, etc. Grace interrupted him. She asked, "Why do you need all this personal information, Spotter? We aren't supposed to share, you know."

He answered, "You asked me for help, Grace, and it is my professional opinion that you've got something illegal going on around that property, and you tell me it's secluded. That's a good place for an operation where business can be conducted without question and nobody would be the wiser. Horse riding and camping may not be the primary objective. You need someone in law enforcement to check it out."

"Who can I call, Spotter? I don't know where to begin," Grace said.

Spotter reassured Grace, "You are not alone in this, Grace. That is too risky. I'll make some calls, talk to some people for you, and then you get ready to have someone call to check it out. You follow the directions they give you. I'll be in touch."

Grace tried to thank Spotter, but he already ended the call. Her hands were shaking as she phoned another member of the group. She thought, *Perhaps* this *one won't be willing to scare the dickens out of me.*

The familiar voice of Pastor answered her call. This man was known as Pastor because he was the leader of the little church where the recovery group met every Thursday. Pastor never missed a meeting. He had arrived at that little church over ten years ago, and now his "little church" had grown from twelve or fifteen people to more than two hundred and fifty. The smaller church couldn't hold the crowd, and a new church was constructed just a few blocks away. However, Pastor insisted his little church be used by twelve-step recovery groups, helping the community where he had started.

Pastor's story of recovery was well-known to the various recovery groups. He told it with delight. He was invited to speak at conventions and seminars held by twelve-step groups all around the state. He laughingly referred to himself as "moving on up," but he never declined to speak of his days as a young man, raised in poverty and sent to prison for crimes against his own people. He said God called him out in that prison to minister to his young cellmates. He saw many of his own young people come in off the streets, already so messed up they would never have a chance to recover.

Pastor was serving twenty years, and God called him to spend his time ministering to the young "brothers." He taught the Bible, taught the twelve-step program, comforted the lost, and preached the gospel. Upon release, Pastor had landed at the first "little church" with nothing but a Bible under his arm. He quickly opened the doors to all twelve-step groups and offered himself as a living witness to God's grace and power. That little church had grown faster than anyone expected, and the bigger church was now full—praise the Lord.

In the recovery meetings, Pastor was tough as nails on what he referred to as dabblers; he called them out for sitting back, wasting time, twiddling their thumbs, just waiting on easy answers. He had been the first to get in Grace's face about "scratching off the meeting list." He told her, "You don't get to intellectualize, you have to internalize, the Word of God. You might be too smart for your own good, Grace."

Grace knew he was right, although she really didn't understand it completely. She could find an academic explanation for just about everything except the question, "Where is God when you need Him?" She didn't question the existence of the Creator; she doubted His involvement with His creation. She and Pastor had a few debates over that issue.

Now, with Pastor on the line, Grace had to ask him for prayer. She sobbed out her story of the withdrawal syndrome and how she had been throwing up and shaking all over. She spoke of the terror she was feeling. Pastor listened a bit, then he laughed as he consoled her. "Grace, I've never been in a place where God sent me that I wasn't scared out of my wits. I still get that way sometimes. I figure it's the same feeling that most all the old stories of the Bible talk about. When God called Moses and all the rest, not one of them felt up to the job He sent them to do. I think if we felt competent, we wouldn't be teachable. God needs us to rely on Him and learn as we go. It's called faith, Grace. Now, what else has got you confused?"

Grace explained her predicament with the old farm. Pastor summed it up in a few words. "Grace, you start with law enforcement and good legal counsel. Don't back down. Now let's pray for strength and power to get you through this." He began his prayer with sincere gratitude and asked God for strength for His servant Grace. Grace thanked Pastor for helping and sincerely thanked God for sending such a dear friend to walk with her.

*****

The old clock on Aunt Lucy's living room wall had Grace believe she had been on the phone for a couple of hours. The praying had helped stabilize her emotions, and her hands had quit shaking. She made a quiet trip to the refrigerator, where she found some leftover chicken and milk. She finished with that, then found a bag of chocolate cookies in the pantry. She was munching the cookies when the phone rang. She snatched the phone so it wouldn't wake her aunt. When she answered, a male voice asked, "Could I speak with Grace Lawson, please?"

Grace replied, "That would be me. How may I help you?"

The man explained who he was and the reason for his call. "We've been informed by a man you know as Spotter that you have a situation we might be interested in, concerning some property that your family owns. Is that correct?"

Grace knew she'd have to answer his questions. These people worked for the government, and they were a seriously demanding group—at least they were portrayed that way. She answered every question he asked as best as she could and made sure to iterate "This is what I know at this time." She made sure he understood about the ownership status of the property. She explained about the boys, Al and Ronnie, and what they were able to find on the premises. She said she suspected the property had been rented without proper documentation nearly ten years ago, when the boys' father was injured in an accident and the family had no income.

The conversation was ending as the man said, "Ms. Lawson, you'll be hearing from law enforcement shortly on this matter. You will be asked to meet with those in charge and show them exactly what concerns you."

Grace thought she'd better inform him about the condition of the road. "You'll need a Jeep or something to access the old farm. There's a creek that has to be forded, and the road is rough and elevated. Ordinary cars can't access the property now."

"Ma'am, we have all-terrain vehicles for just that purpose. We'll get it done. You keep this very confidential. Don't speak to anyone about it until we see what goes on, okay?"

The man said a quick goodbye, and Grace helped herself to some more of the cookies. She began to have some doubts. *What if my reaction is overboard? What if I'm wrong? What if Spotter is wrong?* She recalled Spotter's words, "Don't back down, Grace. You need to get junk like that off the property. You'll never live with yourself if you don't fight for your family legacy. You may be the only one who can."

Pastor's counsel had been, "The Lord calls His chosen people out of their weakness into His power, Grace. You follow where He leads you and don't look back. You'll be amazed where He may take you."

Munching on the last of the cookies, Grace was thinking, *Well, you know, I would be happy to follow God's will if I could understand it. God needs a fax machine, a cell phone, or an overnight message system delivered to the door. I don't have a problem with instructions, I got a problem with walking blind. That scares me. I just want to drink, or eat. Sometimes I feel a need to just yell at God, but I drink instead. Now I'm eating everything in sight. Maybe Pastor is right: if I quit fighting and surrender, be willing to go where He sends me, God will empower me. I can pray for that.*

Grace was giving that idea much thought when the phone rang again. She grabbed it quick and responded, "This is Grace."

A male voice replied, "I'm Sheriff Cosby, Ms. Grace, and we've been asked to look at some property that your family owns. Would it be possible to meet us around daylight in the morning so we can get in and out before the day starts?"

Grace answered, "Sheriff, you will have to bring an all-terrain vehicle, and I'll have to ride with you. I can manage to be ready if you'll stop by my aunt Lucy's place and pick me up. Aunt Lucy lives on the main road just north of Bethel Baptist Church."

"Your aunt Lucy, would that be Lucy Bradford?" the sheriff asked. "Would she be available to talk to us? We might need her permission to examine the property, make sure we don't upset anybody."

Grace answered, "Yes, she'll be available. She gets up early. I'll be sure she is prepared. We'll be waiting."

The sheriff said goodbye.

Grace went into a tailspin of doubt, thinking, *Why so early? Maybe the old sheriff's office is busy and they want to dispense with this little chore before the doughnuts get stale, get it out of the way and move on. Oh well, nothing to do but get ready and let them have a laugh about this.*

On the back porch, Grace found some more of the gardener's clothes she could use, and she laid them out with the borrowed boots. She collapsed on the old bed and fell asleep.

*****

What she didn't know but would quickly learn, the sheriff had been looking all over the county for a source of illegal drugs that had been in plentiful supply for a number of years, and he couldn't find a clue as to its origins. That old abandoned farm way back there in the head of the remote valley might provide a clue. Early morning, on a Tuesday, might be a good time to have a look. The sheriff was gearing up to find out.

The Old Farm Holds Secrets

The old red rooster hadn't left his perch to make his morning announcements before Grace had quietly showered, dressed, and put her hair in a twist on her head. She was trying to make herself look as presentable as possible for the expected company. She hurried to the kitchen and started the coffee. Her recovery friends had warned her about eating too much sugar, and she'd certainly overdone the cookies and ice cream last evening. She'd had a restless night.

Alcoholics and other addicts make the mistake of what they refer to as a "sugar fix." They crave and eat sugary treats to excess, and as the sugar hits the bloodstream, they feel a false high. Then, when the sugar spike is over, they feel an awful crash. This aggravates and undermines their resolve to stay sober. Grace was learning that the hard way.

Badly in need of her toddy, Grace had tossed and turned most of the night. She decided to rid herself of the ice cream and cookies and cook healthy eggs for breakfast. She prepared eggs, whole wheat toast, a tall glass of milk, and some natural honey for the meal. Sometime later, she could worry about gaining weight. Now, at this time, a healthy mind and body would be good.

Aunt Lucy could be heard tapping her cane down the hallway. She came into the kitchen, asking, "What's up, Grace? I'm smelling food. Are we going somewhere?"

"Come on and eat, Aunt Lucy," Grace said. "We're having company around daylight, and we need to be ready, okay?"

Grace poured the coffee and explained to Aunt Lucy who was expected and why they were coming. She said as much as she dared without upsetting the old soul. "Aunt Lucy, somebody has been using the property without permission, camping and riding horses, and they are damaging the whole place. We've got to get that stopped. The sheriff and his men are going to help us put a stop to it. He needs both of us to grant permission for his intervention. I'm riding with him this morning to show him what belongs to us."

The old aunt cheered right up. "Good idea. I could have done that, but nobody told me about any damage. Why hasn't someone mentioned it? They know I won't put up with anybody damaging that property…no way."

Grace didn't have time to respond; through the kitchen window, she could see vehicle lights moving in the backyard. She watched as a big truck pulling a trailer was parking itself between the back porch and the old garden plot, clearly out of sight. The trailer was hauling two large all-terrain vehicles. Grace flipped on the porch lights and waited.

The sheriff stepped to the porch and approached the kitchen door. Grace slowly opened the door as he introduced himself. "I'm Sheriff Cosby, ma'am, and we're here to help you out."

Grace quickly found her voice. "I'm Grace Lawson, Sheriff. I'm wondering why you came to the back door. You had me scared for a minute."

"Sorry about that," the sheriff said. "We don't like to be obvious. We thought our truck and trailer would be out of sight. Too many curious eyes, you know. Is your aunt Lucy up and about?"

"She's having coffee in the kitchen, and she's expecting you," Grace answered. "Come in and help yourself to the coffee. Clean cups are on the counter. I'll find my boots and be ready in a minute."

The sheriff greeted Aunt Lucy in the kitchen, and they were quietly talking away when Grace slipped out the back and left them to their privacy. Aunt Lucy seemed to be holding her own in the discussion, but then she always did.

As she looked at the all-terrain vehicles with their huge tires, Grace thought, *Well, these things are a lot bigger than that old Jeep. Maybe not as scary, let's hope.*

The sheriff's men introduced themselves as Jim, John, and Drake. They were busy off-loading the vehicles while Grace waited for the sheriff. One of the men helped Grace get settled in the vehicle that was positioned to lead the way. The three men loaded up in the second vehicle, suggesting that Grace would be riding with the sheriff.

The sheriff came out the door, donned his hat, and climbed in beside Grace. The vehicles began to roll. Grace was surprised how quiet the big vehicles were. She marveled that the Lexus might make more noise.

As the procession turned north on the highway, the dawn was just barely beginning to break along the eastern sky. The sheriff made the turn into the woods and was maneuvering his way through the rough terrain when he began to question Grace. "How long has it been since you were here? And tell me, why are you back now?"

Grace thought she'd better answer his questions with as much candor as she could, without telling the whole truth. She narrated a short story about her reason for leaving, but on the second part of his question, she just hedged a bit. "As for why I'm here now, I don't really know. I think God must have sent me back, Sheriff. It looks like I'm responsible for a mess that Grandpa Lawson might have left us. I need to clean it up if I can."

All throughout her story the sheriff kept saying, "Okay, I see."

Upon approaching the creek, the sheriff slowed the vehicle. He hesitated, looking it over.

Grace spoke up. "We crossed it yesterday in a much smaller vehicle. It wasn't too bad. It's the bank on the opposite side that might be a bit steep, I think."

The sheriff geared the vehicle and slipped down the bank into the water. He maneuvered to the opposite side without a blip. The second vehicle followed. Soon they were climbing to higher terrain, and the old barn began to appear, looking like a ghost in the morning mist.

Grace thought she'd better remind the sheriff of something. She said, "Sheriff, everything is locked up, and I'm told Lawyer

Henderson is paying Aunt Lucy's family a paltry bit of money to keep it locked. Aunt Lucy doesn't know about that."

The sheriff asked, "And there's no lease or rental agreement that you know of to support his claim that he has it rented?"

"Absolutely none," Grace replied.

The sheriff turned, looking at Grace, then asked, "And you are the surviving heir of your grandpa Lawson, the only grandchild?"

Grace responded, "I am, absolutely. All we need is Grandpa's last will and testament, and Aunt Lucy says he made it before the elder Lawyer Henderson died. She says the young Henderson is just waiting for her to die and get out of the way. Then he can manipulate the younger kids and steal the property. Of course, he never expected me to appear. Now he's all about stealing the property from me. It's not going to happen."

The sheriff responded, "No, that won't work, but you need to be careful. He may be desperate and dangerous."

The vehicles were parked, and the sheriff's men were trying to look around. The sheriff decided to look at the house first, until the dawn might offer more light. Grace was handed a flashlight, and she guided the men to the front porch, where they could access the house through the scuttle hole under the old collapsed porch roof. One of the men, Drake, stopped at the front door and was examining the lock. He played around with it for a few seconds and said, "Sheriff, we got this. Door is open."

Drake and the sheriff gently pushed the door wide open and swung their flashlights around the space before they stepped into the room. Grace was guided through the door by two men behind. As they carefully scanned the room, Grace was surprised to see bunk beds stacked around the walls of the living area. There was no sign of Granny's furniture.

Farther along the north end of the room, the sheriff and his men walked past the old fireplace and headed to the kitchen, in the west end of the structure. Grace moved along ahead of the two men bringing up the rear. They were busy with lights, scanning everything they could see. Grace stood aside when they reached the kitchen while the men made a thorough inspection.

In the kitchen area, along the back wall where shelves were built to hold the food and kitchen supplies, the men were busy sweeping their lights along the shelves. Something had their attention. One of the taller men had pulled up a chair to stand on, and he was peering along the top of the shelves. He announced, "Sheriff, got something. Looks like a stash of drug paraphernalia…bongs, needles, and other stuff."

The sheriff answered, "Okay, get it filmed and leave it right where we found it, for now."

Drake and the sheriff were inspecting a large table that took up most of the floor space. It was covered with a big blue tarp that hung almost to the floor. On the table were candles, oil lamps, and ashtrays. They carefully moved the folding chairs that circled the table and lifted the tarp. One of the men softly whistled at what he saw. Grace heard him say, "Everything a gambling operation might need except slot machines, right here, Sheriff."

Two of the men were on their knees, filming what they had found. Grace stood dumfounded as they completed their inspection, put everything back in place, and cleaned up behind themselves.

When the job in the kitchen seemed to be over, Grace asked the sheriff, "Could we inspect the bedrooms too? I remember where my grandmother used to keep some of her old records, and I would like to see if her things are still there."

The sheriff nodded and began to walk in her direction. He said, "We have to put everything back as we found it, and we'll help you. Just show us where."

After meticulously covering their tracks, the men moved with Grace back through the living area and into a large space on the south end of the house. Grandpa Lawson had built a closet down the center of a large room and divided it into two bedrooms. He did that to accommodate Grace when she came to live with them when she was six years old. The bigger bedroom ran along the front of the house near the porch. Grace's room was smaller and positioned between the room-dividing closet and the back porch, only a small window for light. Grace had to access her room from the porch, but she didn't mind. The old family toilet was located just yards from the porch, secluded by crepe myrtles. Grace could also sneak through the kitchen and snitch some of Grandpa's good cough syrup; it helped her sleep very well.

The sheriff's team set about inspecting the larger bedroom. Strangely enough, the old antique bed was neatly made, with colorful coverings and fluffy pillows. The room was well decorated, nicely arranged, and clean. The men were about to make an exit when one of them leaned down and pushed the small sliding doors on the old headboard of the antique bed. He said, "Well, look at this, Sheriff. What have we here?"

Grace could see the disgust on the sheriff's face as he looked past the fluffy pillows into the old-style headboard, where one might expect to find books, Bibles, medicine, or tissues. Grace looked to see what they were talking about, but the men were filming. The sheriff turned to Grace and asked, "What was it you wanted to see?"

The sheriff listened carefully as Grace explained how the closet ceiling was built of some leftover paneling that Grandpa Lawson used when he had constructed the walls to divide the room. On one end of the closet, nearest the living area, the paneling could be pushed straight up to provide an entrance to the attic. Grandma Lawson had used that access to the attic to store some of her valuables and put her quilting frames away in the summer. Grace wanted to look in the attic to see if she could locate an "old pickle churn" that Granny used to store her papers and the mementos from her heritage. That pickle churn had been broken around the rim and wouldn't work for pickles, so Granny had turned it into a place for safekeeping. Grace described the churn as a ceramic jug about thirty inches tall, grayish in color, and tied around the top with an old plastic bag covered with a burlap scrap.

The younger men, not sure what a pickle churn might look like, asked Grace if she could stand in the closet access hole and direct them to where this might be located.

Grace pointed out the paneling that could be pushed straight up. The sheriff's men moved in to remove some large boxes that blocked the end of the closet. As they moved the boxes, they discovered the stash of alcoholic beverages the young boys had been snitching. The boxes were full of different brands of booze. The men grabbed their cameras. After filming, they stacked the boxes to serve as something of a ladder so they could access the closet and the attic.

One of the men carefully stepped up on the boxes, pushed the paneling straight up, and moved it to the side. Some loose insulation fell around his feet as he lifted himself into the black hole and scanned with the flashlight. He said, "Come on, Ms. Grace, show me where to look. It's spooky up here. And bring a bigger flashlight too."

Grace followed his lead, but she didn't stop at the opening. She lifted herself through the black hole and grabbed for the wooden posts she knew were there. She stood on the rafters, holding on to the overhead crossbeams, balancing herself. As her companion manned the big flashlight, she wiped at the cobwebs and carefully made her way from rafter to rafter until she came to a place where she thought she might find something. She scratched the insulation away from a couple of spots, but nothing showed up. Grace was convinced that the old churn would be somewhere close. As she looked down, on her way back the way she had come, she noticed a strange lump under the insulation that she had missed in her haste. She stooped, trying to brace her feet, stretched herself across the space between the rafters, and pulled the insulation away from the strange lump. The old pickle churn appeared, still clad in its burlap cap, looking a little faded and worn but appearing to be intact. The man who had been tracing her steps with the light and watching her carefully just whistled quietly. That brought the other men, and she heard the sheriff ask, "You two all right? What do you need?"

The filming was done with Grace lying on her stomach, stretched out over the rafters, staring at the old churn. She was trying to hold that position, but the men had to come to her rescue. They picked her up by her arms and helped her stand, holding on to the crossbeams overhead. The old pickle churn was handed off, and Grace was about to leave the space when she noticed that something had fallen into the space where the churn had been resting. She bent down to see a small metal box that she recognized as her grandpa's toolbox for his small wrenches and screwdrivers. The box was well rusted, but Grace handed it to one of the men. She noticed a dull thud sound in the box when she handed it over.

As the team helped Grace exit the attic, they carefully replaced the paneling and arranged the boxes of alcoholic beverages back in the space exactly as they had been found.

The sheriff was looking at the old pickle churn. He asked, "Do you want to look at this now, see what you've found?"

Grace took the hint and began to pull the old burlap off the mouth of the churn. She poured out the contents. Granny Lawson had stored her birth certificate, the history of her Cherokee heritage, and some old pictures of her original family along with a few mementos of her tribal customs. A few loose coins were in the bottom of the churn, but nothing else of interest except the beloved granny's keepsakes.

The sheriff handed the metal toolbox to Grace. He had been running his knife blade around the rusty edges of the lid on the box. He said, "Here, this belongs to you. You get to open it."

Inside the rusty toolbox was a long envelope wrapped in a plastic bag and tied with yarn. The sheriff and his men were watching as Grace carefully untied the yarn, unrolled the plastic, and pulled the envelope out. On the top left-hand corner of the envelope, Grace read, "The Law Office of Robert T. Henderson, Esquire." The letter was addressed to Thomas A. Lawson and mailed to his address.

The men gathered around as Grace unfolded the legal-size papers. She began to read, "The last will and testament of Thomas A. Lawson." She began to cry. The men were cheering her on. The sheriff interrupted, saying, "Ms. Grace, this is wonderful, but we'll have plenty of time to read the whole thing later. Let's get the job done. Daylight's breaking. We need to be out of here before too long."

They made a quick inspection of the second bedroom, Grace's old hangout, and then turned their attention to the barn.

While two of the men were assigned to the barn, the sheriff and Drake followed Grace to the springhouse. Again, Drake made fast work of the lock on the door and the two men stepped in. Grace waited outside, but she noticed the sheriff was kicking at some dried grass and leaves on the floor. Ice coolers had been stacked to the ceiling all around the walls. The men quickly backed out of the little building and put the lock back in place.

The sheriff was shaking his head in disgust as he looked at the waterfall and the old spring hole. Drake had pulled his radio off his belt and was listening as he walked toward the overflow branch that ran from the spring down through the overgrown pastures. He motioned to the sheriff, saying, "They have found something. They're coming right up this branch."

The sheriff remarked sarcastically, "I just bet they have."

Surveying the property, the sheriff could see that the branch was running down a ravine surrounded by the mountains to the west and hidden behind the overgrown trees and bushes to the east. The sheriff and Drake walked a few yards down the branch, and someone whistled from below. Drake answered the whistle with a birdlike warble. Soon the men were seen coming up the branch, following a trail. As they approached, the sheriff and Drake walked to meet them. Grace stood by the old springhouse feeling weak, but curious.

The sheriff was wiping at his forehead when he came up the hill. Grace had to ask, "What have they found, Sheriff?"

With a pained expression, the sheriff said quietly to Grace, "There's a farming operation going on, marijuana growing all along this branch. These men followed the trail through the back of the barn, across the bottomland, and straight to the branch. These coolers in the shed are used to store and transport the stuff when it's harvested."

One of the men came to show Grace what they had found. She stared at the pictures, but they looked normal to her. When the man flipped to the close-up frames, Grace could clearly understand what he was seeing. The man said quietly, "It's a big operation, and a perfect place, secluded from the world, water flowing right through, free of charge, beds for the workers, entertainments and plenty to enjoy—all the perks. I couldn't have done it better myself."

Suddenly, the men seemed to be in a hurry to leave. They loaded up, and with Grace holding on to her treasures from the attic, they turned south toward the exit. On the way out, the sheriff summed the whole thing up for Grace: illegal gambling, suspected prostitution, illegal alcohol and drugs, marijuana farming and transportation, and the illegal use of private property.

And of course, anything else that could be found. He warned Grace that she would have to keep very quiet and give them a chance to work. "You can't talk about this to anybody, Ms. Grace. Give us enough time to make our investigations and put the place under surveillance. We need to lock the place down whenever the action is going on, then we get everybody at the same time."

Grace assured the sheriff that she would not talk to a soul. The sheriff handed her a pen, saying, "Write down this lawyer's name and take that stuff you found into him immediately. I'll call ahead and tell him you are coming. He'll be quiet about it until he hears from me. Do you think you can work this out without telling your aunt Lucy?"

"Oh, mercy, we can't tell her—she'll have a heart attack!" Grace replied.

*****

Back in the yard at Aunt Lucy's house, the men made a hasty departure. Grace watched the truck turn south and then quickly turn east through some backwoods that Grace knew would lead to town. She thought, *Well, they certainly aren't interested in being seen on the main road. This is more serious than they thought, than any of us would have thought.*

Grace picked up the old pickle churn and her metal toolbox and went in to share with her dear aunt Lucy. She'd have to be careful how she shared the good news.

After she read the envelope and the title of the document in the toolbox, Aunt Lucy jumped for joy, danced around her cane, and shouted, "Praise the Lord! I told you! I told you, didn't I tell you? I knew that thing would turn up. Where did you find it?"

After giving Aunt Lucy a rundown of the excursion in the attic and how the men had to rescue her from the attic, Grace slowed down and made an excuse to go to the bathroom. Aunt Lucy had bowed her head by that time and was giving her thanks to God for

THE ROAD TO HELL IS PAVED WITH... WHAT?

His blessing. Grace just needed to collect her thoughts about how to approach some part of the truth without disturbing the frail old praying soul too much. In the bathroom, Grace tried some quiet praying of her own. "Dear Lord, help me with this. I can't lie to her about these things. I know, Lord, You sent me here to help clean this outrageous mess up, but I simply can't lie to Aunt Lucy. What do you want me to do? What to say? Please help me here."

The telephone was ringing, and Grace bounded out of the bathroom before Aunt Lucy could start gabbing and tell anything. She made it to the kitchen, where she heard her aunt say, "Grace, it's for you. Someone wants to talk to you."

A female voice informed Grace that she would be expected at 2:00 p.m. for her appointment, as recommended by Sheriff Cosby, at the law office that afternoon. Grace grabbed a pen and jotted down the directions, assuring the caller she would be happy to be there.

Grace couldn't believe how fast the law enforcement people worked in this part of the world—didn't waste a minute, apparently.

Poor Aunt Lucy had rejoiced, whooped, shouted, and praised her Lord until she was worn out. She picked up her cane and started making her way to bed. She said, "You get yourself together and go see that lawyer, Grace. I'm going to bed. Too much excitement for me. I need to rest. We got up too early. But God is looking out for us, praise His name."

Grace was so relieved that she wouldn't have to explain anything further to the old aunt; she kissed her old face and grabbed a glass of tea. She headed out to the old toolshed by the garden. That old antique trunk that was "stuck to the floor" might provide some much-needed distraction. Grace needed some time to think and try to wrap her mind around the big picture that seemed to be emerging. She would have a couple of hours to relax before her appointment at the lawyer's office. She would also need to eat something nutritious; that seemed to be good for her shakiness and her emotional crazies. She had made that trip with the sheriff and held together well. She was pleased with her performance.

The old trunk in the toolshed would prove to be much more than a convenient distraction. That trunk held some secrets of its own, changing Grace's life dramatically.

The Old Trunk and Its Treasures

The old metal garden shed had a small concrete ramp in front of sliding doors, and it served to house the garden tools. Grace pushed the doors aside and stared at the jumble she found inside: old mowers, rakes, hoes, shovels, buckets, and barrels. There were boxes of canning jars and several old churns. Spiderwebs were hanging over the walls and from the ceiling. Apparently, the dear old blind one had given up gardening some time ago, but having experienced the era known as the Great Depression, she saved everything that might be "of some use" sometime.

The jumbled mess was discouraging to Grace. She sorted through the jumble until she found what might be one of the sturdiest lounge chairs and made her way to a shady spot where she could sit, sip her tea, and collect her thoughts. Perhaps the old trunk that was allegedly stuck to the floor would wait until another day. With her legs stretched out on the lounge, Grace wanted to relax and enjoy the morning. The old red rooster and his hens were scratching around in the garden spot, and birds were singing overhead in the trees. Hawks could be seen quietly circulating around the ridges, looking for prey. The western ridges were glistening as the sun crept higher in the morning sky. All was so quiet and peaceful.

Grace had forgotten how serene the country life could be, or maybe she just hadn't noticed it when she was young. As a young girl, she'd desperately wanted to escape, go anywhere else. Now she compared the peaceful scene to her present reality, the expensive lifestyle in the big metropolis she had come to despise.

She lived in an exclusive, gated community of condominiums replete with the requisite clubhouse and swimming pool. Despite the suggested seclusion of the complex, Grace had to sometimes suffer with the tenants in more than one hundred other units. Some of the neighbors were intolerable at times, especially with their pet litter and trash. When the pool was open for the season, the noise factor became a nuisance; drunken brawls were not uncommon. Midnight disagreements among family members could be loud and profane. The cops had to be called regularly. Grace, of course, could always depend on her nightly toddy for her escape.

Often, Grace wondered if she could just sell the condo and buy a small house in the suburbs, but she'd be too far from work and there would be traffic jams. In the condo complex, she could simply walk a few blocks to campus, leaving her car safely in the garage. On days when the weather allowed, she donned her sneakers and walked to work with her dress shoes in her bag. Sometimes her friend Professor John, who lived in the same complex, walked with her. He had been one of her professors during her studies, and they had become neighborly friends.

As she sat by the old shed, the morning peacefulness began to intrigue Grace, and she wondered what it might be like to get up every morning and just enjoy the quiet—no rushing off, no demanding job, no traffic jams, and no having to meet deadlines. In two years, she would be able to retire and draw on her investments without penalty. She thought about selling the condo and bringing herself back to the mountains. Living way up on Grandpa's old farm might be a wee bit too isolating, but a small house on the main road would be perfect. Grace began dreaming about that possibility, and her spirits lifted; the idea seemed exceptionally appealing.

Nearly an hour had passed before Grace brought herself back to reality. She jumped up, folded the lounge chair, and was putting it back in the shed when she said, "Now, where is that old trunk? I've got to hurry. Don't want to be late."

In a corner of the old shed, almost hidden by a large wooden cabinet, she spotted an old antique trunk. The thing looked beaten and battered, and the ants had built their sand dunes all around the base. Termites had invaded the big wooden cabinet that sat next to it. Grace couldn't believe it. She said, "Oh, my soul, I'll have to take the contents out of this thing and see what we can do with it."

She retrieved an old quilt that was stacked on an overhead shelf and spread it out for the contents of the trunk. She piled a jumble of papers, old Bibles, and pictures on the quilt. As she stared at the bottom of the trunk, she realized that the ant and termite intrusion, along with water damage, had destroyed it. The trunk had been constructed of cheap boarding covered with a thick vinyl, held together with metal edges glued to the frame; the satiny material in the lining had mostly rotted. Grace decided to shovel the whole thing out to the trash barrel and burn it, but she would need Aunt Lucy's permission. She carried the quilt with its contents to the back porch and dumped it where she could sort things later. As she stepped back into the shed to finish her job, she picked up a flat shovel, hoping to pry the trunk off the floor. She pushed and pried around the outside edges, but the thing would not move. She opened the lid to try prying from the inside, hoping to make some progress. As she was tugging at the lid, she noticed the satin lining in the lid was sagging as though a weight might be pulling it down. Grace felt along the sag and realized that papers were jammed between the lid and the old silk lining. As she inspected the lining, she realized that there was a slit at the front of the trunk lid where it wouldn't be noticed. She fished the contents out through the slit, and to her amazement, she found what appeared to be two old land surveys and a letter addressed to Grandpa Lawson.

The land surveys depicted the old Lawson farm when it was owned by her great-grandfather Lawson. The older, somewhat-faded survey showed the old farm in its original dimensions. The newer survey showed the farm when her great-grandfather had divided the farm among his heirs: Grandpa Lawson, Aunt Lucy, and their brother, who had later died in the Civil War.

Grace was amazed at what she'd found. There appeared to be more than eight hundred acres in the original farm. She thought, *These are invaluable. Grandpa had them well hidden. How long have they been in there? Oh my goodness!*

She carefully put the folded old papers in a plastic bag and put them aside to consider later. She was looking at the remaining letter addressed to Grandpa Lawson and realized it was of more recent vintage. The return address was not familiar; Grace opened the letter and began to read:

Dear Mr. Lawson:

My name is Greg Meadows, and I'm searching for my birth mother. I was adopted from your area in 1960. I've been told that my mother might have been your granddaughter. My birthdate is October 10, 1960. If your granddaughter could have been my mother, please let her know about me.

My adoptive parents are now deceased, and I would very much like to meet the original family. Please let me hear from you.

Prayerfully,
Greg Meadows

Grace staggered to the door of the shed and dropped to the concrete ramp. She couldn't believe her eyes. She stared at the postmark; the letter had been mailed about two years before Grandpa Lawson had died. She was stunned. Why would Grandpa hide this, just put it away? What was he thinking?

Some time passed before Grace could collect herself. She put the letter back in the envelope and held it to her chest. She was praying, "Lord, if this is my son, please help me find him. He could still be around. He's not quite forty years old. I need to know about him."

For most of her adult years, Grace would hear a baby cry and flinch. Her baby was taken from her while he was crying, and Grace had nightmares about that for years. She was told it was a healthy boy. That was all the information she'd ever gotten. Whenever memories of that experience came through her mind, she simply focused on the hard work in front of her and dismissed the thoughts as irrelevant. She'd had a lot of experience during her childhood that she'd had to dismiss by focusing on the work. The method worked well, to a point, and then she could depend on her "medicine." Workaholism and alcoholism, the twin turbo engines of self-destruction, had Grace's life in a gradual flight of eventual wreckage, but she didn't know.

After she had collected herself a bit, Grace quickly took the letter to her bedroom and put it away in her luggage. She put the old land surveys with her rusty metal toolbox containing Grandpa Lawson's last will and testament; the attorney would be interested in all that.

*****

Within the next hour, Grace made lunch for Aunt Lucy, showered, dressed, and was out the door to find the attorney's office. She marveled at how fast time could simply vanish when she became distracted. She wondered if that might be another symptom of withdrawal. Could she be getting dementia already, maybe blackouts? She remembered that none of her recovery friends seemed to have any symptoms of brain damage; in fact, they were all quite astute. She gave herself a stern lecture, "No negative thinking, Grace. It undermines recovery. You know that."

Trying to dispel the negative thoughts, she began to make the suggested gratitude list. She had been taught to override the negativity with things to be thankful for. She spoke aloud, saying, "I have just found Grandpa's last will that clearly leaves the old farm to his next of kin, and that is me. The old survey papers can clearly define the boundaries of the property, if there is any doubt. But most of all, I might have a son that would like to meet me, and he can be found if he's still alive. God is on my side, I see that, and I'm grateful for that. Lord, thank You."

*****

Grace pulled into a parking lot of a very modern three-story building housing the assigned attorney. The lawn around the building was beautifully landscaped, and the building directory was displayed just inside the door. Grace was taking the elevator to the second floor and breathing deep to calm her nerves; she knew that attorneys, like some professors, could be intimidating.

A young receptionist greeted Grace, glanced at the rusty old toolbox in her hand, and promptly rang her boss. "Ms. Lawson is here. May I send her right in?"

The man who came to greet Grace was a huge fellow, well over six feet tall, and had muscles bulging through his shirt. He was graying a bit around the temples but otherwise appeared to be exceptionally fit and healthy. His handshake was very firm as he introduced himself. He showed Grace to a chair and opened the conversation with, "Okay, Ms. Lawson, let's see what you have found. Sheriff Cosby has filled me in on your situation with the property, but he wants us to understand that we must keep the whole thing confidential until we hear from him again. He says it may take a couple of weeks. In the meantime, show me what you found."

The attorney slowly looked at the rusty toolbox, and with an amused expression in his eyes, he said, "Somebody went to some lengths to stow this away and keep it hidden. Sheriff tells me he has some good film footage of you sprawled out across the rafters, trying to dig this out of the attic. Is that right?"

Grace tried to match his amusement with her response, "Yes, and did he tell you his men had to rescue me from that predicament? I couldn't stand up after that ordeal."

After he had thrown his head back to have a good laugh, the attorney said, "Ms. Lawson, that is one for the record books. Not too many women would have had the guts, and the odds of finding something like this in an old rusty box, in the attic, under the insulation…that's a story for the news. Unfortunately, we'll have to save that story for another day."

Grace watched as the attorney carefully untied the old yarn and spread the papers out on his desk. He began to read with intense focus. As he flipped to the last page, read through, and flipped it

THE ROAD TO HELL IS PAVED WITH... WHAT?

over, on the back was a shorter page of paper that had stuck to the legal-size page in front of it. It was stuck so well that Grace had not noticed it when she read the document. The attorney began running his letter opener around the edges, trying to loosen the shorter page. Grace watched the pages begin to separate with very little damage. Apparently, the pages had stuck together from humidity in the tin box.

The attorney stared at the short page and announced, "Well, what we have here is a receipt from the law office of Robert Henderson Sr., made to your grandpa Lawson, for the preparation of his will, notary fees, documentary and recording fees. Your grandpa paid to have this thing properly filed and recorded. Did I understand that there is no record in the clerk's office of anything ever being recorded?"

"The clerk's office says that there is no record of it," Grace answered.

The attorney seemed puzzled as he said, "The original copy of these documents usually got filed at the clerk's office, and any copies were stamped across the top in red ink with the word *copy*. This one appears to be the original. Look at the notary stamp. Somebody made a mistake and mailed the original with the attached receipt to your grandpa, assuming, perhaps, it had already been recorded."

Grace thought of something he should know. She said, "Lawyer Henderson was very sick during his last few months, I'm told, and maybe his office staff didn't know how to handle it properly. He died around that time, and Grandpa Lawson died some months later. My grandpa wouldn't have known if it had been property handled or not—he just stuck it away. The young Robert Henderson tells me there is no record of any will that was ever prepared in that office."

"He may be telling the truth as he knows it. This looks like the original document to me, and he may have found nothing to prove otherwise," the attorney replied.

Grace asked, "How does that affect the directives of my grandpa's will now?"

The attorney answered, "Well, with this evidence, the witness statements, and the notary stamp, I don't think it will be affected. Are there any more children or grandchildren besides yourself?"

"No," Grace said. "I've been away for about forty years, and I had no idea the property might belong to me. That property has been abandoned until now. My aunt couldn't find my grandpa's will."

"We'll get the title cleared, Ms. Lawson," the attorney said. "What we can't do right now is alert anybody that we are working on this until the investigation by the sheriff's department is over. It is crucial that we keep this very quiet."

Grace tried to reassure the man. "The sheriff has suggested that I go back to my home, keep my head down, and wait until he informs us. I'm happy to do that."

The attorney gathered the paperwork and left his office to make copies for Grace as she made out a check for retainer fees for him. She was thinking, *I do not care what it costs me. I'm going to clean that trash off the old farm, not only for myself, but also for the poor, hardworking people who came before me. I will do my part. I've been gone too long. I owe a debt here. I may be the only one left who can see this through.*

The attorney returned, and as he folded the copies into a folder for Grace, he asked, "Ms. Lawson, do you know how much that old farm could sell for today in this county?"

Grace admitted she had no idea. He smiled at her and asked, "Would you be happy with around twenty to twenty-five thousand an acre? That's about the average for virgin property these days, depending on water sources and accessibility. The views are important too."

She didn't flinch. Grace quickly replied, "It won't be for sale, not if I own it. I love the old virgin mountain land, and it won't go for development, that's for sure. Money won't be able to buy it. Not from me."

The newly retained attorney stood, handed Grace the folder with her copies, and with his arm around her shoulders, led her to the door. On the way, he said, "Ms. Lawson, I'm glad to hear you say that. We think the same way. We'll make a good team."

As Grace shook his hand at the door, he teasingly said, "Now, Ms. Lawson, please, no more adventures in dark attics unless you are accompanied by a rescue squad."

THE ROAD TO HELL IS PAVED WITH… WHAT?

Walking away smiling, Grace thought, *He's big enough to intimidate the saints in the courtroom, but he has a kind spirit. It looks like I've been blessed.*

*****

Before she left town, Grace grabbed some groceries and filled her car with gas. She had promised two young boys a drive in the Lexus. She noticed that her hands were not shaking, she wasn't feeling sick, and she didn't feel the need for a drink. In fact, she was feeling unusually lighthearted. She wanted to sing and dance. She thought, *I'm turning into Aunt Lucy!*

On the way up the valley toward home, she remembered the letter in her baggage. She began to pray, "Lord, please help me find this man. I want to know if he is my son. I don't care who the father is. I just need to know my son."

Her prayer would be answered. In the next few weeks, her son would find her and bring about the biggest surprise of her life. She would be forever changed. And so would he.

Aunt Lucy's Ethical Testimony

Following the example of Sheriff Cosby's team, Grace parked her Lexus behind Aunt Lucy's house near the porch entry; the car couldn't be seen from the highway or the driveway. Both the sheriff and the attorney had warned her to "lie low" and be very careful. Aunt Lucy never locked her doors until bedtime. Grace resolved to find a way to convince her old blind aunt to change that careless habit. Grace knew a blind elderly lady with unlocked doors wouldn't last long in the city.

As Grace was putting the groceries away in the fridge, she heard the dear old aunt coming down the hallway, tapping her cane. Grace went to meet her and was giving the old one a hug, when Aunt Lucy whispered, "That man was at the door, Grace."

"Who? Who was at the door? There's nobody there now," Grace said.

"That Lawyer Henderson. He was asking for you, Grace, and I told him you had left. It wasn't exactly a lie. I just didn't mention that you'd be back. He didn't get a thing out of me. I told him you had business and had to rush off to take care of something. I didn't say where."

Grace asked, "What on earth did he want?"

Aunt Lucy said, "He wanted me to tell you to call him. He had some papers to discuss with you, go over something. I told him you'd get the message."

"Are you sure that was Henderson?" Grace asked.

"Oh yeah," Aunt Lucy replied. "He has stopped here before, and he calls me Lucille. It was him, all right. He's a big horse's butt. I'd recognize him and that attitude anywhere."

Immediately, Grace locked the doors. She remembered the sheriff had said Henderson could be dangerous; she wasn't taking any chances.

"Aunt Lucy," Grace said, "I'm going to have a new intercom system installed on your door so you can speak to people without unlocking the door. I know you aren't used to that, but it's too dangerous to leave your doors unlocked when you can't see who is outside. Where I'm from, the trusting souls like you wind up being victimized, sometimes over pocket change."

With phone book in hand, Grace quickly found a locksmith and explained her concerns. The technician agreed to arrive early the next morning and help with that problem.

While she had the phonebook, she turned to her dear old aunt and asked, "How long has your antique piano been out on that back porch? And why is it tied up with quilts and a rope? Why is it out there, anyway?"

With a long sigh and a pained expression, the elder one said, "Oh, I fell over the piano stool some time back, and the kids moved the whole thing to the porch so I wouldn't hurt myself."

"Aunt Lucy," Grace asked, "don't you miss playing? Wouldn't you just like to keep yourself company sometimes by playing and singing like we used to do? It was always your playing that brought so much comfort in my early days. You can still play well. Why don't we move that piano back inside? We can arrange it so you can maneuver without falling over it."

The old one answered, "To be honest, I'd love to have it back in the house. I've missed the thing. I think it might need a good tuning, and no telling what else. The cold weather may have damaged it. It may be ruined by this time."

Grace scanned the phone book. She dialed the closest music store and explained what she needed.

A male voice responded, "I'm pretty good at tuning. I could come after work and have a look, see what is needed, see if it's worth the effort. Most of the old antique pianos, especially the old uprights, aren't worth repairing anymore, but we can give it a try."

THE ROAD TO HELL IS PAVED WITH... WHAT?

"When might we expect you?" Grace asked. She didn't want any strange men coming to the door too late in the afternoon.

"I'll be up after closing time, around five thirty. I'm pretty sure I can find you. I've tuned the piano for the Bethel Baptist Church a number of times in the past," the man said.

Grace had been watching her aunt Lucy's face during the conversation. The old dear was delighted with the idea and had a look of pure joy on her face. As Grace put the phone down, she thought, *No matter what it takes, I owe her. She'll get her piano, or she'll get a new one. Imagine being blind and having your one great pleasure taken away. I can't bear to think she can't play for herself.*

*****

The evening meal was over and the leftovers had been stashed when the doorbell rang. A tall man with a balding head stood at the door. He was clad in a shirt decorated with musical notes, and he was carrying a toolbox. As Grace opened the door, he stepped in to greet Aunt Lucy. "Well, Aunt Lucy, I'm Charlie. How are you? I've tuned that old church piano for you several times. You're the one who helps when it's out of tune, and you're right, always right."

Aunt Lucy laughed and responded, "Why, of course I remember that. You're the best piano tuner around here. We want to see what you think of my old antique piano. Grace will show you where it is."

Grace led the man to the old piano, and they carefully uncovered the old treasure. Charlie whistled as he looked. He said, "Wow, this is certainly an oldie, a piece of art, and the carvings are beautiful. I haven't seen one like this in years. It still has the original stool. This is an unusual sight, ladies."

Aunt Lucy looked as though she might shout and dance around her cane again, but Grace grabbed a chair and helped her sit down.

Charlie opened his toolbox, and with careful handling of the old piece, he began his inspection of the working parts. Every inch of the old piece was examined before he rendered his verdict. "Ladies, the good news first. This can be restored, and I'd be delighted to do it. It's too valuable to be discarded. The artwork itself is worth the effort. But the bad news is, you can buy a brand-new piano for the same money. Of course, you won't get the vintage value. Some more bad news is that you need to move this into a temperature-controlled area. Otherwise, it will not be worth restoring—more damage will occur, and the repair costs will be out of reason."

Grace had to ask, "How much would you estimate it might cost to repair it?"

Charlie tapped at his hand-held computer as he looked over the old piano slowly, muttering to himself. He made his pronouncement, "I think about fifteen hundred dollars might get it to a good place, and then on the resell market, it might be worth around four thousand. At this point, you might get fifty bucks if some dealer wants to take it. We can restore it for a better deal than that if you ever want to sell. It's a vintage piece."

Grace had another question, "When do you think you could get it repaired?"

"Well, it'll take about two weeks or more to locate some of the old parts and the keys, but within a couple or three weeks, we can have it sounding good. I'll even clean up the wood, and you won't be unhappy with the way it looks. It'll be a museum piece, but I have to warn you, it has to come back in the house immediately."

Aunt Lucy moaned as she said, "It took four grown men to take it out. We can't do that. That thing is too heavy and awkward to move around."

Charlie was quick to reassure her, "Yes, we can. I have a wheeled dolly, and we can roll that piano anywhere you want it. It's not that hard to do."

Aunt Lucy turned to Grace. "What do you think, honey? I'm not willing to spend money on things that are apt to last longer than I do. Nobody else plays, and the kids will just move it out again. They have no interest in playing the piano. They never did."

As Grace responded, she winked at Charlie and said, "Aunt Lucy, I might want to learn to play. Why don't I pay for the repairs and you can leave the piano to me when God calls you to play in heaven?"

Aunt considered that a done deal, and Charlie wrote up his work order. Grace was making out his required deposit as he bounded out the door to return with his dolly, a jack, and some rope. Within minutes he and Grace had the old piano jacked up, the dolly in place, and were lining it up with the door. With Grace pulling and Charlie pushing, the old piano rolled right up a small ramp and it was positioned in a place of honor in the living room. Its location in the front corner of the room would allow Aunt Lucy to play without stumbling over the stool.

Grace helped gather the tools and thanked Charlie for his help as she walked him to his van. When she came back to the living room, she heard the old piano coming to life. Aunt Lucy was playing away and praising her Lord with an old hymn, "How Great Thou Are." The old piano was not at its best, and Aunt Lucy's voice was crackly and weak. Grace thought to join the racket, but she couldn't get the words to come past her throat. She went to the kitchen and rummaged through the shelves, looking for something to take away the pain. She came up with nothing, completely empty-handed except for some pickle juice, straight from the jar. She knew that would not suffice. She let the tears pour as she sat with her head down at the dining table. Her whole body began to shake, and she felt nauseous. The DTs were happening again; her emotions had triggered the physical symptoms of withdrawal.

"Why are you crying, chile?" Aunt Lucy asked. "What's the matter?" Aunt Lucy pulled out a chair and sat across the table from Grace.

Realizing she couldn't be dishonest, Grace just simply told the elder one the simple truth. "The truth, Aunt Lucy, is that I'm having withdrawal symptoms from an emotional disorder and a physical disease that has plagued me for years. Sometimes it's too much to handle, especially when I'm under stress. I break down and all I want is a good, stiff drink. I'm not drinking anymore, but the urge is overwhelming sometimes. I'm told the symptoms will subside over time, if I don't allow myself to have any alcohol at all."

Aunt Lucy was silent for less than a minute. She cleared her voice, straightened her shoulders, and spoke with a firm voice. "Does that surprise me, Grace? No, it doesn't, chile, and you shouldn't let it weigh on you so heavy. You were raised to the habit of drinking, just like I was. All the men in the family and some of the women drank regularly. In my granddaddy's day, they made their corn liquor and depended on it for medicine. Some drank for the fun of it, made a habit of it, some because it runs in their blood. They're bred to it. You and me, we inherited their blood, and we got the tendency to do the same thing."

Grace asked, "Why have I never seen you drink, Aunt Lucy?"

The old one didn't hesitate. She said, "Well, when I had my children way back then, I decided to leave the stuff alone and not make matters worse. I quit, except for a cough syrup now and then, if it was needed. That was rare, because I saw how crazy that stuff made the others when they got soused up."

The elder paused for a deep breath and continued with her answer, "The poor folks kept getting worse off. The kids were hungry. The families couldn't get a leg up. I made up my mind that I wouldn't let that happen in my home. I put my foot down, but despite that, the men and some of the women just liquored themselves into a bad end. It's good that you have quit, chile, but it's not all your fault. Your grandpa spooned that stuff in your mouth when you were just a baby. I told him to quit that, but he didn't listen to me. I've been wondering all these years if that just ruined your life and you didn't want any of us to know. Praise the Lord, it seems to me that you've done well despite the awful thing that happened to you and the awful injustice that was done. Don't you have a good education and a good job? It seems to me that the good Lord has been looking out for you right good over the years."

Wiping at her face with some handy napkins, Grace quickly decided to ask the hard questions that had haunted her for years. She took a couple of deep breaths and posed her first query. "Why did Grandpa just send me away when I told the truth? He should have defended me."

Aunt Lucy never hesitated with her answer. "Well, to be as truthful as I know how, it was clear that your grandpa didn't want to raise you after your mother put the insurance money from your dad's

THE ROAD TO HELL IS PAVED WITH... WHAT?

death in a trust for your education. Your grandpa wanted that money for his debts. He was my beloved brother, but even our Pappy used to say, 'He won't amount to much.' That's why Pappy Lawson left the bottomlands to me and my eldest brother, and he left the ridges and the wetland to your grandpa. He knew your grandpa wouldn't work the land. Your grandpa drank too much and fooled around with the wrong people. He was not interested in making crops that much."

Grace was listening, and she was intrigued. She encouraged Aunt Lucy to talk.

The aunt went on. "Your grandpa was two different people. He could teach and preach the Bible with the best of them, but he couldn't stay on course with what he taught. He drank, and he couldn't leave the ladies alone. Your granny wouldn't go to church with him because she said he was a hypocrite, and she was right. Many a time he would bring you to church and stop here to get some strong coffee to sober up. You must remember some of that. You were a young child, but you can remember that, can't you?"

Those old memories came back with a chilling effect on Grace; she began shivering, but she couldn't give up. She remarked, "So Grandpa got rid of me because I was not only too much trouble for him but he was also not going to have a baby in the house to embarrass him in front of the church? It was the easiest thing to do?"

Aunt Lucy paused for a deep breath and continued, "Not exactly, Grace. The man was in debt and about to lose the farm. He contracted with some lumber people to cut the pulpwood on the east ridge. The boys that harmed you were hired hands, but your grandpa was afraid of losing his contract for the lumber. He just thought it best to shut the whole thing down before he lost his butt. He didn't stand up for you, Grace, because he would have lost the farm. So he put you out of sight with the money your mother put in the trust, and he saved the farm. That is the gospel truth, as far as I know it, Grace."

Grace responded, "Thank you, Aunt Lucy, for your honesty. I know that was hard to tell about your own brother. It speaks of strong character, and it certainly helps me to understand. I have one more question: Who killed the men that molested me on the ridge?

I can't believe anyone would do that to avenge me. I was gone when that happened. The sheriff came to question me at the school, but he could see I was not able to do that. Who do you think did it?"

A pained expression came over the elder one's face, and she hesitated. Slowly, with a quiver in her voice, she asked, "Who do you think? Who do you remember, chile, who did all the shooting when the animals had to be slaughtered for meat? Your grandpa couldn't hit the broad side of the barn with a shotgun. Who was the quickest and the most merciful when taking the lives of the animals, even the chickens and wildlife? Who was the best marksman in the family? You think about it, Grace."

Several minutes passed while Grace struggled to breathe and find her voice. She closed her eyes and tried to remain calm; she already knew the answer. She heard Aunt Lucy crying. Several more minutes passed with the old family clock ticking loudly in the silent house.

At last, Grace took a deep breath and tried to defend the obvious. "She would never hurt a thing…not even a snake. Said they were God's creatures and we didn't have any right to harm them. She had so much respect for the land and the creation. I can't believe she would murder God's people no matter what happened."

Aunt held her position. "Think about it this way, Grace. When your daddy was killed, he was running some of your grandpa's corn liquor around to sell, trying to help your grandpa make some money. Your granny was mad about that, and she blamed your grandpa for killing her only child. Then you came along, and she took you in. That made Grandpa mad at her. When you got molested and he sent you away, your poor granny went mad—at least that was what he told me. Your grandpa said, 'Anything I do that displeases her, she threatens me with a gun or a knife. She looks like a cornered wildcat sometimes. She's scary.' He thought she was losing her mind. She died within the year after you left, the doctor said, of heart failure, but your grandpa said she poisoned herself. We'll never know the truth there."

Both were crying by that time. As Grace wiped at her eyes, she asked, "What did she ever do to deserve that? She was a good person,

THE ROAD TO HELL IS PAVED WITH... WHAT?

and she knew she'd have to face God. Maybe she did try to punish herself, or maybe God just simply called her."

Aunt Lucy said, "It's a funny thing. She requested that we put her in the graveyard next to her son, and she wanted the words 'He hideth my soul' on the gravestone."

"Did you do that? What do you think she meant by that?" Grace asked.

"Grace, it's an old hymn that she liked. I think she wanted us to know that she'd been forgiven. That's all I can think of."

Their conversation went on for another hour before Grace noticed Aunt Lucy was tiring. Grace had one last question. "Why did I not receive even a Christmas card from anybody? I sent several cards and letters, and not one soul responded. Why? Aunt Lucy, tell me why I didn't deserve even one note."

"You did, honey, but your grandpa wouldn't allow it. He blamed you for your grandma's plight by saying the whole thing was too much for her and caused her death. He didn't want you around, and I think he burned your letters. He was struggling with his drinking and his debts, and he made a lot of bad moves. The church had to replace him, and he blamed that dismissal on everybody and everything, never accepted a fault of his own."

Grace stood and took the old aunt's hand as she said, "Come on. We've worn you out with this washing of the family laundry. You need to go to bed. The locksmith is coming early. After that, we'll get out and go do something fun. We'll leave the old bones buried tonight. I want you to know how much you've helped me understand a lot of things that have haunted me. You are so special, and I thank you for everything."

The elder one laughed and said, "This has been what the younger generation calls an ethical testimony. That's where the plain truth is told to the next generation so they can watch out for the bad stuff, take the good parts of the history and make something better out of it."

Aunt Lucy went to bed praising her Lord. She would reveal some more of her thoughts in the days to come.

The sheriff's office would prepare Grace for her role in their plan of action.

Grace would get staggering news about her son, a most unexpected revelation.

The times, and the perspectives, were indeed a-changing.

Confrontations in the Graveyard

After a training session with the new speaker system on her doors, the safety and security technician emphasized to Aunt Lucy that her outdated habit of leaving the doors unlocked was dangerous. He had arrived as scheduled and had worked several hours installing safety locks and intercom speakers on both front and rear doors. He also showed Grace a way to secure the old windows. As he prepared to leave and handed his invoice to Grace, she made a quick lip-zipping motion at him to be quiet about the costs. He quickly folded his notebook and bade the ladies goodbye. He was out the door before Aunt Lucy could inquire about the expense. Later, when she did inquire, Grace downplayed the expense, saying, "Oh, locks aren't all that expensive, and I'm paying for them so you can be safe. It's the least I can do. You've provided me with lodging and good company. I'm doing something to help you."

To distract her aunt further, Grace was quick to ask, "Now, where do you want to start today? We've talked about visiting with your grandson, riding through the mountains, spending time in the cemetery visiting some graves. Where do we start?"

With a childlike eagerness, Aunt Lucy cheered right up. She said, "Well, it's almost lunchtime. Tell you what? Let's pack some food in the ice cooler and ride through the mountains first. We can eat our lunch at the scenic vista at the top of the mountain, where the new highway cuts across the old west ridge. The housekeeper likes to take me up there, and she says it's well worth the view. Then we'll stop at the cemetery, if I can hold out, and we'll run by to see John and the boys after that. Before seven this evening, we need to be at the prayer meeting. We got a lot to be thankful for, Grace. We need to go praise His name."

Grace didn't fancy the prayer meeting thing, but she reflected on how she had survived the Sunday service without a meltdown; she could do it again. The little ice cooler was packed with good finger foods and Aunt Lucy's favorite moon pies. A thermos of sweet tea was included, and the picnic lunch was complete.

As they pulled out of the driveway, Grace asked, "Aunt Lucy, you'll need to direct me. This highway was not here when I was young. Which way do we turn?"

"Take a turn northwest toward the old west ridge. It overlooks the whole valley. The road will wind up the mountain to a look-off point. The whole Lawson farm can be seen from that point if the trees haven't put on leaves just yet. You'll recognize the valley when you get there. Just drive on up the mountain until you see the scenic overlook on your left, nearly at the top of the ridge."

As she maneuvered the car around the deep curves in the steep mountain, Grace began to feel nauseous. The mountain was steeper and sharper than she knew how to navigate; she held her breath and drove right on. Aunt Lucy was happily humming along; she didn't seem too concerned. Right before Grace felt her last nerve would snap, she spotted a sign that read, "Scenic Overlook Ahead: Visitors Welcome." Grace let out a loud sign of relief, and Aunt Lucy chuckled. She said, "Oh, come on, you ain't that citified, are you, Grace? It's gonna be worth your trip. You'll see."

Pulling into the parking lot, Grace was not about to park her new car close to the edge of the mountain. She chose a spot nearest the highway and tried to ignore the huge bank of layered rock that towered above the road. She was feeling a bit shaky, until she got a good look at the incredible view of the valley below and realized how far above the scene she was perched.

"Oh, my word, Aunt Lucy. This is beautiful! Everything looks miniscule from here, but it's picture perfect. You are right, it's well worth the trip."

Aunt Lucy was placed in a wheelchair and rolled to a picnic table with her ice cooler in her lap. Grace placed the food on the picnic table and a blanket over the aunt's shoulders. As the old dear began to enjoy her food, Grace grabbed her trusty camera and began snapping pictures. She could see the various roads running south through the valley toward the little town in the far distance. She could see the entire Lawson property to the north with the old rusty barn roof, the creek flowing south through the property, and the old east ridge towering over the creek.

Some thoughts began to occur to Grace as she stared at the old Lawson farm way up in the valley. *Oh my lord, no wonder Henderson wants the farm so bad. It's worth a fortune. What did that attorney say? Twenty or twenty-five thousand an acre for virgin mountain land with water and views. That's a staggering amount! Aunt Lucy says there should be nearly three hundred acres—that's millions of dollars. Oh… my…lord.*

She staggered to the table, where Aunt Lucy was munching her bananas and peanut butter, thoroughly enjoying the moment.

Grace said, "Aunt Lucy, this is breathtaking. I'm overwhelmed when I see the entire farm from this view. Your house can be seen—it looks like a tiny little dollhouse. The church and its steeple make a beautiful sight. This is a gift! Thank you for bringing me up here. I'm so happy to see the old farm from this angle."

The elder one smiled and kept munching her lunch. Grace joined the picnic, but she continued to stare out across the valley. Soon, Aunt Lucy was dozing in her chair. After a few more snapshots, Grace rolled the old soul back to the car and belted her in. That road down the steep grade and back onto flat land might be a challenge. Grace had never driven on steep curvy mountain roads, and she was grateful that her share of the road was near the side of the mountain as she descended.

*****

At the next stop, the cemetery parking lot, Grace jumped out of the car and took a few deep breaths. Although she'd enjoyed the experience, that trip up the steep mountain, and down again, would not get to be a daily happening, she hoped.

As Aunt Lucy began to stir, Grace asked, "How do we manage the cemetery? Your wheelchair won't work on this hill."

Aunt Lucy had the answer. "You fold the wheelchair under one arm and let me lean on the other arm, and I walk. I can walk. I'm slow, but I get it done. You place my chair between my son and my late husband, right in the middle, where my grave will be, and I'm good."

The wheelchair was anchored between the graves of George T. Bradford Sr. and George T. Bradford Jr., where Aunt Lucy could be close enough to touch the tombstones on each side. She began happily greeting her beloved ones as though they had been expecting her. Grace walked away, saying, "Aunt Lucy, you yell if you need something. I'll be within hearing distance." As Grace walked away, she thought, *That old dear will welcome her own death one day, just so she can join her beloved people. She is remarkable.*

*****

Strolling through the cemetery brought Grace to her grandpa Lawson's grave. His grave was not placed with the family, as one might expect. He was placed on a different row, away from Granny Lawson and their son. Grace's dad and mom were placed together with Granny Lawson on the side of her son. Grace thought that peculiar, but she would ask her aunt Lucy about that sometime later.

At this moment, however, Grace was overcome with feelings she had so wanted to express to Grandpa Lawson for many years. She straightened her shoulders and began. "You didn't want to bother with me, Grandpa, and you made my young years torture for the most part. I had to be your personal slave. 'Do this,' 'Do that,' 'Earn your keep' was all I ever heard from you, never a word of encouragement or praise, just abuse and thrashings if I didn't measure up. Then, when I was raped and needed your help, you sold me out for your own gain. You put me out of sight, and that nearly killed poor Granny. And maybe, in some ways, it did."

Shaking with rage, Grace paused for a minute to feel the pain. After some deep breaths, she continued, "I'm sure, Grandpa, that you hid that last will and testament where nobody would look except me. I'm the only one who knew about that old churn, and you put that box there just in case I might come back and look. You didn't make it easy. Aunt Lucy believes you were trying to make amends. You didn't treat me and Granny right, and maybe you meant to atone for that—at least Aunt Lucy gives you some credit. So here I am, and I will honor your intention. You sent me away, but my life has benefited greatly. I have a good education, a good job, and I think I can find my son. It may have worked for his benefit too. The Lord has called me to take care of the old farm, and I'm following His guidance. You rest in peace. I'm free now, and you are forgiven for the hardships you caused. May God forgive us both for our human weakness. We might have been set up for destruction by our genetics, and we didn't have a choice. We had a disease that smothered our spiritual awareness, but God still loves us both."

Grace walked toward the cluster of graves where the other members of the family rested. She said hello to her dad, whom she barely remembered. She thanked her mom for watching over her and appearing in visions to encourage and lift her spirits. As she came to Granny Lawson's grave, Grace felt a stabbing heartache. On the tombstone was the inscription 'He Hideth My Soul.' Between sobs, Grace asked, "Granny, did you avenge me? If you did, I'm so sorry. It cost your sanity and your life. I pray that God has forgiven you, and I believe He looked beyond your insanity and saw your love for His creation. He saw the dreadfully hard life you had to endure. You rest in peace, Granny, and wherever he 'hideth' your soul, please know that I'm back and I'm okay. I can go from here, and I will."

Grace bent to kiss her granny's tombstone, then she decided to walk up the hill toward the pauper's end of the cemetery. Aunt Lucy had warned her, as they made their slow trek up the hill, that she shouldn't wander into the back of the old cemetery. When Grace asked why, the old one replied, "Grace, your old ghosts are buried up there, the three men who hurt you, and the place is grown up. Sometimes the church cleans it up, and sometimes not. The free graves are supposed to be maintained by the families, but you know how that goes. The church is expected to pay for that too. That part of the cemetery is way up there near the edge of the woods, out of sight, anyway. Just don't go there. You'll have nightmares, like you used to."

Aunt Lucy was carrying on a happy conversation with her beloved son's grave when Grace checked, so she just walked on by and started up the hill. Toward the top of the hill, she noticed that weeds and brush had taken over a large portion of the cemetery, and the graves were almost obliterated with vines. Grace looked around for a cluster of three graves, and she spotted a large plot with a rock border. She went to investigate. She was barely able to read through the vines and weeds, but she saw the names: Andrew G. Colson, James B. Colson, and John D. Colson. Andy, Jim, and Johnny Boy, the three boys who had raped, humiliated, and damaged her, body and soul, on that east ridge over forty years ago.

Grace stood very still, looking around. The weeds and vines had nearly obscured the graves, the groundhogs had burrowed into the ground around the plot, and it appeared that the graves had long been forgotten. She shivered to think that animals would burrow into human remains. She tried to speak, but her mouth would not work; words didn't come out. She was having trouble breathing.

After several attempts to speak, Grace heard herself whispering, "Guys, you had your fun and it cost you your lives. I'm sorry that you made such a poor choice. I was just a young girl. You had been tooting your horn and waving at me for days. I thought you were just being friendly. Now I realize you had the whole thing planned, even brought along some booze to celebrate the catch. When you thought I'd passed out, after you each had your turn, I got up and ran. I knew how to get through the laurels and across the creek before you could catch me. You lied to the sheriff, told him I was soliciting money for sex. You almost got away with that."

As she talked a bit, her voice began to strengthen. She continued, "The one thing I find so hard to accept is not the harm you guys did but the thought that Granny Lawson had to take your lives to avenge me. I hate that thought. She didn't need to do that for me.

And we may have a son. If we do, he will hear the truth about his origin. I will be sure he understands the circumstances of his birth, not to blame you, but to forgive you for the pain you caused all of us. I've accepted the experience as part of a larger plan that I don't understand. God doesn't owe us an explanation. I need to forgive you, all of you. Rest in peace. We'll get this mess off your graves for Memorial Day, out of respect for God's greater plan and His mercy and grace."

When Grace walked back to check on Aunt Lucy, the old dear had one hand on her husband's tombstone, her head resting on her chest, and she was sound asleep. Grace slipped down to the car and grabbed her trusty camera. That beautiful scene of the old one sleeping so peacefully with her men would be priceless when her time came to join them; it would comfort the grieving for sure.

Several photos were snapped before Aunt Lucy stirred. Grace reminded her of their last stop. "Come on, let's go. You wanted to visit with your grandson and the boys, then we can get to the prayer meeting. Let's hurry."

"Yeah, that's right. Did you find some graves you remembered?" Aunt Lucy asked. "How did Grandpa's and Granny's look? Do they need flowers? Memorial Day is coming, and we need to decorate, bring pretty flowers and remember to honor all our loved ones."

Grace promised, "I'll bring some flowers when I get back for the holiday, and we'll visit your dad's grave too. I understand it's in a Confederate space. Is that right?"

"Yes, and it's been a long time since I've been there to talk with him. I'll be glad to do that. He was a Confederate soldier, and we need to honor him and his service."

*****

From the cemetery, Grace drove south for a short distance and turned in a northwesterly direction following Lawson Creek. A turn toward the east, over a bridge spanning the creek, brought them out in a clearing that Grace guessed might be within yelling distance of Aunt Lucy's cottage. They had just made a wide circle. Only a strand of trees obscured the highway in front of Aunt Lucy's cottage; a visit would be easy—just simply walk through the trees.

The grandson John was sitting on the porch of a double-wide trailer in a wheelchair, cigarette dangling from his mouth. The boys, Al and Ronnie, ran to help their granny up the handicap ramp that served as steps. Grace was greeted by their mother, Helen.

"Come in, Grace. We're glad to meet you. Would you like a glass of tea?"

Grace politely declined the tea, but she asked if she might use the bathroom, saying, "Your granny has kept me so busy today. I'm in need of some quick relief."

As Grace was finding her way to the bathroom, she quickly scanned her surroundings. The place was reasonably clean, but the furnishings were old and worn, some threadbare. The whole thing smacked of meager means and lack of resources. Grace thought, *I see why one hundred fifty dollars a month might have been so appealing to them, and Henderson took full advantage, that's for sure.*

While she washed her hands, she noticed pill bottles lined up on a shelf above her head. Apparently, someone in the house had need of lots of medications. She made her way back to the front of the house and noticed a large flat-screen television taking up the front corner of the living room. She was happy to see they were not cut off from the rest of the world like she remembered being.

Grace had promised the boys a turn with the Lexus, and they had worked out their plan. The boys would chauffeur the ladies to the prayer meeting and bring them home. Grace had a different plan; the boys would come practice with the car before their Granny Lucy would be the rider. They got their agreement high-fived all around, and Granny and Grace headed for home.

A strong motive began to materialize in Grace's heart. She decided maybe prayer meeting might be a good place to ask God to show her how to help the young boys. Grace wanted to make them a project, help them have hope and aspirations. She felt the pain of their poverty and saw their dismal hope for the future. She'd start with God's plan; that would be best. She'd ask God for help.

THE ROAD TO HELL IS PAVED WITH... WHAT?

Indeed, God had His plan for the boys, but for today, God had His focus on Grace. He was turning Grace herself on a different path. She'd be astonished—an unexpected calling from God was coming her way.

An Unexpected Calling

The lights around the church were shining brightly, welcoming the community to the regular Wednesday-night prayer meeting. Two dozen or more assorted vehicles were parked around the area as Al and Ronnie chauffeured their riders to the church door. The boys jumped out and held the doors open for the ladies to disembark from the rear of the Lexus. The young lads were having so much fun with their role—even their Granny Lawson was laughing.

Earlier, Grace had allowed the boys, under her supervision, to take the car on a trial run around some of the back roads. She had no intention of putting her old aunt in the back seat until they had practiced. She watched their every move because the younger lad was not yet licensed to drive. The older one, Al, said, "Oh, don't worry about him. He drives like an old lady."

After Grace and Aunt Lucy had been properly escorted up the steps and into the sanctuary, Grace took a few deep breaths and tried to calm her nerves. The oversight of teenage boys might be a bigger challenge than she could bear. She decided to pray about that.

Greetings and handshakes were exchanged all around the church, and soon the piano announced a tempo of joyful praise. The congregation rose to its feet and joined in song, praising the Lord. As the song quieted down, the pastor led in prayer and offered a few warm words of welcome. With the congregation seated, the pastor welcomed one of the older men to the podium and introduced him as Brother Bishop.

Brother Bishop, apparently the treasurer for the church, was to bring a very "brief" business meeting to order. He began by reviewing the past month's financial changes, the money collected and expenses covered. He quickly discussed the electric bill, the heat bill, and other small miscellaneous payments. Grace listened to the report and noticed that the poor little church was seemingly well managed.

After the treasurer's report was accepted and approved, Brother Bishop took his seat, and the pastor introduced another, much younger man, apparently a liaison between the mother church downtown and the satellite churches around the county. He came to inform the business committee of a decision being considered by the larger church to allow a group of twelve-step folks to rent a room in which to hold their meetings. He explained that the twelve-step group had outgrown their old meeting space and needed a larger, more centralized place to hold their meetings. Traditionally, the church had not permitted outside groups to utilize their premises for anything but church-related meetings.

The young man explained that the satellite churches could have a say in the matter and would have a month or so to deliver their vote. He went on to explain that the local twelve-step group would be working from their own program and would not interfere with the church's activities; they would meet on a Thursday night, be careful to clean up behind themselves, lock up carefully when they left, and do no eating or smoking in the church. There would be a rental fee charged for the accommodations.

It was explained why the church was considering such a move. The young man said, "The twelve-step ministry, for some of you who don't know, is a group of alcoholics and addicts that meet regularly to support one another in their efforts to abstain from the use of alcohol and drugs. They help one another find strength through dependence on a higher power.

"They learn to believe in a higher power instead of their use of self-defeating chemicals. The twelve-step program emphasizes a strong belief in a spiritual power to overcome alcoholism and drug addiction. Some of the regular participants come to believe in God and go on to become great spiritual leaders. It's a movement that our churches need to pay attention to. We can't explain how the ministry works, but we know that it is effective—the numbers speak for themselves. I'd like to see our church support the cause. They're not asking for much. Are there any questions?"

Before the young man could catch his breath, one of the ladies sitting close to the front of the church spoke up. "Why don't the alcoholics and addicts just attend church with everybody else? We got a higher power to tell them about, and we do it every Sunday. Don't they know about that? Why do they need a special time and place of their own? I say we don't need such people around our church. My vote will be no."

The man thanked her for her comments, and looking across the congregation, he asked, "Would anyone else like to comment before we close the business meeting?"

One of the older men near the front slowly rose to his feet and began to address the audience. "It's been my experience over my lifetime that the people who indulge in alcohol and drugs to an abusive degree oftentimes won't listen to the church and its religious approach to their problem. They often accuse the churches of spouting self-righteous ritualism as the way to God, and they say that approach doesn't work for them. They say their addiction is not a conscious choice, and they believe the churches don't understand the problem and have the wrong focus. I'm retired from working in a prison, doing chaplain duties. I hear it from the people. I say if the local twelve-step ministry needs more room, let's praise God and help them out. They may teach us something we need to know. I've found some of our most troubled people are our best teachers. Let's think about this before we judge."

Grace was listening intently as the differing opinions were batted back and forth across the aisle. Some people were adamantly opposed to any group that didn't associate with the church, and some just wanted to help all of God's people with an accepting and loving heart.

The age-old battle between the self-righteous right and the liberal, open-minded left raged on for a few contentious minutes. It was a replay of the battle between the recovery movement and the traditional churches. The recovery ministry tried to focus on the spiritual development of each of God's people, one at a time, while the religious group seemed to focus on the masses, religious ritualism, church attendance, and works. Although the two sides claimed to be seeking the same goal, they differed in their approach to the point of hostile argument and division. The twelve-step ministry had been spreading around the world for well over fifty years, saving lives as it went, but the churches wanted to label it a "cult." The churches, for the most part, had ignored the cult, and the twelve-step ministry went on without their support. Two different missions espousing the same goal were in conflict over their respective methods of reaching God's precious people.

Grace had not made a practice of attending church since she left the girls' school many years ago. That primitive religious practice and its required sacrificial duties had not been of benefit as far as she could tell—not to speak of the hypocritical leaders of the church who voted to exile her through no fault of her own. She had maintained a scornful rejection for most of what she considered the sanctimonious nonsense of the modern-day church.

She had always believed in a God of love and compassion, but Grace wasn't convinced that such a God believed in her. She'd always been on her own, comforted by her beloved medicines when life got too stressful. Where was such a God when her parents were taken from her, her baby had been taken away, her dear Granny Lawson had died, and she'd never received one word of encouragement or love from any of the Lawson family about that? While she was being battered emotionally and mentally, where had God been? Did he forget about her? What did she do to deserve such oversight?

As she sat quietly, clenching her teeth, Grace knew she couldn't have anything to say; it was a business discussion, and she was not a member. She was just visiting.

The differing sides were clearly drawing battle lines. The older "gray hairs" of the church were not necessarily in the conservative camp, and some of the younger people were leaning toward the conservative. One of the young women spoke up. "I'm not in favor of any group that tolerates addicts of any kind for any reason. I've got three children, and I'm working two jobs because their daddy won't keep up his custody and child support payments. He's down in the jail right now, picked up for violation, driving drunk again. He will plead with me on bended knee to take him back and promise God that he'll do better, but he goes right back to his habits as soon as I let him back in the house. I'm sick of such people, and I don't think the church should support them. They'll take advantage and go back to their ways. I vote no."

Grace had endured her closemouthed position about as long as she could stand it. Just before she raised her hand to speak, Aunt Lucy rose to her feet to be recognized. A respectful quiet settled over the entire church. Aunt Lucy was apparently a voice to be reckoned with; everybody calmed down.

She slowly began to speak. "I have the privilege of being the oldest member of this church. I've seen plenty of years, praise the Lord, and I've witnessed how alcohol has been Satan's best weapon against our people. My own family has been tragically influenced by using what our Bible calls strong drink. We were making 'home brew' for medicine when I was just a girl. Some of us took it up for pleasure, to enjoy it, and it destroyed any good works we tried to do. Some people are born into it, some learn from habit, some learn from the example of others, but it all comes to a bad end. It's the children who are left to suffer, and the cycle victimizes them, all over again, generation after generation. The Bible has lots to say about the 'sins of the fathers' and how they are visited on the children 'unto the third and fourth generation.' Some, I think, are caught in a bondage to their human weakness, and they don't know how to get out. If any group, twelve-step or otherwise, can help set them free, I say we welcome them, if not for ourselves, then for the children, the younger people. We've all got these young people to consider."

Aunt Lucy sat down, and there were many around the pews who responded "Amen."

Grace had her hand up, and when she was recognized, she stood and said, "My name is Grace Lawson. I'm not a member of the church, and I know that I don't have a right to speak. However, I want to offer something for consideration. I'm familiar with the twelve-step movement. It has been a major influence in my life. My own life was on a self-destruction course until I learned that none of us are exempt. No matter how much we think we know, how educated we are, how religious we try to be, alcohol and drugs destroy our minds and eventually our bodies. I was raised here on Lawson Creek, and I'm familiar with the customs of the culture.

"I was drinking alcohol before I left here at the age of seventeen, and I kept up the habit for years. For reasons known only to God, I've been occupied with studies through an extended education, then I had to work for a living. That slowed the process of destruction somewhat, but Satan didn't give up. He tempts me every day, even today. I'm a qualified professor at one of our distinguished universities. If the church needs someone to explain the twelve-step ministry and what it believes, how it helps God's people, I'll find the time to do some educational sessions and work toward that end. I can also help the church to understand alcoholism, its genetic influence and the mental and physical deterioration it imposes on the body. Our medical experts have known for decades that overuse of alcohol and drugs results in mental dysfunction, physical disease, dementia, and death. I'm offering my services to educate the people of the church so that we don't become a hindrance to God's plan for His people. Thank you for allowing me to speak."

The young liaison from the mother church thanked everyone for their input and left the podium. The pastor began taking prayer requests. Grace sat stunned. What had she done? What had she committed herself to do? Just a few short months into sobriety and she had become an expert? She was horrified, thinking, *Oh my lord, relapse can happen anytime, and it often does. I've simply hung myself. What was I thinking?*

The prayer requests were taken, and people began to gather at the altar for prayer. Grace found herself leading Aunt Lucy to the altar. As they knelt to pray, a young woman slipped in, kneeling close to Grace's side. The people took turns with oral prayers, and that went on for several minutes. The pastor took over when the oral prayers were said, and he spoke the closing prayer. The prayerful group stood to their feet and sang an old song, "To God Be the Glory."

The young woman who had knelt by Grace was clinging to her hand and whispering, "We need you to help us, me and my kids.

We don't know where to go for help. My husband will be in prison before long, and I would like to know how to help him. If you can help people like us, please do."

Grace embraced the quivering young woman, and with a surprisingly calm voice, she said, "Of course, I'll be glad to help if I can. I'll be back in town for the holiday. Call my aunt Lucy's number and we'll see what we can do to help you. In the meantime, we'll pray."

The young man who had instigated the lengthy discussion and debate came to Grace to shake her hand and said, "Thank you, Professor Lawson, for your input and your offer. We're blessed to have someone in our midst who is willing to help us understand better than we do. With your permission, I'd like to suggest to our church that we host a seminar and have you come to speak with a focus on the topic of addiction. Our society is suffering and getting worse all the time, and the church could help if we understood how to be of help. We're lost in our ignorance, and I think we need someone to help educate us. Debates and conflict don't help anything. Thank you for speaking up. You'll be a blessing. God has sent you. I know He has."

Grace shook the young man's hand, and trying to buy some time, she reminded him to schedule any seminar during the summer months, between semesters, so she would have the time to come. He thanked her again and walked to the door smiling.

Before Grace could walk away as well, she noticed that Al and Ronnie had captured their granny and were escorting her to the door. Grace tried her best to follow, but several people came up to talk with her, mostly about their relatives who "drink too much and cause trouble."

She tried her best to be reassuring, understanding, and compassionate, while inching herself toward the door. As she found herself shaking the pastor's hand at the door, he said, "Thank you, Ms. Grace. I thank the Lord for bringing you to us. I've prayed for years for someone to bring some help to this old valley. You're an answer to prayer. I thank God for sending you."

The boys, Al and Ronnie, had backed the Lexus right up to the steps of the church, and Ronnie was holding the rear door open for Grace. Grace slid in quickly, happy to be escaping. She felt Aunt Lucy grab for her hand. The boys were asking if they could make one more trip with the car before they had to give it up. Aunt Lucy poked Grace in the ribs and said, "Could we drive over to that ice cream place and get a treat? I'm ready for a good ice cream. It helps me sleep. What do you think, Grace?"

Grace felt numb, and she could only nod. The boys were happy to keep up their chauffeuring act; they drove away to the ice cream store, where they got their treats, and sat outside on the patio. The cold chocolate ice cream seemed to settle Grace's nerves a bit, and she began to relax. The boys and their granny were having so much fun Grace decided to join the moment, despite her frayed nerves. She began to enjoy herself immensely. A strange peace began to settle in her mind.

*****

Later in the evening, with the boys off to home and Aunt Lucy in bed, Grace let herself crash on the old living room sofa. The day had been exhausting, but strangely enough, she felt victorious. She couldn't explain it. She'd scared herself with her self-doubts about her unexpected commitment to the church. But then she asked herself, who is more qualified to teach, who has the experience, and who has the compassion for the people more than herself? She remembered the words of a dear friend in recovery who said, "Grace, I've never been called of God to do anything that didn't scare me. We walk in faith, never doubt. God calls those He knows He can use, and He's always got your back."

Before the brain circuitry could shut down for the night, Grace remembered to think back over the day and make a "gratitude list" for the blessings. Quite a list of things came to mind, the most surprising of which was the realization that alcohol had played no role in the happenings of the day. She'd handled herself with strength and purpose, even on that steep mountain road that rattled her nerves. Before she dozed off, she was smiling about how God had called her to teach after nearly twenty-eight years of a teaching profession she thought of as a job that paid well.

Grace was sleeping peacefully while Sheriff Cosby and the various law enforcement agencies planned their strategy. Tomorrow they would assign Grace a role to play in their plan and she'd get a crash course in how undercover agents work. The appointment with Lawyer Henderson would test her ability to "stay calm and carry on." The spiritual enemy would not give up easily. Grace was breaking her chains.

Grace Goes Undercover

Dawn was being loudly announced by the old red rooster as Grace began to stir. She could hear Aunt Lucy fumbling with the coffeepot out in the kitchen. As she pulled on a robe and headed toward the sound, she thought, *I can't believe I sleep so soundly, and all night without interruption. Maybe the recovery gang is right. Maybe my mind and body are trying to rest and heal. Maybe my chemistry is changing for the better. Hopefully, the physical symptoms will stop soon. Maybe abstinence does work after all. I feel surprisingly good.*

Grace spent the morning cleaning and tidying the little cottage while Aunt Lucy played hymns on the mangled old piano. Time was passing quickly. Lunch was prepared, and they were bowing their heads to say grace when the phone rang. Sheriff Cosby called to instruct Grace; she needed to appear around an hour before her appointment with Lawyer Henderson for a briefing. He suggested she try to wear a loose-fitting blouse with a light jacket over the top. Also, he instructed her to park behind the sheriff's office and not on the street side of the building. He didn't explain his instructions and was gone before Grace could ask. Grace took his attitude to mean, "Do as you're told, no talking, no questions. We're in charge."

Over lunch, Aunt Lucy thanked God for His bounty and asked for His guidance on the next leg of their journey. She asked for the strength to "stand against the evil" that had tried to destroy the Lawson legacy. Grace, in her turn, thanked God for His intervention, for her sobriety, and for protection. She humbly thanked God for His call to a greater purpose for her life and asked for strength to accept her responsibilities with humility and gratitude.

Grace went to her room to locate the appropriate clothes for her visit to the sheriff's office. With permission to look through Aunt Lucy's closet for a jacket or cape that would hang loose and free, she located a lovely, dark-colored cape that would hang well and match her blouse. As she dressed, she couldn't help feeling a bit shaky, but she also felt determined.

The Lexus was loaded, and Grace gave her dear old aunt a goodbye hug. She said, "Aunt Lucy, you be safe, and I'll be back in about a week. Your housekeeper will be here to help until then. Remember, the piano man is coming soon. I want to hear that music when I get back."

*****

On the long ride into town, Grace tried to make a mental note of all her recent commitments. She repeated them to herself: "I'm committed to help Aunt Lucy. I'm committed to reclaiming and restoring the old Lawson farm. I'm committed to helping the boys, Al and Ronnie. I'm committed to finding my son, no matter where he may be. I'm committed to the call of God to teach about addiction in this community. I'm committed to do God's will, and I'll have to stay sober. I'm committed to staying sober. Otherwise, none of my commitments will work."

Deep in her heart, Grace knew she had committed to giving up her lifestyle in the city and taking on the hard work that would be required to accomplish her new assignments. The hard work wouldn't be a challenge; she'd had hard work most of her life. The recovery group had suggested some time ago that she needed "purposeful and meaningful" work to fuel her motive to stay sober. This purpose and meaning would not leave room for careless and muddled thinking; she would need all her faculties clear and focused. Grace felt strongly motivated and strangely empowered. She had no intention of turning back; she had come too far already. This felt right.

*****

THE ROAD TO HELL IS PAVED WITH... WHAT?

After parking the Lexus behind the sheriff's office as instructed, Grace walked toward the rear door. Someone she didn't know opened the door and motioned for her to enter. A young woman introduced herself as Lydia and said, "Come in, Ms. Lawson. I'll be working with you. Come in and meet the gang."

Grace quickly responded, "Thank you. Just call me Grace, if that is okay. If not, I'm comfortable with Ms. Grace."

Lydia led the way to a large conference room where a group of men were seated around a table with Sheriff Cosby. Grace was introduced as Ms. Grace as the men stood to shake her hand. She was given a seat at the end of the table. The sheriff spoke first.

"Ms. Grace," he said, "we have several different agents here today from the various law enforcement agencies who are here to help us with our plan to clean up your property. We're working out a strategy, and we need your help to gather some information for us. You have an appointment with Lawyer Henderson at three thirty this afternoon, and that gives us enough time to talk about some questions we'd like you to ask, some things we'd like you to bring up. Do you feel up to some good training on how to work undercover and get the man to talk?"

As Grace looked around the table, all eyes were on her. She chuckled. "How can I not, with all this expertise to coach me? I don't have a problem with training, just remembering what the man tells me. He talks fast, and he lies even faster. I can't stand the man, and I may forget what he says."

Quickly, one of the older men assured her, "Oh, don't worry about that. Lydia knows how to fit you with a recording device, and you won't need to remember. You need to concentrate on the information we need to get. We'll be listening. You establish trust with him right away, act interested in any offer he makes you, chat away about the riding clubs, laugh about the good old days...things that will loosen him up and get him to talk. Turn on the charm if you need to. Act naive and let him make you an offer you can't refuse. Just don't sign any papers."

Another of the men offered input. "Ms. Grace, there are serious violations and crimes being committed on that property, and it's been going on for a long time. We are asking you to help us, not only to clean it up, but also to prosecute the offenders. It's going to affect the whole community if we do this right. You are an important player in the strategy at this point. Lawyer Henderson appears to be the best place to begin, and he'll give up some useful information if he thinks you are a vulnerable woman, interested in free money. If he thinks you are as money hungry as he is, you can play that angle and he'll sucker right up, pull you right in."

Different agents offered suggestions as Grace listened intently. She was to keep Henderson talking until he dropped his guard, then appear to go along with his manipulations, acting innocent and interested, playing dumb when necessary and asking naive questions.

Lydia was directed to arm Grace with the wiretap and show her how to activate the audio. Grace removed her cape, and the technician armed her body with a concealed recorder. A lovely fake flower was attached to the front of the cape, and Grace was shown how to discreetly operate the device without being noticed. She was also given a couple of small wireless magnetic transmitters to plant in hidden spots in Henderson's office if the opportunity presented itself.

The sheriff assured Grace that she would be monitored, and the men would be close if anything threatening should occur. One of the men offered gum to chew to help keep the nervousness out of her voice.

About fifteen minutes before the appointed time, Grace left the sheriff's office and headed out for her debut as an undercover sleuth for the long arm of law enforcement. She was smacking her gum and rehearsing her "points of focus," as explained by the instructors. Taking deep, calming breaths, she thanked God for her training as a teacher, someone who could stay on course with important segments of a lecture despite distraction. She knew she was being tested, and she was determined to give it her best.

*****

Lawyer Henderson was waiting, and he met her at the door. "Come in, come in, lovely lady. I didn't know if you were gonna make it. Your aunt Lucy said you'd had to rush off."

While trying to avoid his hands, Grace stepped around him and went straight ahead of him to his desk. On the way, she said, "Oh, Aunt Lucy doesn't understand that I need to work, and I have to come to the library to use my computer or my cell phone. Those things don't exist in her world, you know."

Henderson responded, "Well, I'm glad you're here. We can make some progress on that old farm. Did you get a chance to look at the shape it's in? Did you get up there to see how it's falling into ruin?"

Grace evaded his questions by saying, "Aunt Lucy's housekeeper was off this week, and I had to cover for her. Aunt Lucy is blind and can't help herself if there's no one looking out for her. She's a full-time job, and she needs to be in a facility. You can bet she's not ready for that. I've been tied up trying to keep her and work at the same time. The boys, Al and Ronnie, say the place is grown up and dangerous and the road won't accommodate my car. They tell me I'll need to learn horseback riding before I venture up there too much."

Henderson chuckled. "Well, that's a good reason to sell that ragged thing to me and forget about it. I'm talking to some people about going in with me to offer you a good, fair price for the whole thing, as is."

"Well, I don't know if I really own that property," Grace replied. "You say there's no last will and testament left by my grandpa, and I'm sure Aunt Lucy would throw a fit."

"Oh, don't worry about that. That property has been abandoned by her and her family. You are the next in line, direct descendant. We have ways to establish your ownership of that property," he said.

Grace tried to look innocent and thoughtful as she asked, "How much do you think it might be worth?"

Henderson jumped right in. "Oh, gosh, there's two hundred acres, more or less. It needs a good cleanup, lots of work, and a new road. We might get it appraised for perhaps seventy-five hundred dollars an acre. I would be willing to do the paperwork for free. That's a million and a half, Grace. That's a darn good deal. You need to take that and forget about the whole thing. Your aunt Lucy got her share years ago, didn't she?"

Grace ignored the question and tried to look impressed with the numbers. She straightened up in the chair, put her hand to her mouth, and stared at Henderson. "You said one and a half million? That's a lot of money, my friend. I certainly don't earn that kind of money."

While she was doing her best to look stunned, Henderson pushed some paperwork across the desk in her direction. "You can retire and go to Florida, forget about earning money, just enjoy your life, get out of that big city and leave that college behind," he said.

Henderson shut up too fast. Grace realized that he knew where she had been living all the time and he never mentioned that to Aunt Lucy or her family. She reached for the papers and pretended to scan while she calmed her emotions.

While pretending an interest in the paperwork, Grace noticed that an LLC corporation would be making the offer. She looked confused and naive as she asked, "Why would a corporation pay so much for a place to ride horses and camp? I don't understand how they expect to make a return on their investment, especially when they have to spend so much on cleanup and repairs?"

Henderson hesitated, but he didn't hedge when he said, "Grace, we don't ask about their business. They wouldn't make an offer if they didn't make money. What they do is their business, and you can take the money and forget you ever came back here. That's the way it works. We don't ask questions."

Grace remembered her instructions. She smiled at Henderson and teasingly asked, "How about you and I go into a business like that and split the profits? We can rent the old place to these people and keep some of the profits for ourselves. What type of business would we need to do?"

Henderson started stuttering, "Uh…well…uh…Grace, you and I could rent to these people, but they will ask for upgrades and repairs. They want a helicopter pad down in that old lower pasture, they want a locked gate on the entrance, and they want bathrooms and water, you know, like a deep artesian well. That would all be expensive and lots of hard work."

THE ROAD TO HELL IS PAVED WITH... WHAT?

With a coy, curious expression, Grace winked at him and asked, "Okay, tell me the truth. I'm a big girl. If there's a secluded old farm with a helicopter pad, a locked gate, what kind of business are they in? You're right, it's none of my business, but I'd like to be far removed from this area with my money in hand if it's not legal. I'm only interested in covering my butt, not talking about any 'business' going on around that old farm."

He hesitated, but he lowered his voice and stammered with his answer. "These people...they come in here from Columbia, Grace. They need a private, secluded place to conduct business without having anybody interfere, especially the law enforcement dummies here in this little county. If they don't bother anybody, who cares what they do?"

Grace asked, "Does the local law enforcement 'dummies' just intentionally ignore them or what?"

He answered, "No, not exactly. That old farm is considered not accessible and off the grid. They don't bother with it. It's perfect for the purpose it serves. People pay to use it, have fun, and make some money at the same time. The local sheriff doesn't even look. Never has."

"Okay, how much rent do you collect?" Grace asked. "You need to let me in on that. You've been renting a long time, apparently. Who gave you the go-ahead? Aunt Lucy would never do that if she thought it might be illegal."

He looked annoyed, but he countered with, "No, Aunt Lucy is not responsible. I do all the scheduling and catering. I take supplies, food, and whatever the people want. I earn a good dollar and keep the people coming back. Your aunt's kin get paid, but they won't do a thing, they never have. They won't do much for themselves. They get paid good for nothing."

Grace knew she had him cornered, but she'd need to give a little ground to set the trap further. She shrugged and said, "Well, the old farm has been good for somebody while it has been sitting there going to ruin. I can't say that I wouldn't have done the same thing. So tell me this: I'm going to be retiring soon, and if you and I form a partnership and do the catering and rent the place to these people, how much could you and I make together?"

He looked down at his desk for a few minutes, scratched his chin a bit, as if in deep thought. As his expression suddenly brightened, he said, "You know, Grace, I'll have to think about that. If you own the property and I do the scheduling and catering, we could just split the profits as you said. We could finance the improvements as needed and pay as we got paid. That way, we can charge more and come out on top. You know, Grace, that might be a good plan. At some point, then, we could sell the whole thing and walk away, no risk involved. That sounds like something we could work out."

Pretending to give the whole idea some thought, Grace slowly tightened the snare. "How much do you think we could make in, say, a month? I like to think in numbers, especially when we would need to borrow money to finance improvements."

Scratching away on his legal pad, Henderson appeared to be in deep thought. He tapped away on a calculator, and Grace kept silent, watching him sweat. He was looking over the figures when he said, "It looks like I might have collected about sixty-five to seventy-five thousand last year, not counting for the bad-weather months. If we put in a helicopter pad and the other improvements, we ought to be able to triple the profits and make a lot of money for both of us. We can work together to work that out."

Grace felt her emotions going bonkers as she quickly did the math. That rascal had been renting the old place for years, making huge amounts of money, and paying Aunt Lucy's family exactly one hundred fifty bucks a month, eighteen hundred dollars a year, not even 3 percent. What kind of person would do that?

It was difficult to keep her composure, but Grace became more determined. She dismissed her rage and reverted to her intended focus. She prodded into the business of catering. "What kind of catering is needed, and how could I help with that to make money?"

Henderson jumped right in with, "Oh, food and wine, beer and pizza, horses and equipment, female companionship—you know how the men are. They like girls, and they pay well for the girls. The younger, the better. We can supply whatever they order. We got some good working girls around here."

Grace widened her eyes, looking at Henderson as though she loved the idea. "Well, that is interesting. I'm intrigued. I know a few classy college girls that would be good for that, add a little flavor to the mix and charge more. Let me think about that for sure."

Having heard about as much as she could endure, Grace knew she needed to escape before she lost her focus entirely. She diverted the conversation with, "Could I have a copy of this offer to take with me? I like to weigh all my options, and I'll be back next week with my answer. You and I might have something to talk over. I'll stay in touch. Do you have a group coming for the Memorial Day weekend? I won't bother you if you are going to be busy with that long weekend. You make all the money you can. Don't let me get in your way."

He gathered the paperwork and moved toward a copier in the back of the room. He chuckled as he said, "You bet I'm gonna be busy. I got twenty-five or more people coming through over the weekend. Memorial Day weekend is one of the busiest and most profitable weeks we have. It starts the whole ball rolling for the rest of the season."

While he had his back turned, making copies, Grace installed one of the magnetic transmitters under the framework of her chair. She pretended to be scratching her foot as she secured the thing where no one would be able to see it. Then she got up, stretched, and walked around his desk to view some pictures on the bookshelf behind his chair. She slipped another transmitter between the bookshelf and a metal file cabinet standing next to it; one would have to look hard to find it.

She was amusing herself with the pictures on the shelf when Henderson returned to his desk to staple the papers. Grace kept looking at the pictures of the Bobby Henderson she had known from their high school days, the football star, the heartthrob of all the girls. She gave Henderson a big grin and said, "Those were the days. You were the catch of the town. Who finally caught you? Anybody I'd remember, anybody from around here?"

He smiled broadly as he handed the paperwork to Grace and said, "Nope. I tried a few times to settle down, but it wasn't my thing. After three bad marriages, I'd had enough. I like to drink some, but my wives wanted to label me a drunk and put me in rehab, cause trouble with my legal profession. I'm better off by myself. Don't mean I don't like good female companionship, but I don't put up with rules about my casual drinking. I enjoy a good drink, always did, always will, I reckon."

Grace pretended to notice the time and exclaimed, "Oh, heavens! I'm gonna be late. I need to be back in the city before eight, and I've got to hurry. It's a long drive. You make some good money this week, and we'll go out to a nice dinner. We can talk about our plan. I've got to rush. Bye, bye."

She was out the door before he could get his lecherous hands on her body. Her little Lexus sped away while he was still standing in the doorway. Grace didn't dare to look back. The law enforcement team would be waiting for her at a secluded spot she still needed to find. She hoped she had covered the bases well enough, and she hoped to leave undercover sleuthing to the professionals. Maybe, just maybe, the sheriff wouldn't ask again.

*****

At an old warehouse on the outskirts of town, where the sheriff's team was supposed to be waiting, Grace turned into the parking lot, swung the car to the right toward the end of the building, and was making her way toward the rear when she noticed she was being followed by another vehicle. Her heart was thumping in her ears. She made the turn around the building and found herself in a very secluded spot—no way out except the way she had come in. She didn't dare shut the engine off until she saw someone she might know. As she was looking straight ahead, someone came from behind and tapped on the window. Grace nearly jumped out of her seat as she whirled to see Lydia looking at her.

"Oh my lord, Lydia, you scared me! This place is spooky! What do you want me to do?"

Lydia said, "Sorry, this is our temporary headquarters, concealed from the public. You come in and we'll take that wire, and the

THE ROAD TO HELL IS PAVED WITH... WHAT?

boss will instruct us further. You did really well. We were listening. You're okay now. You're with us."

Grace trailed Lydia to a private area, and the wiretap was retrieved. Then she was taken to a makeshift office where several familiar faces were waiting. She was offered a chair, and she sat down with an exhausted plop. The sweat was popping out on her forehead; the men offered her a cold drink and let her rest. She had to gather her strength before she could talk.

Shortly, the sheriff came to congratulate her. "Ms. Grace, you did it, got what we needed. Lady, you are good at this kind of thing." He grabbed her arm and held it up in the air, symbolizing a champion. The guys all cheered.

Grace sipped at her soda and tried to breathe deeply to stop her hands from shaking. She managed to ask, "Did I cover everything? I can't focus well when I'm mad, and I was getting outraged. He's been cheating my aunt's family for years. He is disgusting! How can anybody be that deceptive with poor people who can barely survive their circumstances?"

One of the older men spoke up. "Ms. Grace, I don't know how you remained as calm as you did. I wanted to laugh at how easily you trapped him and he walked right into the trap. You're good at this, lady, and you need to give yourself some credit. We're happy with you."

The sheriff had his usual instructions, "Ms. Grace, when you come back next week, we'd like you to trade cars. Your Lexus is too easy to spot. Rent something less showy, maybe something that will navigate that old farm road. We may need you to help us. We're planning to lock the place down after the holiday. You'll need to be available. Also, park behind your aunt's house, not in front. Be quiet and keep a low profile. Don't take any chances until we tell you, okay?"

After shaking hands all around, Grace happily left town for her condo in the big city.

Grace didn't know that her role as a mole would bring fame and notoriety around town; she would become a celebrity to the locals in the next couple of weeks. She didn't give it a thought; she just wanted to go home and feel safe with her beloved friends.

Deception of the Self

On her way home to the big city, Grace was happily singing along with her satellite radio, tapping her fingers on the steering wheel and feeling quite pleased with herself. Much had been accomplished over the past few days, and her spirits were up; she was feeling pleased with the progress. She had a lot to tell her recovery friends, and they would be proud of her; she just knew she'd receive accolades all around.

This happy mood lasted about an hour. The second hour of driving grew tiresome, and when the big city began to appear with its traffic snarl, Grace began to sweat. Multiple lanes of traffic, normal for late afternoon, gnawed at Grace's nerves. The pace of traffic, the noise, and the big city rush were simply too stressful for Grace to maneuver. She was feeling nauseous, and her hands began to shake. She needed to stop.

Leaving the mayhem of the freeway, she made her way to the nearest quick stop. After a trip to the restroom, she wandered into the store to find something that might calm her nerves. There seemed to be very little available, so she asked the attendant, "Where is the nearest liquor store?"

The attendant pointed his finger toward the street and replied, "Go to the street, turn right, and the store will be about two blocks on the left."

Two blocks later, Grace had purchased what she knew would quell her nerves, a big bottle of bourbon. She gave no thought to sobriety or her upcoming progress report, due at 8:00 p.m. at the recovery meeting. She was back in the car and heading into the traffic before it dawned on her that she could not be drinking and driving;

she'd have to wait until she got home. When she arrived at home, she realized that she had to face the traffic again and make her way across town to the appointment. She certainly couldn't talk with alcohol on her breath; she remembered that. At home, she delightfully placed her big bottle of treasured relief on her nightstand and told herself that it would be waiting; she'd get some much-needed relief at bedtime.

Grace didn't notice the subtle trap that she had set for herself in her own thoughts. She also didn't notice the fact that she had handled the traffic perfectly well as soon as she made the purchase. She didn't notice how calm she had become just knowing her trusty old medicine would be waiting. She made her way across town to her meeting quite calmly and efficiently, without a blip. Her psychological dependency was well embedded. She thought she'd simply hurry home after the meeting and have the problem solved.

The recovery friends had been watching for Grace to appear. Their meeting was already in progress when she slipped in quietly and took a seat. The moderator took notice of her presence, and during a pause in the conversation, he spoke to Grace. "It's good to see you, Grace, and we're all eager to hear what you have to share. We'll dismiss the regular meeting at the usual time, and you can have the floor. Those who want to stay and hear Grace's progress report are all welcome. It always helps to share experiences. We get to learn together."

The regular meeting went on for another half-hour. Grace was silent, not paying much attention to what was being discussed. She was thinking how she might cut her time short and leave; she badly needed her relief. The day had simply been too long, too stressful, and she was hungry and tired. She'd had nothing to eat since lunch. She could solve her dilemma at home by herself, the sooner, the better.

The closing prayer was said, and the regular meeting ended. Those who could stay and hear Grace's report kept their seats. Four men and three women were eager to hear Grace's account of her journey into step 4 of the program, that "fearless and searching moral inventory" of herself. They had sent her on her journey with a couple of Bible verses to remember.

> Be alert and of sober mind. Your enemy, the devil, prowls around like a roaring lion, looking for someone to devour. (1 Pet. 5:8)

> Let us examine our ways and test them; and let us return to the Lord. (Lam. 3:40)

Grace did not understand the intent behind the fourth-step self-examination. The recovery group had pushed her to investigate her background, so she started with the backwoods community from which she had been exiled, in a spirit of rebellion. She wanted to get the obligation to self-examine over and done with, the faster, the better. Many addicts start their recovery with just such an attitude; it's easier to deny their own moral flaws and simply point fingers.

*****

Step 4 requires an honest effort to find the moral failures of oneself without casting blame—no naming, shaming, claiming, proclaiming, or pointing fingers. The question of blame becomes insignificant while the self-examiner has an honest look at "one's own behavior." Was there oversight, neglect, lack of responsibility on the part of oneself? How did one's own attitude and behavior contribute to the discomfort and difficulty? Can an honest, objective analysis reframe the experience, and might there be both "good and bad" aspects of the experiences of one's life?

This "searching and fearless" effort can reveal the roots of self-destructive behaviors and attitudes that have perpetuated and promoted dysfunction. Despite what might have been bad behavior on anyone else's part, patterns of dysfunction can be identified and accepted simply as "it was what it was, and it is what it is." Acceptance brings change, and recovery can begin.

It takes personal courage to fearlessly search, forgive, and take responsibility for change. Recovering addicts support one another through this journey. With a willing heart and a humble spirit, miracles can happen. Troubled souls find their way out of confusion and into a spiritual light; they begin to look to a higher power's purpose for their lives. In this way, they break the cycle of dysfunction that has hounded them for years; they pass on what they learn to the next generation. Generational curses can be broken in the process.

*****

As the recovery group listened to Grace's brief synopsis of her five-day journey, they kept the questions coming and tried to keep the story moving. Mostly, they prodded her with, "How did that make you feel? What would you want to change about that? What would you like to have happen there?" They were trying to encourage Grace to think through the issues for herself, seeking a vision of purpose in the orchestration of God's greater plan.

The members were particularly interested and joyful as Grace talked about her sense of "calling" to educate and enlighten the church community about the disease of addiction. The group came to its feet in praise, thanking the higher power for guidance toward that goal. Then the members brought up the final question, and it stunned Grace. "How much did you drink while you were away? Did you succumb to your cravings? How much did you bring home so you can throw a party for yourself and celebrate, now that you've accomplished so much? Where did you hide the stash?"

The group sat silent, waiting for Grace's response. Her jaw had dropped, but she managed to stammer, "Why do you think I'd do that?"

One of the older fellows just smiled sheepishly, and with a chuckle, he said, "Because we've all done the same thing, get a little progress under our belts and blow it all away with our presumption that we're home free. It's called relapse, Grace, and it happens right at a pivotal point in our spiritual journey. It's designed to undermine our own efforts without giving it a thought, then we're back where we started. The enemy knows when to strike, Grace, and I can tell from your demeanor, your body language, and your attitude, you want to get this little accounting over with and done. So tell us, how much have you got waiting, or did you plan to run into a nightclub on the way home?"

Grace knew she was trapped; everyone was staring at her. She looked around at the different faces. There was no denial—they knew. She took a choking breath, dropped her face in her hands, and began to sob. One of the ladies, Stella, came to her side, patted her back, and pulled Grace into a bear hug as she said, "Honey, we've all been there. You're being tested. It's an expected part of our journey. You can tell the truth. We'll understand and help you. What exactly did you do?"

When her sobbing slowed, Grace managed a weak response to their questions. "I was so frustrated with the traffic, and I guess I snapped. I bought a single bottle of bourbon, but I didn't drink any. I had to drive, and I was expected here. I saved it for later, for bedtime."

The next questions came. "Was that the only bottle you saved? Are you stashing bottles anywhere else? Are you planning to celebrate at a nightspot later?"

Not a soul in the group was surprised that Grace had fallen on her face; they were more surprised that the bottle was still unopened. They praised Grace for having some restraint despite her discomfort.

Stella spoke to Grace. "Honey, I've been right where you are, a dozen times or more. I'm thinking you could use some company tonight. I'll pick up my things and meet you at your condo. I love to stay there. It makes me feel wealthy. I'm not coming to guard you or your beloved bourbon. You need to decide that for yourself. I'm gonna make myself available to talk and listen. I can help you with your perspective. You need the support, Grace, and I am available. I know how to put that old devil, alcohol, in its place."

Grace dabbed at her face as she thanked the group for their insight and for pointing out her self-deception. They reminded her of a prayer in Psalm 139:23–24, "Search me, O God, and know my heart; test me and know my anxious thoughts. See if there is any offensive way in me and lead me in the way everlasting."

Pastor said, "You memorize that prayer and keep it in your heart, Grace. God will empower you when you are tempted. You know that Satan won't give up on you. You are too valuable a resource in God's greater plan. He'll try to destroy anything you try to do for God's people. Satan has had you under his power for way too long, and he'll put up a good fight. God has called you out of bondage. You've already seen where he can use you. Remember, you've got a son. What kind of miracle is that? God is on your side, and you are being called for a great purpose. Believe that and listen to your conscience, not feelings, not cravings. Walk with God, Grace, walk in faith with God."

*****

At the gated entrance to Grace's building complex, Stella waited for Grace to come home. She was determined that Grace would hear the truth about her reliance on the bottle, taken from Stella's own experience.

Stella had befriended Grace from the beginning of her association with the group. Stella often referred to her days "on the street" and how she had endured poverty and hunger during her young years. She openly shared that she started selling her body for food and clothes before she was out of puberty. Her teenage years were spent as a "young working girl" on the streets, working for money to help feed her younger siblings. She had started her drinking habits, first with her customers, and then by herself, to shut out the shame and humiliation of her job. The things she was expected to do to earn money were painfully shameful and humiliating. Eventually, she turned to drugs to dull the pain and found herself supporting both an alcohol and drug habit with very little money to help herself. She was arrested several times for prostitution, and she had little money to bail out of jail. She wandered into a twelve-step group and never left.

Grace had been fascinated with Stella's story and noticed her plain-spoken way of addressing others in the group with love, compassion, and understanding. Stella just plowed right into denial and justifying behaviors with persistence, and she wouldn't let up, but she did it with love. Stella was much admired for her honesty, her spirit, her "street smarts," and her experience. Grace considered Stella a great asset and her best friend.

*****

The two women were sharing a late-night snack in Grace's condo when Stella asked, "Okay, Grace, where's the stash? Where did you hide the devil's poison? Bring it out and let's see what you think is so vital to your existence."

Grace retrieved the big bottle of bourbon and placed it on the table in front of Stella. Stella promptly pushed it across the table to Grace, saying, "I'm not here to stop you, Grace. I'm here to convince myself that a woman of your intelligence, your status, your talents, and your good fortune, a woman as blessed as you are, would reject God's protection, His abundance, and His calling to help His people, would give it all up for a stupid drink of this poison. It appears to me that God has been at your back a long time and you have been on a long pity trip, whimpering. You're so full of self-pity. You need your bottle, like a baby does. I know about that because I have been there myself, desperate for relief, in bondage to a lifetime of pain and misery. The day this changed for me, I came to believe in a power greater than myself, and stronger than my bad habits. From that day forward, my life has changed in miraculous ways. God's abundance started showing up, and I've never had time, or the desire, to whimper. I'm too grateful for deliverance. You have to drop the denial, Grace, and do your part."

Grace had to ask, "So you think I'm just feeling sorry for myself when I drink, and I'm having a blackout about how God has blessed me so far in my life?"

Stella went on with her lecture. "Girl, what on earth keeps you stuck in your old resentments, the old pain, when God has blessed you beyond measure? Yes, you got the bad end of the deal when you were a child. You didn't get to choose your circumstances—nobody does. We all got families like we got, dysfunction and all. It becomes our place to make the best we can of the circumstances, not to sit and whine for years. You got sent away to have your baby—unjustly, yes—but look where it took you, a free education with housing, later a good, guaranteed income in a high-dollar job. But all that time you wanted to stay stuck in the resentment, the anger, and feel sorry for yourself? All these years, Grace, while you've been on a pity party, I've been hustling, selling my dignity and self-worth to just survive, drinking to drown the shame and humiliation. I developed so much self-hatred I wanted to commit suicide. I couldn't endure the thought of another man using my body in such shameful ways. You, Grace, could have been just like me, and many others, if your family hadn't sent you away so you could have a better chance. Can't you see that?"

Grace took Stella's pleading tone in thought as she answered, "I guess I really never thought about it from that angle. It would have been a miserable life, being a young woman with an illegitimate child in that environment. The young women didn't have a chance when they started having babies early, just poverty and hard going. Some that I grew up with are still there and poor as church mice. I'm one of the lucky few who got out of the cycle. You're right, I'm blessed and there's no reason to be mad at anybody now. They're all dead, anyway. I see what you mean. I'm drinking out of habit to escape what doesn't exist now. God is calling me to get over it and help others. I'm capable of helping break the cycle of dysfunction and poverty in my old community. I really want to commit myself to that."

Stella responded, "Grace, that's right, and you can't get the job even started if you are dependent on your old habits. You'll lose before you get anything done as long as you drink, and you're trying to turn into your grandpa Lawson. Do you want to follow his example, his reputation, his legacy as a drunk? Do you intend to lose the old farm because he sold you out to keep it? Do you want your son to find that his mother is an alcoholic? Ask yourself how you want others to think of you when you're gone."

Grace was quick to respond, "Not like I remember Grandpa for sure. I want to do something admirable with my life, something better than he managed to do. Grandpa was a talented man, but he couldn't stay on focus with his talents without undermining his own good intentions. His personality was split, and his drinking brought out the abusive side. He didn't relate to the pain others might have.

He didn't act like he cared. He knew God's Word, but he couldn't live it. I often wondered why. Now I guess I know. The alcohol took out his controls, and he lost his way, just like I'm doing. You're right, Stella, I'm following him. I've lost sight of how protected and blessed I have been. I never really thought of my reaction as being self-destructive. I just escaped, like Grandpa did, shut everything out."

Stella glared at Grace, and she grabbed the bottle of bourbon, holding it up for Grace to see, saying, "You have been brought to this point for a reason, Grace, and you don't have any more time to give this old bottle of death. Now, don't you need to be at work early tomorrow?"

"Yes, I have to catch up. Can't wait for Monday. There's a ton of work waiting, graduations to work on, students to grade and grades to post…busy week ahead. You're right, I don't have time to wallow around with this poison. My mind will need to be clear and focused. Besides that, Stella, I dare not offend the regulators, and they are watching me." Grace dropped her head in shame.

Stella answered, "Don't give the regulators any reason to fire you, Grace. You play the game close to your chest, then you can retire and go on with God's plan for the rest of your life. I've got to get some sleep. I have to be in the restaurant before 7:00 a.m. You take this bottle to bed with you or you can make another, more sensible choice. It's up to you."

The bottle never left the table as Grace doused the lights and headed for the shower. She said a quick prayer asking for forgiveness for her pity parties and her immature attitude.

Stella was dressed and ready to leave when Grace appeared the next morning. Stella gave Grace a hug and said, "Congrats, girl. You slept without your tonic, and I heard you snoring. You don't need that old junk. Now, just repeat that behavior, one day at a time, until you can ignore the stupid stuff and praise God for His abundant blessings, okay?"

Grace hugged her dear friend, and as Stella left, Grace was reminded of how God had turned that little streetwalker Stella into a renowned chef and caterer at one of the most prestigious restaurants in the city. Despite Stella's busy life, she never missed a meeting with her beloved recovery group on Thursday nights. She helped her community and brought many young girls off the street, sometimes buying medical care and contraceptives for their protection. She had become a messenger of God's love and power. She told her own story with humility and gratitude. Grace said a prayer of thanksgiving for her dear friend Stella and considered her to be a gift of God.

The bottle of bourbon sat unopened on the table as Grace left for work. The spiritual enemy would have to find another opportunity, at least for now. Relapse is a common occurrence, and Grace was by no means exempt. She would be a valuable, gifted soldier in God's army, and the enemy would not give up easily. Grace would have to fight to break her bonds; the war was not over by any means.

An Angel on Assignment

It was Friday, and Grace had been in her office, working in a Spock-like mode all day, no feelings, just logic and cold judgment. Dispensing grades at the end of the semester brought out the best in some students and the worst in others. Some Grace referred to as the "entitlement hounds," those who argued for grades they simply didn't earn. Professor Lawson didn't hear arguments; she simply gave them a choice: earn the grade you want and you'll get it; otherwise, don't waste time. She was known to be tough and didn't pamper anybody. Those who made it through her class with good marks were exceptional, and she let them know that. She could be very patient with the slower learners but had little tolerance for the "entitled" group. Spoiled, overpampered, lazy, and indulgent kids didn't get any sympathy; sometimes she'd just smile and ask, "Did your grandmother die again? How many times has your poor grandmother died? Bring me an excuse I haven't heard." Not many challenged Professor Lawson.

Her workday was almost over when she heard a knock on the door. Thinking it might be another whiner, another entitlement hound, she barked, "Come in!"

Professor John Larkin, her neighbor in the condo complex, hobbled in and plopped wearily in a chair. "Thanks, Grace. I'm trying to escape, and I saw your car. Could I get a ride home? I walked in this morning, and I'm too tired to walk home. I don't want to bother you. Do you mind giving me a ride?"

"Of course not," Grace said. "I'm trying to escape myself. I'm going by my favorite deli to find some food. Want to join me? I'm starving."

John Larkin was happy about that. He said, "Indeed I do. I hardly had time for a break all day, and I'm bushed. Good food would help, and good company. We can forget the day's miseries. Talk about retiring. I'm all in."

*****

Professor John Larkin had been Grace's guide and counselor since she had arrived at the college years ago. He was about five years older and had been at the job of advising new teachers, overseeing their progress, and keeping tabs on their performance for most of his career. He had helped Grace with the purchase of her condo when she had finally saved sufficient funds to buy herself a home. He was also on the regulatory board that had disciplined Grace for her alcohol habit.

Grace had admired her advisory professor for his fairness and had no problem with him at all, until her drinking had gotten out of hand. Even then, he never mentioned it outside the campus, at the condo complex, or on the many occasions when they walked to work together. He always maintained a strict professional relationship. Grace had grown comfortable with "Professor" Larkin.

Professor had never invited Grace to his condo for any reason, so she was quite surprised to hear him say, "Grace, let's eat together tonight. I badly need the company. Would you like to join me in my place, or would you be more comfortable at your home?"

Grace covered her surprise as best as she could and said, "Let's eat at my place. It's convenient to park in the garage and bring the food into the kitchen. Helps to keep the place a bit neater."

They made their way into the kitchen, and Grace was clearing the dining table when she spotted the big bottle of bourbon. She reached to remove it from the table. Professor was watching. There were yellow sticky notes attached to the sides of the bottle. Stella had attached notes to the bottle earlier that morning that Grace hadn't noticed. On one side Stella had written, "Grandpa's poison," and on the opposite side, "You're next!"

Grace stared at the notes for a moment, and realizing Professor was looking at her, she simply said, "You know already about my struggle with this stuff. My friend Stella, who is also my sponsor in my twelve-step program, is testing me. I'm not going to drink this. Do you drink, Professor? Do you know about alcoholics and how crazy some of us can get when we drink?"

Professor didn't hesitate. He said, "I've had some experience with the stuff myself, so yes, I know the struggle. I was fortunate that I never had time to take it too far. My job simply wouldn't allow it. The board must hold some high standards for the students and staff. Had it not been for the need to hold my job, who knows where I'd be at this stage? My family had some susceptible genetics, and some lost the genetic lottery and wound up with the full-fledged disease. I'm fortunate that it didn't happen to me."

Grace tried to make her guest comfortable at the table, and then she sat down to eat. Professor reached for her hand and asked, "Grace, do you mind if we say a word of thanks?"

In his prayer he spoke of gratitude for the food and the wonderful presence of good friends with which to share it. Grace had only heard sincere and genuine prayers from her Aunt Lucy, so she followed his "Amen" with one of her own. She felt truly blessed to have him at the table.

During the meal, it occurred to Grace that there were rules against "fraternizing" with coworkers, especially superiors in charge of overseeing one's career. She was enjoying his presence but felt she'd better make herself clear: the man might just be testing her. One violation was all he'd need to ruin her professionally; her distrust of men in general kicked into high gear. She had to ask, "Professor, are we breaking the rules? I'm tired tonight, and I didn't think about the socializing and fraternizing thing. Are we violating the rules of conduct?"

Professor laughed, and with a broad smile, he said, "No, Grace, we can eat together, walk to work together, live in the same complex, even swim in the same pool. It's the personal behavior that is not allowed. We need to behave professionally, and we've always done that. Besides, I'm retiring this summer, so who cares if you and I have a dinner together? If it's comfortable for you, I'd welcome your friendship. I'm not going to be your superior officer much longer. I'm happy to retire."

Surprised and alarmed, Grace said, "Oh my gosh, if I can't come to you for help, what will I do? Whom will I depend on?"

He answered, "I suspect Margo Lemons will be nominated. She's been after a seat on the board for a long time. She will probably be filling in this summer, and she'll get her hooks into the right people. You know how that goes, politics, alive and well."

Grace was speechless. Professor Margo Lemons was a pain in everyone's backside, and she was one of Grace's biggest critics. Two more years at the college would leave Grace on a tightrope, and Lemons would see to her dismissal if Grace even so much as wobbled. Yes, politics would be alive and in control. Grace felt a sense of despair.

Professor John already knew politics would put Grace in a predicament, and he began to offer some suggestions. "Grace, why don't you submit your retirement plans? By the end of the fall term, you could be out of sight and away from the pressure."

Grace asked, "What about my pension? I need to be careful that I don't risk my income. I'm only fifty-seven years old, and I need to work as long as possible to maximize my retirement income, and in another two years, I can access my accounts without penalty. My personal retirement funds need to build up, if they can. I'm certainly not interested in another teaching job at this point. I've got too much to do, and lots of expenses up ahead."

"Maybe you could ask the board if you could serve on the advisory committee for your specialty for another year or so, then you don't have so much classroom work, but your salary continues with benefits until you officially retire. Could you work another year, stay out of trouble, not let Margo Lemons have any reason to push you out, then take the last year as a much-deserved sabbatical? You've never taken much time off, Grace, and you're due a sabbatical every seven years. I don't see that as a problem with the board. These people admire your work ethic, your stamina, and your devotion to the job. It's something to consider. It might work. It's something to think about."

Grace responded, "I wonder, Professor, what might happen if I choose to retire now. How would that affect my income? I'm sure my pension would be reduced considerably, but I'd be willing to adjust my expenses and survive if it's not extremely tight. I'm needed in my old community with what's left of my family. I'd love to go now. I feel a strong conviction to go there and teach for the community. I know I'm being called to go. I'm just not sure how to manage the finances that will be needed to make the change. I know God provides for His servants, but I'm weak, and poverty scares me to death. That's one of the reasons I'm having trouble with alcohol. My recovery friends are trying to support me, but this old bottle of bourbon has its appeal. I'm scared. I'm fighting some health problems too, but I feel a need to go back to that old farm and answer God's call on my life, while I still can."

Professor John said, "Tell me about your calling. Can you share that with me? I'm interested, because I'm retiring with no plans, no sense of direction, no conviction, and nothing calling for my time. I certainly don't want to write any more books, or grade any more research papers, or read not one more doctoral thesis. I want nothing to do with educational endeavors, but I don't know what it is that I do want. It's a confusing time for me. After thirty years, I'm burned out, and I'm scared too. What if this is all there is to life? What do we do now? Just get old and expire? That scares me. The old philosopher said, 'Life goes by fast. If you don't stop to notice it, it is gone.' That scares me. You're one of the lucky ones, Grace, to feel something beckoning in your spirit, compelling you to better things. Can you share your sense of calling with me? I'd love to hear your story."

Grace spent the next couple of hours relating her recent attempt at the fourth-step investigation and what she'd found, much to her astonishment, in relation to herself as well as the family of origin. Professor was absorbed in the story and prodded Grace to keep talking. She freely answered any questions but iterated, "That's all I know at this time." She emphasized, "I'm trusting my higher power to help me."

As the story unfolded about Grace's young pregnancy and how it might be possible to find her son, Professor watched as Grace wiped her tears. As he wiped at his own eyes, he said, "I've always known, Grace, that you had some inner turmoil going on. Deep inside you were in pain, but you covered it with an intense focus on work. Your work ethic was admirable, but you seemed to be on automatic pilot, and you never seemed pleased with yourself. A deep inner doubt and lack of confidence seemed to hound you. I can understand it better now. It seems to me you've never had validation from others where you didn't have to perform, jump through hoops like a trained animal, and try to survive. Your personal value was never recognized, just your performance. Your alcohol became your best friend and, in a sense, your lover."

Grace said, "You are right. Alcohol is the only reliable comfort I've ever had. Now it has become the enemy. I want to go back to my home, where I can find myself again, find my son, enjoy what's left of my life, and help my community. I can feel better about myself if I can help the disadvantaged, and I know I can. I want to make amends to myself, my son, and my family. I need to go. God has called me. And look at what He is offering me. Professor, what would you do if you were in my place? How do think you might feel?"

With a burst of enthusiasm, Professor responded, "I'd go, Grace, I'd go! In fact, please don't misinterpret this, but I'd be willing to go with you. I don't have a clue how I can help, but this sounds like an incredible challenge to me, and an adventure. I'd be delighted to support you any way I can, and I'd never expect anything in return. I'm well off with my finances. I don't need a thing. I could help you. You're taking on a lot by yourself. If we could get you retired and focused, you could trust me to help, couldn't you? I'd love the challenge, the change of pace, and I have absolutely no plans for myself except fishing a bit."

Grace stared at her old friend and adviser. She had known him to be honest and trustworthy, never giving her any reason to believe he would hurt her. He seemed particularly interested in the project with the old Lawson farm; he could be a great asset on the farm and a great support for the tremendous volume of chores ahead. She never hesitated as she said, "If you want to help, you are welcome, but when you see the amount of work, you might change your mind.

And pay is out of the question. You decide about that. Let me show you some pictures. You'll see what I mean."

Grace retrieved her camera, and as she flipped through the various snapshots, she explained the images and showed the beautiful scenes of Lawson Valley as it appeared from the scenic overlook from the west ridge. He took it all in with great excitement, even the pictures of Aunt Lucy sleeping at her family graves.

Professor said, "This is precious, Grace. I understand why you need to go, and right away. Your love for these mountains and your love for your family…how can you not? I want to help you with this. I've got a motorhome in storage, and it tows my Jeep. I'm already equipped. You just say when and where. I'll be there."

Grace said nothing; she let him decide for himself. She did, however, place her palms together and bowed her head. God had sent an angel in the form of someone she could trust.

After a few minutes of reflection, Professor offered some suggestions. "Why don't we ask the board members how we can feasibly retire you now with the least amount of pain? You might have to submit a doctor's recommendation, retire for health reasons. Your health could be at stake, that sort of thing. Do you want me to look into that possibility?"

"If that's what it takes," Grace said. "My health is becoming a problem already. My doctors have warned me about a nervous system disorder, high blood pressure, heart failure, cirrhosis, dementia, and death. I'm pretty sure they would recommend a change of pace to preserve my health. Hopefully, they won't suggest rehab again. I've done that. I will certainly ask them about a letter of recommendation that I be retired."

"In all honesty," Professor said, "I believe the board would be relieved to let you go. Some think you are becoming a liability to the school and believe it might be good to get you out. You can avoid any further losses if you volunteer to leave. That will be the best thing for yourself and the school. I'm being honest here. It might work out for the good, after all. Let's work on that angle, okay?"

Grace swallowed hard as she realized the bitter truth; she would be ousted eventually, anyway. Politics and butt-covering by those in power would be her fate. Professor had just given her a way out. She took a deep breath and responded, "Thank you, Professor, for your honesty. It's brutal, but I need to know. I'll speak to my doctors next week, and I'll submit my resignation based on health concerns. If you think of anything more I need to do, please let me know. I want to do what God is calling me to do. I believe that will save my life."

Professor agreed to speak to the board and try to get the process started. As he left for his home, Grace said, "Thank you, Professor. You've been a great help tonight, as usual. You've always been fair with me. I'd give you a hug, but proper protocol doesn't allow for it. You have a good night."

The man winked and grinned at Grace as he said, "Save the hug. I'll collect on that after I'm no longer in position, retired and free, no rules at that point. And by the way, my name is John, just John. I would appreciate being simply your friend John."

*****

As Grace cleared the table, she put the bottle of bourbon back in place and thanked her higher power for friends like John. It seemed very strange how friends like him were showing up all around just when she needed them the most. Certainly, God knew how to pick the best for the circumstances. Grace slept peacefully, dreaming of the day she would be retired back on the old Lawson farm.

John, the old friend and professor who had been at her side for years, would prove to be her guardian angel, assigned to be a mainstay in her life. He would take his assignment seriously, and maybe, just maybe, the lovely lady would catch on. She had so many challenges at this point he dared not dream. He would simply bide his time and pray, leave the outcome up to God.

Conviction Changes the Direction

The weekend was exhausting. Grace spent much of Saturday with her recovery friend Spotter. He had agreed to help Grace find a suitable all-terrain vehicle she could use to manage the rough backcountry road into the old farm. Grace knew the lovely Lexus would be an entertainment for the boys to enjoy, but it would be mostly worthless for the required work. Spotter assured Grace he knew how to handle the auto dealers and keep her out of trouble.

They made several stops at the dealerships and looked at several models, but Spotter did not express much interest in the prospects. Grace might have taken an offer at the first stop, but Spotter shook his head. He said, "We have to get a better deal for your car, Grace. You don't want to lose any more than you need to when you trade. Let me make a call to some lease agencies. They like cars like yours. Maybe they will offer something we like. We might find something a year or two older with some mileage, but you don't want to pay for something new and use it on the old rough farm road."

Grace's approach to car-buying was simple: find what you like and pay for it. Spotter had a much more frugal approach: get a suitable vehicle for the job and pay no more than necessary. After a few nonproductive stops, Grace was ready to give up and rent something. But no, her friend wasn't having it; he was on the phone, explaining to rental agencies what he needed. After a lengthy discussion with one of the largest rental companies, Spotter said to Grace, "See what I told you? Someone wants to see your car. Let's go. These people have one of the biggest fleets in town, and they might have just what we need. If we find something suitable that you like, give me a thumbs-up and I'll do the bargaining, okay?"

The dealership had several vehicles that had just arrived "off lease," and two of them were sports utility vehicles, just what Spotter thought Grace should drive. Grace, of course, picked the lovely bright-wine color with shaded windows. Spotter preferred the all-black with storage racks. Grace was quick to explain that the color black would be a pain in the backside to keep clean on the farm. She said, "I'd have to park that thing in the creek just to keep dust and mud washed off, and we don't have carwashes on Lawson Creek."

Spotter was laughing when he said to the dealer, "The lady wants what she wants. Let's see what kind of deal you can make us on the Lexus."

Within the hour, negotiations were over and Grace had a new ride and twenty thousand dollars in her purse, her Lexus being worth more than the SUV. Spotter had successfully driven a hard bargain, much better at the business of car trading than Grace would have had the patience to do. She gave her Lexie Lady a pat on the nose, said goodbye, and drove away in a much more practical car. Spotter was pleased with the deal. He asked Grace, "How's that for a hard day's work? This is a good-looking, serviceable kind of thing, and you can spend your money repairing the old road."

Grace responded, "I owe you, my friend. I'm not patient enough with the process. I'd have given my car away if you hadn't been with me. I'm such a dummy about vehicles."

"Grace," he said, "I'm trying to help you. You've got a lot to deal with, and I don't want you to lose your footing right here. You need to keep your focus on your goals, one step at a time, one day at a time. Today you get a reliable ride, good for the job ahead, and some money in your pocket to get started with your projects. Things are coming together, and I'm also looking into your son's whereabouts. I should have some news to share by Thursday night. Don't miss the meeting."

"How will I ever repay you, Spotter?" Grace asked. "What can I do to help you?"

"Well, for starters, Grace, I'm hungry." Then Spotter went on, "You can pay for my dinner today, then my grandkids and I are going to bring our tent and camp, fish, and hike all over your property. We might even ride horses. That's all I want, Grace. Let me bring my grandkids to enjoy the backcountry while they're young enough to explore. They're being raised in the city, and they need to experience something else, develop some skills of survival. We'd love to come and stay on the old remote property. That would be quite the treat."

Grace responded, "You're on the calendar anytime you want to come. When summer is over, the cool weather will color the leaves and the temperature will be perfect. I should have the road passable by then, and we'll plan your visit. You can also take the kids to see all the tourist attractions just west of the property. They're all within an hour's drive. The kids will love all the different things to see and enjoy."

Spotter was excited. He said, "Count us in, Grace. I want to see you doing well. You deserve all the help you can get. Think of me as your brother. I'll be on your side whenever you need me."

*****

After dropping Spotter off at his home, Grace headed for her condo. She was tired, but deep inside, she felt joyful and grateful for the day's accomplishment. She began to sing, "To God be the glory…great things He hath done…"

At the condo, Grace sat down at the dining table to sort through her mail; she liked to dispose of what she considered trash before it piled up on her desk. The sorting was going quickly until she noticed the bottle of bourbon beckoning for attention. For years it had been her habit to pour a drink as soon as she came in the door after work. Grace found herself torn between having a single shot or simply enjoying the whole bottle—after all, who would know. She had a new car to celebrate, and she might have to dub the lovely ride with a cute name. The more she thought, the more appealing the idea became. After all, she didn't have to report to work until Monday. She went to the cabinet and reached for a glass. She was happily making her way toward her favorite old comfy chair when the telephone rang.

"Hey, Grace, Spotter here. Did you make it home okay with your new car? I was worried about you managing the traffic with an unfamiliar car. It sits higher in the saddle than you are used to. Did you do okay?"

Grace answered, "Yes, I did fine, and I love it. I like that higher view of the traffic. But, Spotter, to be honest, I'm about to celebrate my good fortune with a big bottle of bourbon, convincing myself that I deserve to relax and celebrate. Is that stupid or what?"

"Yeah, Grace, that's real stupid," he said. "You are undercutting all the good progress you've made already. If you drink tonight, you'll find another excuse to drink tomorrow, and you will be gone from there. Soon you won't have anything to celebrate but shame and disgrace. You have some victories to celebrate, but you don't let that call out self-destruction habits. Find another way to celebrate, Grace. Remember that we are looking for your son. I should have some news by Thursday. You can surely stay sober that long, can't you?"

Grace was crying when she said, "I know you are peed at me after you spent most of the day trying to help me. I need you to yell at me or something. Every time I start feeling good about myself, I fall into this same trap. I don't understand it."

Spotter responded, "That's the prime time to fall into relapse, Grace, when we think we're sailing right along. We drop our guard and get stupidly careless. Shortly thereafter, we get a good kick in the backside and the whole process starts all over. It's stupid, Grace. You've got a lot to lose, but God is supplying you with plenty of friends to help. There's no excuse for betraying yourself. I'm not mad. I'm being straight with you for your own sake."

Grace said, "You're right, Spotter. I am happy with my progress and all my recovery friends. You're all invaluable. I love all of you for your concern for me. That is priceless. I will put this bottle down and celebrate with thirty laps in the swimming pool. That always tires me out, and I can sleep without any help. Thank you for your help, and please feel free to chew my butt up anytime you think I need it. It matters that you care. I won't let you down."

THE ROAD TO HELL IS PAVED WITH... WHAT?

"I'll check with your tomorrow, Grace," Spotter said. "You put that bottle down and thank your higher power for his love and protection. You are not alone. We're all here for you. Good night, Grace."

*****

Grace put the bottle down, donned her bathing suit, and headed out toward the swimming pool. She could hear the noise and splashing from her rear patio. She paused for a minute, turned back toward the door, walked into the kitchen, and picked up the bottle of bourbon. On most Saturday evenings, the residents of the complex were in the clubhouse, partying; not a soul would notice if she deposited the bottle where the drinks were being served. Everyone's attention would be on the huge television screen as Grace left the bottle of bourbon amid the collection of alcoholic beverages. The partiers would love it; they weren't choosy.

Attending some of the Saturday-night parties in the past had taught Grace a lesson. She'd be so strung out on Monday morning she didn't dare drive to work. Sometimes she had to walk, rain or shine, with a splitting headache. Then the day did not go well, and she couldn't wait to get home in the evenings and find some relief, her favorite time of the day. Her liquor cabinet was always well stocked because relief required a full bottle before bedtime some days. She never considered her tolerance level going way up and her bank account going in the opposite direction. She never gave any thought to how her health was being affected. The doctors had pointed to high blood pressure, high cholesterol, heart palpitations, and stress as culprits. Grace had dodged their questions about alcohol. They suggested exercise and a strict diet, gave her medication for the high blood pressure, and sent her on her way with warnings, "You have to take better care of yourself, exercise, diet, get the stress levels down." Grace ignored them, for the most part, because she didn't see the connection to her drinking.

Alcoholics and other addicts block awareness with their denial, and Grace had denied for a long time. Her idea of exercise was a swim in the pool once a week or so. The walk to work twice a week would suffice for the rest of her needs. She felt better just relaxing with her bottle and popping headache pills for any pain. She had no idea what she was doing to herself; she thought she was perfectly happy with her own "medicine."

As for friends, Grace didn't have many friends; she was a loner. She didn't trust men who showed an interest, because she simply couldn't stand the thought of their obvious intention. She didn't make friends with the ladies because she didn't want to be thought of as lesbian. She didn't fit into the college social circles because she didn't have a mate; she felt awkward. Her isolation became the norm, her bottle her friend and lover.

*****

While the clubhouse crowd was distracted, Grace swam thirty hard laps and was too tired to get out of the pool. She was sitting on the edge, trying to regain her strength, when she realized that the children were screaming. One of the young girls had fallen into the deep end of the pool. The child was thrashing, coughing, and strangling. Grace didn't give it a thought; she plunged into the water, swam under the ropes to reach the child. The little one grabbed at Grace's neck and held on tight. As Grace kept the child afloat, she kicked herself toward the side of the pool where someone was holding out a rubber float. The child suddenly went limp, and Grace couldn't lift her over the edge. Grace grabbed for the float; she was breathless and weak. She heard someone yell, "Get the lady out—she's passing out!"

Grace awoke to find someone pushing on her chest and talking to her. She was staring at an EMT; the rescue squad had arrived in time to rescue her. Both she and the child were exhausted but otherwise appeared to be okay. Grace sat shuddering under a towel as the crowd looked on.

The parents of the young girl, having been distracted at the clubhouse, didn't notice the commotion until the rescue squad came through the gate. They claimed they had left the child sleeping in her room. Grace didn't say anything as she listened to their lame excuses, but when they came to thank her and the strong smell of alcohol was on their breath, she couldn't help herself. She said, "You might want to ask yourselves what is more important, free drinks at a football rerun or the safety of your child. You're lucky I wasn't drinking tonight, or you would have lost your daughter. If you care about your child, get a handle on your priorities."

The couple huffed away, dragging the child by her arm. Other residents came to Grace's side, asking, "Can we help you? Do you need someone to walk with you? Can we call someone?"

Grace thanked everyone for their concern and was trying to get to her feet when she heard a familiar voice say, "Thanks, everyone. She'll be okay. I'll see her home." Professor John had come to her rescue. He put his arm around her shivering body and walked with her out of the pool area.

"What happened, Grace?" he asked. "I heard the ambulance, but I thought it might be for the older couple that lives in this section. I didn't really pay attention."

Grace whispered, "It wasn't me. It was a young girl drowning, and I am the weakling that went in after her. I'm exhausted. She nearly choked me before she passed out. I guess I must have passed out as well. I really thought I would be stronger than this."

John said, "Come on, let's get you some dry clothes and warm up. You're okay."

In the condo, Grace headed for a hot shower while John made some hot tea. When Grace returned to the kitchen, she could smell the relaxing aroma of chamomile tea. She plopped in a chair, wet hair hanging around her face, her robe wrapped tightly over her pajamas. She said, "I'm sorry if I'm not presentable. I'm too tired to try. I'm decent—that's all I can manage."

Laughing, he said, "You, dear lady, are the heroine of the complex tonight. Grace, did you see all the cameras snapping? You'll be on the front page of our newsletter this month. You deserve a medal. Have some good, relaxing tea, and you'll feel better in a bit. You just saved a child's life. Give that time to sink in, Grace."

Grace told John what she had done with the bottle of bourbon. She said, "I wish I hadn't done that. I just fueled someone's stupidity with that little pass-off. I should have trashed that instead. I'm sorry I did that."

"Now, now, Grace," he said. "You bear no responsibility for the behavior of others and their choices. You know there is always plenty of drinks at those parties. One more bottle wouldn't have made any difference. Alcohol is permitted on Saturday nights. Some of us argued against it, but we were outvoted. Until the rules are changed, we have no choice but to ignore it."

"I know you're right," Grace said. "I'm mad about the child. I've been a lonely child, watching out for myself while the adults were distracted. It's a miserable life."

John switched the focus by saying, "Let me tell you about my day. I've been busy painting and freshening my condo. I'm planning on having it on the market in the next two weeks. I'll be living in my motorhome soon. I'm going to invest the money from the condo in an annuity to take care of my old age, and I'm out the door, free as the wind, no more hassles and no more pressure. I'm excited to simplify my life, and I'm looking forward to visiting your remote old farm. Let's talk about that, Grace. How does retiring make you feel?"

Grace put her teacup down, placed her palms together, bowed her head, and said, "Thank you, dear Lord, for making that possible."

John was smiling when Grace looked up. He said, "We'll get the paperwork together. You write a letter to the board, and we'll see where that gets us. I think they'll work with you."

Grace said, "John, you know, I'm going to retire one way or another. If I need to take a cut in benefits, so be it. God has called me to do this, and I know He will provide. I'm not destitute. I've just traded cars, and I've got money in my pocket to get started. My condo can be sold. I won't need it. Besides, I've never been happy here. It's just convenient to the campus."

John said, "You know, I've been thinking, if you come and address the board, talk about your health, your family obligations, and your spiritual conviction to go help your old community while you can, the members might be more cooperative. They like a good cause."

THE ROAD TO HELL IS PAVED WITH... WHAT?

Grace answered, "Yes, I'm thinking the same thing. I need to apologize for my past behavior, my lack of insight. I owe them that."

John stood, put his hand on her shoulder, and said, "Good night, Grace."

*****

Grace fell across her bed exhausted, but not before she thanked God for friends like John and Spotter, and her much-beloved sister Stella. Where would she be without them and their support? She asked for strength to prevail in her fight for sobriety. She prayed for the child she had rescued.

The old creek was gurgling along its path, the birds were singing, and Granny Lawson was laughing. She and Grace were swinging in the old porch swing again. Grace was dreaming the same dream that had recurred several times lately. The clarity of the sounds never faded but puzzled Grace. What was Granny trying to convey? Sometime much later, the message would reveal itself and Grace would solve the mystery.

The Strategy of God

As the dawn was breaking on Sunday morning, Grace stirred from her sleep. She had been dreaming yet again; she and Granny Lawson were swinging on the porch, birds singing all around and the old creek gurgling along its path. The dream was vivid, except for Granny's laughter, which Grace couldn't hear, but the happy expression on the old one's face was evident. Perhaps the psychiatrist might say it was a creation of the subconscious, projected as a comforting presence in stressful times. Grace chose to think of it as a more spiritual presence; Granny was simply trying to relay a message pertinent to Grace's journey back home.

Grace couldn't sort it out. She thought to pray and ask God to help her understand. She prayed, "Please, God, help me to understand when the time comes. Please, please don't let me miss whatever it is she's trying to convey. Please don't allow me to hide in my habit. I'm through hiding. I'm trying to 'set my face to Jerusalem,' whatever that means to You. Stay with me. I'm weak, but I'm going. Thank You for your protection. Amen."

Grace finished her breakfast and set about dispensing with the morning household chores. The phone rang, and she thought it might be Spotter. But as she glanced at the caller ID, she pressed a recording button on the answering machine and picked the receiver up slowly. She said, "Hello."

"Good morning, lovely lady. Bob Henderson here. How are you this morning?"

Grace barely had time to respond before he launched into his deceptive spiel. He said, "We've been working on a plan with the people who want to buy your old property, and I need to run it by you. They're interested in buying it straight out and doing the improvements for themselves. They really aren't interested in taking on any partnership, so here's their best offer.

"They'll pay eight thousand an acre for two hundred acres, accept the property as is, with no obligation on your part. That comes to 1.6 million dollars, Grace, and you don't have to bother with it. They're willing to pay the extra if you sign the paperwork now and let them have the title. They're eager to get started planning repairs. I'm willing to drive down to your place, and we can sit down and get the paperwork done before they arrive this weekend. Grace, we won't get a better deal from anybody. We need to work fast. When can we get together?"

Grace was disgusted. Did he really think she would be such easy prey? Where did he find her home phone number, anyway? She kicked into "undercover sleuth" mode and, remembering what the sheriff's men had taught her, said, "Oh my goodness, I haven't had a minute to think about any offer just yet. This is the end of spring semester at the college, grades and graduations to handle. It's all I can do to keep up. Besides, I don't feel comfortable about any agreement until I'm sure I own the property. Give me time to settle that issue, and then we can negotiate, okay?"

He countered with, "Grace, these people are serious cash buyers. We can't stall. They'll get away, and we won't get another chance. They've made a good offer, considering. We're talking big money here, and you can walk away from that [expletive] college. I'm trying to help you here. I don't know if this offer will be any good after this weekend. You don't get a cash offer just any ole day."

Grace took a deep breath to control her need to scream. In her best "professor" voice, she spoke with a calm but firm tone as she said, "When I establish my ownership of the property without question and I am able to sell without recourse, I'll consider the offer. You can tell your clients that I insist, before I accept their money, that the title will be conveyed with no doubt as to ownership." Then to stress her point and annoy him further, Grace added, "I will also be doing the buyers the favor of paying for a survey before any papers are signed. There's too much leeway around that 'more or less' clause, and the acreage should be clearly established. A survey will identify the boundaries, keep any encroachment from occurring in the future. Tell your clients that I'm interested in their protection and I'll work on that when I have a break. I simply can't do it this week. My job is overwhelming right now."

Henderson was not pleased; his voice betrayed his thoughts as he tried to maneuver around Grace's position. He said, "Grace, you might regret pushing people like this. They can afford to buy whatever they want. What if they change their minds? You gonna be happy about that? I'd sleep better with the money in hand. You're leaving it on the table."

Grace rendered a good kick in his backside when she said, "You know, Bob, you're making a substantial profit off a property you don't own, you have no legitimate rental agreement with anybody, and you don't have a thing that should keep you awake at night. You just relax, count your profits, and I'll handle my stresses here at my job. When I get some time, I'll talk about this. In the meantime, I doubt if that property will fall off the earth—it won't go anywhere."

Henderson was not a happy man. He snapped, "Okay, but you're cutting your own throat. You may not get another offer."

Grace couldn't resist a "turn of the knife" she already had in his ribs. She said, "There is an old survey that we have found that shows more acreage than you're talking about, anyway. Until I know for sure how much land is involved, I won't be selling anything. Let your clients know that we may have to renegotiate if the old survey is accurate. They'll be interested in that, I'm sure. The survey suggests there might be at least three hundred acres. Wouldn't that make a difference in the numbers? It seems worth waiting to see, don't you think?"

His goodbye was curt and quick; he had nowhere to go from there. Grace extracted the tape from the tape recorder, put it away in her briefcase, and smiled. The newly acquired attorney would get to hear that, and the sheriff's men would get a good laugh. Henderson was desperate, and Grace was delighted. What a crook he had turned out to be.

Recovery work had taught Grace to stop, feel her feelings, acknowledge the impact, but go on with intention and focus. She took a happy skip, much like a small child might do, and went to her bedroom, where she dressed for a shopping trip. She needed to find good, washable clothes and boots for the farm and flowers for the Memorial Day holiday; she had promised Aunt Lucy. To get herself organized for the long weekend and have hope for her early retirement made Grace feel like dancing. Henderson would get his reward soon enough; the legal and law enforcement people would take care of him. Grace had no time to waste. Paperwork had to be processed, the condo would need to be sold, decluttering would be a job, and well, life had picked up speed faster than Grace could think. Things were certainly looking up, and Grace was happy. God was looking out for his child, at long last.

*****

Shopping was going well and boots were in the bag when Grace spotted a favorite liquor store. The urge to enjoy a few sips became overwhelming; she pulled into the store fully convinced that a few minutes with her old friend in celebration wouldn't hurt a thing. Fortunately for Grace, the liquor store didn't sell alcoholic beverages on Sunday. Grace sat in the car, staring at the door, feeling sheer frustration. She had nothing to do but back out of the parking lot and leave. She remembered to "feel the feelings" and try to keep her focus. She asked herself, "Why do I lose control so easily? I lose my focus and risk losing everything over this stupid stuff. I do it when I'm feeling good about life, and when I'm tired, when I'm teed off, anytime I see alcohol readily available. Why? Is my chemistry so far off whack that I simply wax stupid? Do I blank out or what? This is insanity, just like they told me."

At last week's recovery meeting, she had heard someone say, "It happens when you're feeling the best and when you're feeling the worst. You are vulnerable to emotional swings. You get careless, reckless, and dumb. You can't let emotions run the show like that. You'll relapse every time."

Grace left the liquor store marveling at her own lack of mindfulness. She said to herself, "I know I'm a smart, intelligent, and accomplished woman. How can alcohol have the power to turn me into a total mindless idiot? Will this phase of sudden stupidity ever pass? My DTs and nausea have slowed down. I wonder if this psychological dependency will wane as well. The God Squad will have to explain this. Thank You, Lord, for them. They are my angels."

*****

Later in the evening, while Grace was packing her new farm clothes in her travel bags, she got a call from one of the God Squad members. Stella asked if she might provide the evening meal and spend the night with Grace. Being a little surprised, Grace asked, "Are you okay?" Stella was usually so worn out from her work on the weekends she crashed at her own apartment and didn't stir until midweek. Grace seldom heard from Stella until Thursday's meeting. This change of behavior left Grace feeling a bit concerned.

Stella said, "Yeah, I'm okay. This weekend wasn't so bad, but the weekend coming up is going to be a killer. That's why I need your help, Grace. I need a place to stay close to work, and your place is perfect. I'm working a convention nearby, and if I can stay with you, there's some free food for you and a big bonus check for me. Could I depend on you to help me here?"

"You bet," Grace replied. "You come on over and bring that food. I'm vulnerable when I'm hungry, and your food is the best. We'll work it out. I may not be around much this weekend, anyway, and you're welcome to stay. You'll be safe, and you can housesit for me."

Within the hour, Stella arrived with enough packaged food to last the entire week. She stashed the food in the freezer as she said to Grace, "Your meals will require heating, that's all. You're all set for the week. Let's eat the fresh salad with flounder tonight. Fish doesn't last long, and we can just heat it and eat it now, if you're hungry."

Grace was busy setting the table and Stella was heating the fish when Grace was confronted with a harsh question. Stella asked,

"Okay, Grace, where is that bottle of bourbon? Did you drink the whole thing already? Don't lie to me. What did you do with it?"

"No, Stella," Grace said, "I didn't even open it. But let me tell you what I did with it and what happened after that."

The story of the previous night's pool incident held Stella's attention until the smell of the delicious fish stopped the dialogue. After a brief word of prayer, the ladies chowed down on what would been a very elegant and expensive dinner at Stella's high-dollar restaurant.

Wiping at her mouth, Grace said, "Stella, how much do I owe you for all this good food and the packaged meals? I'm so grateful. Next week is going to be rough for me, and you're helping me a lot. You are not going to afford this by yourself. I can pay for it."

"You don't owe me a thing, Grace," Stella said. "We try to use up all the leftovers at our restaurant. We let the workers clean it up, and I get my share when I need to."

Grace replied, "Well, at least the food is being used, not wasted. That's a good thing for the workers, saves on their grocery bills. I'm grateful too. It's great food."

Stella said, "You wouldn't believe how much food we gather up every day and distribute to the poor people. We have workers whose job it is to come in at night, clean up the good food, and store it in coolers, for delivery the next morning to starving families. We don't allow anything to go to waste if it can be used. Our delivery van goes to some of the neediest communities, and we feed the elderly and the children. Sometimes the kids will be waiting on the street for a plate of food. We alternate routes so we can feed them at least twice a week. The owners of the restaurant get to write the expense off their income tax. You know how that goes, I'm sure."

Grace was astonished. "Do you mean the children are actually that deprived? Where are the parents, the adults?"

Stella answered, "Grace, honey, you were raised in a culture where you had access to good farm food. You never had to go hungry. There was sufficient room for gardens, farm animals, and wild game where you came from. In our big city, where there is no such access, the people are stacked up in housing developments, and it is a very different lifestyle. Sometimes hunger is the biggest challenge, and there's no relief unless those who have food share with the others. It can be a tortuous existence."

"You know, I guess I've never really thought about that," Grace said. "I just assumed that adults would manage to feed their children no matter how meager their means. That's my limited view, I guess. If that old farm could produce it, we grew it and ate it or canned and preserved it for winter. That was grueling work in the summers, and then the colder weather brought out the beef and hog killing, a brutal work. You're right, we were never at starvation's door. Even if the food got skimpy in the winter, we could always hunt wild turkey, deer, and other game."

Stella responded, "Grace, you were blessed with that life in a lot of ways others will never have a chance to experience. These poor city kids are apt to wind up on the streets, stealing whatever they can find, or streetwalking, like I had to do. Some will start trafficking in illegal substances as soon as they can. Survival depends on 'street cred,'… knowing your way around the street. I figure, if a good meal can help some of them have a brighter future, it's worth the effort. I send out every bite of food I can afford, and I sometimes hire some of the older kids to work. Somebody took me in off the streets and gave me a chance. I try to pass that on."

"You've done extremely well," Grace said. "You made a miraculous turnaround in your life, and you still bother with people like me who are lost, trying to come out of our own stupidity. You're a living saint, Stella, as close as I'll ever find. You're welcome to stay with me. Stay for as long as you need. I'm honored to have you and help you. It's payback for loving me."

"Thank you, Grace," Stella said. "I need to be close to work. We need to work a big convention that is coming into town this weekend and that will test my metal, but I'm promised a big commission if we can pull it off. I'm gonna need that money. I'm not renewing my lease on my apartment this month. The landlord won't keep up the grounds, my roof is leaking, and he is renting to some trashy tenants. I've warned him about that. He is gonna lose his best-paying people. I intend to find another place before the first of the month, then he will have to give me my last month's rent back, and I can be gone. I need to be closer to the ritzy crowd that we cater to, anyway. I need to follow the money, you know."

Grace stared at her dear friend for a few minutes before she asked, "Why don't you just stay with me until you find a place? I'm retiring in a week or two, one way or another, and I will have to sell this condo, but you can stay until then. You can housesit for me while I'm waiting on a buyer."

Stella wiped at tears as she answered, "Grace, you won't believe how much that will help! I love this place. It makes me feel so good to be here. This condo living would be the height of status for someone like me, like the palace. The rich people live like this. I'd feel so spoiled. I'd be delighted to housesit, whatever that means."

Grace explained, "Housesitting is merely bringing in the mail, picking up the newspapers from the sidewalk, and answering any management phone calls. Sometimes management calls about security or we have a mishap with the plumbing. They like us all to know what goes on. You get to use the pool. Just try to avoid the clubhouse—there's too much drinking on Saturday nights."

Stella was thrilled. She had to ask, "How much does it cost to afford such luxury? If poor folks could aspire to such accommodations, how much money would it require?"

Grace answered, "Well, a two-bedroom like this would probably be around two hundred fifty thousand. Then there's the monthly dues that take care of the upkeep, the security, and yard maintenance. You don't have any responsibility for outside chores, and the swimming pool is cleaned daily. It's easy living if you have a busy life, as most of us do. Most of us professional people just need a place to shower and sleep. It's convenient to our jobs. We like that and pay two hundred dollars extra a month for that convenience."

Stella looked confused. She asked, "Break it down for me, Grace. If I bought your condo, how much would it be on a monthly basis? I'm simple-minded. Can I afford to pay for it?"

"How much do you make on a monthly basis?" Grace asked. "How much rent are you paying now? All these questions must be answered. If you are willing to give me some of your personal information, I can estimate what you can afford."

*****

The next couple of hours were spent calculating and recalculating possible scenarios by which Stella could purchase the condo. In the end, Stella choked back her excitement and wearily shook her head. "I don't know if I can spend so much on something like this when it seems to be such an extravagance. Poor people are hungry, you know what I mean?"

Grace responded, "I hear you, I do, but you don't have to feel guilty about spending money on yourself when you've earned the right to enjoy something for yourself. Aren't your siblings doing okay now? Your mother passed last year, didn't she? You have anybody else to be responsible for now except yourself?"

Stella responded, "No, just me. But for some reason, I still have the poverty mentality, and I think I'd feel guilty when other people are so needy, especially the little children. I might be trying to live in the past, feeding the children that my poor mother had to raise, but on a broader scale. I've wondered about that. Maybe I'm stuck in my old ways, fear of displeasing God or something. I feel guilty if I pay too much for chewing gum—that's crazy, I know."

Grace asked, "So your hard-earned money is going where? You work like a slave all the time, you make good money, and you can well afford some luxuries, but your focus is on those of us who muddle around in our humanness, and you are trying to feed the masses at the same time. When does Stella get rewarded? I have read in our Bible where God said He would 'restore unto us the years that the locusts have eaten.' If God is trying to restore us, Stella, we need to think outside our old box. I'm thinking you and I need some restoring. We've paid some serious dues. If not now, when? I'm fifty-seven years old, and you are sixty. We need to enjoy our lives before we're too old to be restored. I think if you can afford a nice home yourself, now is the time. That doesn't mean that I need you to buy this condo. There will be others for sale, but if God provides,

I say embrace His provision with gratitude and enjoy. My Bible says that the 'poor will be with us always.' I don't know the purpose of that, but I know I can't play God with that idea. God is reasonable and fair with His servants, I believe, and He rewards us for the work we do. You deserve what you've earned, Stella, and your work with the rest of us speaks for itself in God's eyes. You might be right when you say you are stuck in the past, repeating your codependent behavior because of a loving heart, but we can overdo that. We have to find balance. Otherwise, we burn out, get sick, and aren't able to help anybody, not even ourselves."

Stella listened to Grace's sermon intently and said, "Grace, you won't believe this, but I've been thinking the same thing. I've been saving money, just dreaming of the day I could own my own house, a big achievement for someone like me, someone of my status. After the convention this weekend and the Fourth of July celebrations, I will have a substantial amount for a down payment on something. I'm concerned about the monthly mortgage obligation. It's steeper than I've ever had to pay. I'm too old to take on a thirty-year mortgage. At some point, I won't be able to keep up the long hours. And then what?"

Grace said, "Okay, I see your point, but at that point, you sell, for a profit. You build equity, like a savings account, until you sell. You get your money back, for the most part, maybe even make a profit, and you're out. It's forced savings as you go, you might say. Anytime along the way things get too tight for you, these condos sell quickly, and you are on to other things."

*****

For the next couple of hours, the academically advanced Grace, from the prestigious condo neighborhood, and the aspiring Stella, from the old impoverished neighborhood, had a good laugh about how their alcohol and drug habits had brought them together. And now they were about to switch places. Grace would be returning to her impoverished roots, and Stella would be "moving on up" to heights of affluence. God had prepared them well. They thought it ironic and quite humorous.

The strategic positioning of these two trusting servants would have an awesome spiritual impact on their respective communities and change the course of many young lives. God had brought them together, and they would remain sisters for the rest of their journey despite their racial differences. God had a strategy, His wonders to perform.

A Stunning Revelation

The following week came and went in a blur. Grace and Stella had no time for chatting; they passed each other coming and going, with Stella arriving home somewhere after midnight almost every night. On Thursday she had called, saying, "I'll see you at the meeting, Grace. You be sure to be there."

Spotter called to ask, "Are you coming to the meeting? I have some information to share about your son. Do you want to share with the group, or do you prefer privacy?"

"Is that good news or bad news?" Grace asked. "You need to warn me if it's not so good. We might need some privacy."

"Well, Grace," he said, "you have to decide that, but I think it might be a time for celebration, just to know he's alive and doing well. The group will rejoice with you about that."

"Okay, I'm eager to hear, whatever you got. I'll be there. Thank you, Spotter," Grace replied.

Grace wasn't giving it much thought; her week had been one stressful thing right after another, and she was tired. She had tried to cover her bases at the college with grit and determination, just to put her career behind her with finesse and be done with it. During the lunch breaks, she had spoken with her physicians to request the required letters of recommendation for retirement; both doctors agreed it would be in her best interest. The letters would be sent directly to the board before the end of the week. For good measure, Grace asked her recovery friend Pastor if he would submit a similar letter, as her spiritual adviser, recommending a change of focus to benefit her mental, emotional, and spiritual health. He had said the letter would be in the mail promptly.

As Grace walked to work one morning, Professor John caught up with her. He grinned at Grace as he said, "Some of your colleagues have agreed to help us with your retirement. It's coming together well. Politics and greed are good tools to use sometimes. Nothing else is needed."

Grace didn't dare to ask.

*****

Thursday's recovery meeting was just getting underway when Grace hurried through the church door; she'd been tying up loose ends in the office until the last minute. Her beloved friends were all around the table, welcoming newcomers. Grace tried to offer encouragement and understanding to the new faces, much like she had received in the early days when she'd arrived full of despair and confusion. Grace did her best to reassure the newcomers and offer love and compassion. She temporarily forgot her anxiousness about the news she wanted to hear from Spotter. The hour went by quickly, and the dismissal prayer was over before she remembered.

Plopping in a chair beside Stella, Grace said, "Spotter has some news for me about my son. Hang in here with me, would you? I don't know how this will feel. Don't let me freak out."

Spotter had taken a bathroom break, or so it seemed, but he went to his vehicle to retrieve a file folder. When he returned to the room, there were five of the core members eagerly waiting for his report. Grace glanced at the file folder and braced herself.

Spotter asked, "Grace, do you want the good news first, or shall we start with the beginning?"

Grace took a deep breath and said, "I already know about the beginning, but for the sake of the group, give them a rundown, if you will, please."

"Okay," Spotter said and began his report. "I'll move right along. Grace has shared with us about having a baby back in 1960, October of 1960, when she was only seventeen. The baby was adopted before Grace left the hospital, and now he is almost forty years old and Grace has never heard a word about him. This week, I did some checking, and he has been located. Grace, you'll be happy to know, he lives within a two-hour drive of your old community. He is a well-educated man, has a degree in structural engineering, and runs a trucking company that his adoptive father left when he died some years back. He has two children, little girls of preteen age. His adoptive parents were of modest means, in their early forties when they took him in, an only child. He has had what looks like a good, stable family life, religious parents who are both deceased now, and he has done very well for himself. I recently spoke with him myself, and he is eager to meet his birth mother. Grace, he wants you to meet his girls. I made no promises, said we'd be in touch. It's up to you."

Grace was staring at the ceiling, hands clasped together, tears pouring down her face, whispering, "Thank You, thank You, dear Lord. Thank You." She couldn't find her voice.

The group let her have a few minutes to collect herself before Spotter spoke again. "Would you like to see some pictures, Grace? These are taken off the printer, but they look pretty good." He pushed a copied photo of two little girls across the table. Grace dried her eyes and blinked at the tall thin gangly limbs and the straight black hair on the sisters; the photo was clear enough to see the girls resembled Grace's young self. Grace said, "Oh my word, they look like me when I was that age. And that hair is Grandma Lawson's Cherokee heritage! They are definitely related to me and her."

Spotter handed two shots of school pictures, taken last year, across the table as he said, "Here, take a look at the features. I think you're right. Genetics don't lie."

Grace took a good look at the photos and handed them around the table. She asked, "Am I right, or am I dreaming? Do these girls resemble me or not? Be honest. Am I dreaming?"

The members all agreed that the girls could pass for Grace's grandchildren, no question. Grace was thrilled. She turned her eyes to the ceiling again with praise to her Father.

Spotter gave the group a minute to settle, and then he dropped a bomb that he knew would shake Grace to the core. "Grace, here is the girl's father when he was a college boy and when he served his country during the Gulf War."

Grace stared at a very good-looking, dark-haired college boy with beautiful, smiling eyes and a well-decorated, handsome military man whom she felt she should know; he looked familiar, but she couldn't place the resemblance. She said, "Well, he is definitely a good-looking man, but I can't think who he looks like. It's not my dad, not Grandpa, but he's familiar."

Spotter handed the last of the photos across the table. He said, "Look at these. Maybe you could think about when this boy was born. Remember, October 1960, and nine months before that, remember that period."

A puzzled look came over Grace's face as she sorted through the pictures. Among the photos, there was a picture of her old high school flame, Bobby Henderson. Grace snatched his picture and compared it, side by side, with the picture of her son; the resemblance was undeniable. The two men could have passed for twins at that young age. Grace put her hand over her mouth and gasped. Stella moved in close to put her arm around Grace.

Grace was feeling chills, nausea. Finally, she managed to ask, "How can this be? I was raped…how can my son look like him?" She pointed with disgust at Henderson's picture.

Spotter spoke slowly as he explained, "Grace, your son's birthday was October, early October. You were raped in March. Either this child was premature or you were already pregnant. Did you have a relationship with Henderson?"

Grace suddenly shoved the stack of pictures across the table. She was mad. She said, "I can't believe this. I was told my baby was healthy. Nobody said he was premature. I didn't know I was pregnant. I was just a girl…scared to death. I didn't think about it…" Her voice was getting louder, and she noticed Pastor had raised a finger, indicating she should keep her voice down. Grace shut up and simply shut down for a few minutes.

A few minutes of silence passed, and finally, one of the women, Carolyn, spoke up. She said, "Grace, you wouldn't have known about these things at that age. Some girls are well along before they notice their symptoms. You might think about what you were doing in early January of that year and see if that makes sense."

Grace had her hands over her eyes, her head down; she was shaking and sobbing. Most in the group were silently praying.

"Come on, Grace," Stella said softly. "Let's give it some thought. If you were already pregnant, then at least you know who the father is, and that's not all bad. Your son got the good looks, the intelligence, and the education. He's turned out well. The girls take after you. It looks like a miracle to me. I'd be proud of that and ignore the rest. God above has His purpose for it. Trust His hand here and He'll help you."

After a few minutes, Grace began to recover. She squared her shoulders and took some deep breaths. Her hands were trembling as she reached across the table to retrieve the photos. She dried her eyes and looked through the collection again, slowly. The group waited, praying. After a few minutes, Grace began nodding, and looking around at her friends, she said, "I'm okay, guys, but this is a shocker. I never expected this. All these years I thought the men who raped me produced this child, and now I can clearly see they didn't. It was me and my old boyfriend, Henderson. We had a careless love affair, yes. We were guilty and reckless, got all wrapped up in our newfound fun. It's a bitter pill to swallow."

She picked up the picture of her son, looked at him, and said, "I'm proud of this young man. He doesn't need to suffer for the mistakes we made, our stupid behavior. I want to meet him and his girls. Spotter, you can tell him that. Just don't tell him who his father is. You know I'll have to help prosecute Henderson. How on earth can we keep that secret?" Grace put her face in her hands as she admitted, "I'm not thinking straight right now. Please, somebody say something. Help me."

Carolyn spoke up. "Grace, I've been following your story, and I usually don't say much. I'm still learning, but I want to help you here. My husband, father of three children, has been in prison for about ten years now. I've had to raise the children myself with help from my parents. My husband was a heavy drinker, and when the kids were babies, he made some dumb mistakes.

"He was selling stolen merchandise—fencing, they called it— for his friends when he was caught. We lost a good business and all our income. He was charged with trafficking, not only hot merchandise, but drugs as well. I had to move back in with my parents. It was such a depressing time. I got hooked on alcohol and drugs myself. My parents had to take over the children, and they put me in the street. Living on the street is the greatest teacher. It didn't take long for me to realize that alcohol was the problem.

"I went home and begged my parents to let me have enough time to get a job and pull my own weight. I promised no more drinking. I've found that the only way I can stay on track is to trust God and keep one foot in front of the other, and to tell the truth.

"My kids are in high school now and will graduate in the next few years. I don't hide the truth about their daddy. We go see him at the prison, and they send cards and letters. The man loves his kids and they love him, but they know he made his mistakes, and he doesn't deny that.

"We have agreed that our kids need to know the truth now, not after they find out the hard way by making the same mistakes. Family genetics don't have to rule over these children, Grace. It matters that the family tell the truth about the risks and build awareness in the kids early on. Lies and cover-ups don't help. Your son is an adult. He'll understand if you are open and honest with the truth."

Carolyn paused to take a breath, and Pastor spoke up. "Grace, she's right. How much pain have you suffered because you didn't know the truth? You're just now beginning to understand how dysfunctional patterns, learned in family, can affect your adult life. Do you want to pass on deception and ignorance, like you've been given? Think about the adage 'The truth shall set you free.' You've been in bondage a long time. Do you want to pass that on to these little girls?"

Grace had been moving the pictures around, gazing as she listened. Carolyn took another approach. She said, "My children got a lot of good traits from their daddy. I think we need to look past the human blunders and look at the gifts. Your son is extremely good-looking. He's educated and accomplished, raising two beautiful daughters. Someone did that raising job for you, Grace, when you wouldn't have had a chance to do so well. You need to thank God for that. I hope to live long enough to see my children turn out so well. I envy you, Grace—your education, your job, even your expensive clothes and that fancy car. God has had your back for a long time, it seems to me. You can't let feelings toward your son's father stop you here. God has a much better plan. Ask Him to help you see it."

Grace looked around the table for a few minutes and, with a trembling voice, asked, "Okay, Spotter, you are my brother. What do you think?"

"Well," Spotter answered, "it's been already said pretty well, but I'll offer you this. Your son won't hold you responsible for Henderson's choices, but he will be interested in the outcome. He'll appreciate that you gave him up for a better chance than he would have had otherwise. You won't regret being honest. He was raised to respect the truth, and he may be a lot like you, Grace. You can't deny the girls look like you, and maybe he got the better genes from both sides. Henderson has turned into a louse, but it's not because he's stupid—he's not. You are a highly intelligent woman, highly thought of in academic circles. Maybe your son got a mix of both of you to his advantage. I think if you two get to know each other, it could bring out the best in both of you. Give it a chance, anyway. Don't hide the best by covering up the worst."

"What do you think, Stella?" Grace asked. "You're not one to withhold an opinion."

Stella didn't hesitate as she said, "We don't get to pick and choose our kith and kin. We are assigned our place according to God's plan, and our role is to do the best we can with what we get for family and try to further God's purpose. If we accept what we can't change, we have the power to focus on what we can change, and we're not bogged down fighting with reality and wasting time. This is your son and precious little girls who don't have a paternal grandmother. I wouldn't waste my time worrying over their grandpa. You can't change that. Give them the best of their Grandmother Grace. God is handing you a gift, several fine gifts, in fact. Let God deal with Henderson. You love this little family and enjoy the blessings. That's what I think."

Grace dried her tears and thanked her friends for their wisdom. She said, "I guess I'm stunned, but I hear you. I know you are all on track. This just feels so unexpected, and I'm totally off balance. But it's better to know who the father is than to not know exactly. You're right, Henderson is a talented man. He told me his drinking had cost him three marriages. I suspect he forgot to say anything about his obvious 'womanizing.' He likes to twist things in his favor, justify his own behavior. Maybe together we did produce a good mix of genes when we were young, before bad habits and choices blew us away. I want to believe that. Maybe our son missed the poor conditioning that brought out the bad stuff."

Grace choked up for a minute, crying. When she found her voice again, she continued, "I think we might have been blessed here. This is my only child, and Henderson never had children. He said he was too busy for what he called pesky little whiners. It gives me a lot to digest, but maybe, in the end, we'll all benefit here. I'm leaving early tomorrow to go help law enforcement do their work to prosecute him. All of you need to pray for me. Thank you, all of you, for your wisdom. I'm so grateful, Spotter, for these pictures and this information. You are an angel."

Spotter handed the file folder across the table and said, "Phone number is included, Grace. It's up to you. You make the next move."

The group closed the meeting with the usual Lord's Prayer. Grace gave each one a grateful hug. On the way out, Stella said, "Grace, I'm right behind you. No stopping to rethink yourself. It's been a heavy day. We're going to bed and rest. Tomorrow we start again."

Grace turned out of the parking lot and turned toward home, Stella right behind her. As Grace traveled, she noticed how the bright lights from every bar and liquor store in the city were blinking at her, beckoning, tempting, calling her name. She thanked God that Stella was behind and watching; she was emotionally wiped out. She wanted to escape, just for a few drinks. Instead, she set her face toward home.

When they arrived at the condo, Stella had a plan. They would swim a few laps, drink some good, relaxing tea, and be in bed before eleven. Grace didn't have the energy to object; she just thanked Stella for being by her side. She packed her car for the morning trip, set the alarm, and collapsed in bed. Tomorrow would be coming early.

*****

Grace was on the freeway, headed out of the city, the next morning before the monkeys started chattering in her head. Grace's thoughts were going berserk, and she knew Stella was not on her tail. She began to look for some relief along the way.

Addicts, especially those struggling with withdrawal, are subject to bouts of hyperactive mind-chattering thoughts, feelings, and reactionary behaviors. They simply want to chill out and escape; their nerves are on overload. Relapse offers relief, at least for the moment. Instant gratification is the cure for what ails them, and they don't think about the consequences.

The monkeys were chattering, but Grace kept driving, thinking of the son and the little girls God had given her. They were located just two hours away, close enough for frequent visits. She tried to remember what she'd been taught. What was that HALT thing? That "hungry, angry, lonely, tired" thing? She pulled into a morning coffeehouse and ordered coffee with a big egg-and-cheese sandwich. Her appetite appeased, she drove on. She was thinking, *Funny thing how stupid I can get when I'm too hungry, angry, lonely, and way too tired—I'm all of that.*

Grace prayed the Serenity Prayer. She added, "God, please grant me the wisdom. I can't do this by myself. Please stay with me. I need wisdom, wisdom. There's a lot I can't change, but I'll do what I can. You grant me the wisdom. I'm trying to listen."

The mountains of her old homeplace began to appear in the distance. Grace drove on to her calling, back there in the valley known as Lawson Creek.

Another Curveball

Her old hometown was bustling alive with traffic when Grace arrived at the grocery store. She grabbed her purse and headed toward the entry, hoping to make her aunt Lucy happy with some fresh-baked pastries. Before she made it to the entry, she heard a man's voice coming from behind her, say, "Good morning, Ms. Grace. It's good to see you this morning."

Grace turned to see Sheriff Cosby. Apparently, he'd been right on her heels. She stammered, "Oh my goodness, Sheriff. You scared me. It's too early to sneak up behind me. I'm jumpy already."

"Sorry about that," he said. "I'm glad to see you in town. Have you had any trouble with Henderson this week? We've been keeping an eye on him."

"No, nothing but a phone call, which I recorded," Grace said. She rummaged through her purse to find the tape. "Here, you can get a good chuckle out of this. The man is unbelievable."

"All right, that'll entertain us over doughnuts and coffee this morning," the sheriff said. He laughed as he continued, "That boy thinks we're all dumb as rocks around here. You be careful, keep quiet, and listen. You'll probably hear some noise on the old farm this weekend. You don't have to be involved. You just listen and let us handle the rest, okay?"

In the store, Sheriff Cosby went one way, and Grace went in a different direction; she didn't see him again. Grace was relieved—not good to be seen talking to law enforcement right before a roundup.

*****

With her groceries and Aunt Lucy's favorite pastries in the car, Grace headed north toward Lawson Creek. She was thinking how she might tell her dear old aunt about her son without revealing the truth about his father. Aunt Lucy would not welcome that revelation; she might be overcome, and her health would be in jeopardy. Grace decided to limit the news by skipping the part about parentage; maybe the old one wouldn't ask.

Dear Aunt Lucy was in the kitchen, fumbling to feed herself cold cereal and jellied bread, when Grace arrived. "Oh, Aunt Lucy," Grace said, "let me make you some hot breakfast and some good coffee. I have your favorite pastries too."

Aunt Lucy said, "Wonderful! Yes, I'm so tired of cold stuff, but I'm getting too shaky to risk turning on the stove. I forget to turn it off and I burn myself, and the coffeepot is too hot to handle. You make whatever you want. I'll enjoy it. And make a big pot of coffee. We can catch up. We got lots to talk about."

Grace set about stirring up a good, nutritious breakfast while she filled her aunt in about the son and the granddaughters. Aunt Lucy's response was a periodic "Praise the Lord," "Thank You, Jesus." When Grace described how the young girls resembled herself with their tall thin builds and the black hair, Aunt Lucy clapped her hands with laughter. She was delighted with the story.

The dear old aunt was thoroughly enjoying her hot food as Grace looked on. Grace could see that her dear aunt needed a sitter; it was getting dangerous to leave her alone. Grace decided to hire someone to stay with the frail old dear as soon as she could.

Soon the meal was over, and Aunt Lucy was sipping her coffee when she asked, "Who does your son favor, Grace?"

Grace was at the sink, washing the morning dishes; she dried the last pan before she turned to answer. She said, "Well, the pictures are not real clear. It's hard to tell. We have to guess about that."

Aunt Lucy didn't let up. She started probing around with, "Is he a big man, like some in the family, or does he resemble the short, stocky side? If the girls look a lot like you, he must have some of the family traits. Does he look like your daddy, or your grandpa?"

THE ROAD TO HELL IS PAVED WITH... WHAT?

Grace answered with, "No, I don't think he looks like the Lawson family."

Aunt Lucy tried again. "Grace, you seem so proud of this man and his children. If he reminded you of the boys who raped you, I would think you'd find that hard to swallow. You wouldn't be so eager to meet him. But you seem excited about it. I don't understand that."

Grace poured a cup of coffee for herself, warmed Aunt Lucy's cup, and sat down across from her aunt. She knew the truth would come out sooner or later. She took a deep breath and began, "Aunt Lucy, the truth is, the boys who raped me didn't father this man. I was already pregnant when that happened. I'm sorry, but that's the ugly truth."

Aunt Lucy was quiet. She put her head down in a prayerful pose. For a few minutes, neither of them said anything. Soon, Aunt Lucy lifted her head, held her hand up in a sign of praise to her God, and said, "Way back there your grandpa told me he had a letter from that girls' school where you had that baby. The letter announced the baby's birth and your transfer to school to begin your education. I told him then that the baby was too early. It might have died. He never mentioned it to me again, but I often wondered if old Lawyer Henderson helped him ship you out of town in case the baby belonged to his son. I've always thought, especially when the baby was too early, that something didn't stack up right there. Is that your baby's father, Grace, Henderson?"

"Looking at the pictures, I'd say, yes, it is," Grace said. "Of course, Henderson will deny it, but I'm convinced. Their young school pictures are so similar even I have a hard time picking out who is who. It's not what I wanted to see, but I've decided it's better than not knowing who the father is. That old rape incident still makes my stomach hurt. I don't want to be reminded of that every time I look at my son. At least I know Henderson's history, much as I dislike the man, and that helps me accept this man as my son. He's very much like Henderson used to be, a handsome man."

"I agree with you," Aunt Lucy said. "The men who raped you were outlaws, thugs, drinkers, and brawlers...good for nothing. Henderson, thief and liar that he is, had a good family background, hard workers and good family. He got off to a good start, but he got greedy and forgot about God's laws. He was spoiled by his family, and that's not good for children of prosperous people like his family. I think you need to welcome his son no matter what Henderson does or thinks about it."

"Thank you, Aunt Lucy," Grace replied. "I intend to put aside my feelings about Henderson and get to know the girls and their dad. I'm not sure how to tell my son that I'm prosecuting his father—that's a predicament I don't like to be in. We need to think that over and ask God for His guidance."

"Prayer is a good tool, chile. We'll pray over it and see what happens," Aunt Lucy said. "And…we'll let God show us the best thing to do."

"Oh, by the way," Grace said, "I ran into the sheriff, and he says something will be coming down on the old farm this weekend. We are to stay out of the way. We will do that."

Trying to steer the conversation in a less-stressful direction, Grace brought in the flowers she had bought for Memorial Day. She said, "When you feel up to it, we can visit your dad's grave and take these flowers. You will have to remind me where it is. It's been a long time, and I've forgotten. I brought enough flowers to decorate all the family plots and then some."

Aunt Lucy got excited. "Wonderful! Let's go before lunch while I'm feeling good. I get tired toward evening. It seems to me that you might be worn out, Grace, and you might need to relax and rest some yourself. You're pushing too much these days. What did the old writer say about 'the spring always comes, and the grass grows by itself'? You might need to slow yourself down a little."

"Well, yes, I know you're right. I'm going to be retiring soon," Grace announced. "I can't stand another year at that college. I'm handing in my resignation next week. I need to be here taking care of you and following the Lord's call."

Her aunt smiled and said, "I was hoping you could do that pretty soon. There's something I want you to do for me if you come back anytime soon. We'll talk about it on the way. Let's get going. I haven't been to Poppy's grave in a while. I'm eager to visit again."

*****

The Confederate burial ground was an hour's drive south. Grace stopped to fill her gas tank before they left town, and as she pulled out of the station, Aunt Lucy began to talk. "Grace, I want you to listen to me. You know I can't stay by myself much longer. In fact, my heart is telling me that I won't be here much longer. I don't have anybody to depend on. John is disabled, Helen needs to work all the time, and the boys, Al and Ronnie, are too young to take on their old granny. I've been thinking, if I let you have my house to stay in as long as you need, can we put me in the nursing home in town, where most of my old friends are? You can keep the house and then sell it when you don't need it anymore. The nursing home bill could be paid along the way, and if I don't last long, and I can't, then you could have the house. Is there a way we can borrow enough money to just keep the bills paid until I've passed? I'd like to not be a burden to the family if we could find a way to work that out."

Grace asked, "Are you sure you wouldn't want to stay in your home?"

"No, Grace," Aunt Lucy said. "I'm ready for a change while I've still got a choice, but I can't afford the nursing home by myself. I'm paying my housekeeper about a thousand a month, and the nursing home costs about three thousand and then some. If you'll help me figure a way to afford that, we can sell the house to you on paper, take out a loan to pay the nursing home, and you can have the house when I've passed. I doubt if I'll last another year, anyway. Would you be willing to do that? It would provide you a place to stay until you get the old farm in shape and decide what you want to do with that."

Grace was surprised. She asked, "Won't that insult your family? Won't they throw a fit? They'll think I've coerced you somehow and pushed you out of your home."

Aunt Lucy was shaking her head. "No," she said. "They'd probably be glad to let you do that. They can't afford to help me, and I'm sure, as soon as I'm gone, they'll sell their part of the land, which I've not allowed them to do. I gave them the land to live on and reserved the right to say what they do with it while I'm alive. When all the developers started coming through here, they wanted to sell, and I said no. They've been sore-tailed about that for years. I told them they didn't pay for it, my Poppy worked hard for it, and I wouldn't allow it to be thrown away on easy spending. I've told them, the longer they hold it, the more it will be worth someday."

Grace was listening closely. She asked, "You want me to put it in my name, make the payments to the nursing home until you are no longer with us, and then, I will have ownership, free and clear—is that the way I'm to understand this?"

"That's right, Grace." Aunt Lucy went on, "If you can work that out, use the bank's money or something, you'll be helping me, and I'll return the favor. What's left will be yours. My kids won't be able to take care of it, anyway, and they'll let it run down to worthless. You won't do that if you live here. If I should outlive its worth—and I don't see how I can—you can put what's left of me under Medicaid or something. You can ask about that. I don't believe it will even come close to that. I'm too far gone now."

Grace's mind was racing. She asked, "How much do you think the place might be worth at this point?"

The old one answered, "The tax man says about one hundred fifty thousand. You know how that goes. The market says more than that. That could keep me about three or four years, but I can guarantee you it won't be that long before the Good Lord calls. My bell will ring in the next year or two, and I'll be summoned. I don't see how you can lose, Grace, and I'll not be a bother to anybody."

"Aunt Lucy," Grace said with a firm tone, "we can hire somebody to come in and stay with you, right in your home. I can rent something until I get the old farm up and going. I won't disrupt your home. If you want to have someone come in and help, I can help pay for that."

Aunt responded with a determined voice, "I'm in touch with some of my friends who live in the nursing home. They like the good help, the social things they get to do, and the entertainment. They are happy. They have church and lots of activities, lots of visitors. I think I'd like a change of pace. It gets lonely around here. I want to play piano for some of my old friends like we used to do. They would like that. I've been thinking about this for a long time."

"Okay, Aunt Lucy," Grace said, "but I'll need to work on the financing, see what can be worked out. I do need somewhere to stay, and if you're sure about this, I'll certainly help. You will need to explain it to your family, though. I do not want to fight with them over this."

Aunt Lucy chuckled. "They will be happy to get me off their plates. Watch what I tell you. They don't fancy taking me in, not with John disabled and Helen running her legs off. The boys don't need to babysit their old granny. This is what I think will help all the way around, and I'll be happy with that."

At the Confederate cemetery, Grace parked her old aunt beside her Poppy's grave and slipped away as the old one started chatting with the long-dead ancestor. Grace was trying to think through the offer she had just been given, to ask God for direction. Aunt Lucy needed to be in a facility, for sure, but Grace didn't want to take advantage or cause trouble with the family. On the other hand, the offer made sense; that little cottage would be ideal until improvements could be made on the farm. At that time, the little cottage could be a good rental property.

On the way home, Aunt Lucy was happily humming an old gospel hymn. She stopped long enough to say to Grace, "You know, chile, you have helped me more in the past two weeks than my family has been able to do in years. You are restoring my old piano, you put in the security system, and you've located the lost paperwork. Now you are straightening out your grandpa's property mess. If I'm right, you'll get that old farm back in shape as soon as you can. You'll be a good influence on this little community, and you'll help the church. The boys are proud of you. They say you're a good sport. If there's a way to get them educated, you'll help with that. They want to be able to afford what they say is a 'cool ride' like you got. You help me, Grace, and I'll leave you what little I got. Just help the boys if you can. God has sent you back to us, Grace, and I don't want you to feel guilty if I'm gone within the year. You go right on with God's calling for your life. My family will benefit from that."

Grace's response was, "Thank you for that. I'm definitely planning to be here, and your house fits my immediate needs perfectly. I'll have to get the financing worked out to our best advantage and get all the legal paperwork drawn up, then we'll know where we stand. But you remember, if you are not happy, we have other options. You just say so, anytime, okay?"

"I'm sure," Aunt Lucy said. "I want to sit with my old friends and tell tall tales, like we used to do, you know. We old folks enjoy the old stories and the old ways of talking with each other. We don't much like the new ways with telephones and such."

*****

Aunt Lucy retired to her bed shortly after lunch, and Grace lounged on the screened-in porch, sipping tea. Her mind was chattering, the monkeys coming alive. What if…what if…what if…what if the old one lived another five years or more? What if the money ran out and the nursing home filed a lien? What if Grace should die first? These what-ifs were pounding at Grace's mind; she had a strong compulsion to shut down, get a good, strong drink, and let the fear pass. Instead, she felt the fear, ignored the panic, and talked to God. When she couldn't sit still much longer, she got up and started walking around the yard. She began to look at the condition of the little cottage, the framework, the roofing, and the windows. She found the building that housed the water supply and gave it an inspection. She asked herself a question: How much money would it take to make a nice little home, comfortable and functional, for the time it might be needed? She decided to get some help with that.

Grace walked around the entire property, making mental notes to herself. It seemed to make sense that the smaller home could serve as temporary housing, providing a good place to sleep and eat, while the larger, more expensive projects around the farm might take a while. Aunt Lucy had just handed her a convenient blessing, and God had surely inspired it.

Grace noted how close she would be to the church, within walking distance. Aunt Lucy could come visit and play her the old piano for the family gatherings. Grace smiled about that.

Friends in recovery had warned Grace, "Don't jump ahead of God. Don't allow emotions to push you ahead of God's plan. Take your time and the plan will reveal itself to you, then you'll see God in the whole thing. Be grateful for His provision and His guidance. Relax, knowing that He'll provide the wisdom."

Grace returned to the lounge chair on the porch. She stretched out and relaxed, musing about how God had thrown another curveball in the game plan, something she certainly didn't expect. The birds were singing all around, tomorrow would be another day, and more surprises were on the way, no doubt. Grace fell into a much-needed restful sleep, smiling as she dreamed.

A Revelation and a Raid

Early Saturday morning, Grace was in the old cemetery with rake and clippers, helping the church clean and clear the property for new memorial decorations for the holiday. Several people were pushing mowers, carrying trash, disposing of faded old flowers. Some of the older ladies were in charge of ice, water, drinks, and snacks. Sometime before noon, the whole landscape would be trimmed and cleaned, ready for Sunday's memorial tribute. After Sunday-morning church, the residents would turn out to memorialize their beloved families with new flowers and decor, a cultural tradition highly respected and celebrated.

After raking and cleaning the Lawson family grave sites, Grace picked up her tools and walked up the hill toward the paupers' graves. She was surprised to find several people were trimming and piling brush; some had wheelbarrows with fill dirt to repair the sunken graves, and some were brushing the trash and mud off the tombs. Grace went to the back of the area, where she knew her old enemies would be found. She was busy pulling the wild vines and briar bushes off the plot when she heard a man ask, "Do you know these fellas?"

Grace looked up to see who asked. Two men had walked up, carrying rakes and an ax. Grace felt a bit leery, but she tried to cover as she said, "Not really. They've been here a long time, and the plot needs some work. I'm just trying to do what I can."

The older of the men, perhaps middle sixties, said, "I'm Bill, and this is my son, Jeff. We're members of this church, and we try to help with this part of the graveyard. It gets run over right quick. Are you from around here?"

Grace tried to keep her hands busy as she answered, "I was raised here, but I've been away for some time. I'm thinking of moving back. My name is Grace Lawson, Lucy Bradford's niece."

The men were quiet, too quiet. Grace looked up to find both men staring at her. She asked, "Did I say something wrong?"

The older Bill pointed at the graves and asked, "Do you know whose graves you are cleaning? If you are that Lawson girl, Grace, that these boys raped years ago, how can you work on their graves now?"

Grace tried to hide her surprise that somebody actually remembered her name and that awful old story. She shrugged and said, "It's about trying to find peace through forgiveness, you know. I've let that old story circulate through my brain for too many years. I'm trying to put the whole thing in perspective, put it behind me. They've been punished. I need to move on, not hold anything against them now."

Jeff, the younger man, spoke up. "Lady, Ms. Lawson, that's more than I could do. Dad has told me about these fellas and how they used to grab young girls right off the road and nobody ever found them again. You can count your blessings if you made it out alive. These were some dangerous people, brutal and bad to the bone."

Bill cautioned his son, "Now, son, let's not be too judgmental here. These boys didn't have a good raising like most of us. My older brother told me these boys were pretty messed up from the time they could walk. The daddy beat on them and their mother when he was drunk, and they nearly starved to death. They had to fight to survive and had no church training at all.

"They started stealing and robbing people when they were just kids. The three of them would gang up on people and take what they wanted. They had no way to learn anything else."

Grace kept pulling at the weeds and vines, listening as the men talked. The men slashed the heavy brush, piled the vines, and put the stone border back in place. When the plot was looking much better, filled in and restored, the three of them sat under a shade tree and enjoyed some ice tea the ladies were passing out. Grace had to ask, "Bill, who do you think might have killed these men? I've always thought someone avenged me, but I don't know who that would have been. The sheriff never arrested anybody, did he?"

"No," Bill said, "but the rumor got out that the daddy of one of the missing girls had done that job. He was a military man training to go to Vietnam when his little girl went missing. He came home, and when he couldn't find her, he figured these boys had done something with her. They lived in the area and drove right by her school bus stop on their way to a job. After it hit the papers, what they did to you, he went up on that mountain and waited on them. He took them boys out with a single shot to the older ones and two shots while the younger boy was running. They didn't have a chance. Sometime later in the spring, some little human bones were found in the burn pile where they had been working. If that soldier did that, nobody wanted to prove it."

Grace asked, "Who found the bones?"

Bill answered, "Some hunting dogs. They kept sniffing around that brush pile, and the hunters dug the bones out. The sheriff couldn't build a case against dead people. That military man took care of that for him."

Jeff spoke up. "Ain't that man still around, Dad? He's getting old now, but didn't they take him to a nursing home over in Brownsville? He came home from the war with lots of wounds, didn't he?"

"Yeah," Bill said. "My brother told me that the man was wounded pretty bad. He's probably around seventy-five about now."

"Do you think," Grace asked, "they killed his little girl and just burned her right there in their brush fire?"

"Uh-huh," Bill said. "My brother said the girls around were scared to death of these boys. The oldest one was married to a fifteen-year-old girl, and she had two children by him. She left him, took the children, and went somewhere to hide, said he was like living with a snarling dog. Didn't trust him around the kids, and they were always hungry. She couldn't take it, and she moved out of state somewhere."

Jeff stood up, looked at Grace, and said, "Ms. Grace, you got away. You could have been in a fire just like that other girl. Don't let this old stuff drag you down now. It's history, and you're still here. You've helped clean up their graves. God saw that. He'll give you peace. Com'on, Dad, we got company coming for dinner. We'll see you at the church, Ms. Grace."

Bill gave Grace a pat on the back as he said, "You let these old memories go. They won't serve you now. You might want to check with the nursing home and ask for Brandon O'Neil. If he's still there, he may be able to tell you something about what he remembers about these boys. And you can ask old Sheriff Tate. He'll be in the nursing home in town, sharp as a tack, I'm told. You make peace by getting another side of the story, you'll see."

The men picked up their tools and headed toward their truck. Grace exchanged a few pleasantries with the other workers, thanked the ladies for the tea, and loaded up her own tools.

On the short drive home, she shuddered as she remembered the awful morning when she was repeatedly raped by the three brothers. Grace remembered going limp with pain, closing her eyes to die. The boys left her for a few minutes to pile brush on their fire. Grace heard that fire crackling, and she pulled herself together and ran, with no clothes or shoes. She got away before the boys noticed, and they couldn't find her.

Grace had learned from Granny Lawson how to hide in the laurel bushes and be quiet; Granny often did that to trap wild turkey or deer. Granny also taught Grace where the old creek could be crossed on foot; the boys didn't know about that either. Grace simply outsmarted them, thanks to Granny's skills.

Granny Lawson heard Grace screaming as the naked, bleeding girl came running into the yard. Grace couldn't talk much for hours, just lay shivering and crying, her face turned away in shame. The sheriff came to investigate later in the evening, but Grace could only point to the east ridge and say, "They're up there…they hurt me… I'm gonna die."

Weeks later, she still hadn't returned to school. She was vomiting and sick, having awful nightmares. When the doctor pronounced her pregnant, she was dispatched to the girls' school, nearly two hundred miles away.

Remembering the trauma, Grace, now forty years later, was feeling proud of her young self. A peculiar peace seemed to surround her memories. She thought, *Gracie, you were a courageous little thing. I'm proud of you. I still have that courage, that strength. I'm not giving up, not hiding in a bottle anymore. I've come home. Thank You, dear Lord.*

*****

At the kitchen table, awaiting her lunch, Aunt Lucy said, "I've been listening, Grace, and all I hear is little extra traffic, and I suspect most of that is neighbors working on the cemetery."

Grace answered, "I got a feeling, Aunt Lucy, that the sheriff's team will come in at night or early one morning, when they get ready to move. Nobody will know a thing until it's done."

"How did the cleanup go? Is the cemetery ready for visitors?" Aunt Lucy asked.

Grace answered, "Well, it's looking good. We all worked hard." After a pause, Grace asked, "Do you know Bill and his son, Jeff Patten? They gave me some information about the Colson boys up in the paupers' graves, and I wonder if it is credible or just hearsay."

Aunt Lucy said, "Well, they're good people. They come and help every year and do their part for the church whenever we need repairs. They build houses and do some farming. The community thinks highly of that family. I would say that whatever they told you might hold up. They wouldn't tell something they didn't believe. What did they say about the Colson boys?"

Grace related the information the Pattens had given her, the old aunt listening with rapt attention. As the story unfolded about the military man who lost his daughter, Aunt Lucy was nodding. She said, "You know, I remember something about that. By the time he was being looked at, he was shipped out to Vietnam. They didn't want to charge him with it, being a soldier, you know."

"And nobody wanted to pursue him for murder, especially after he lost his daughter, and her bones were found after the boys were already dead?" Grace asked.

"I think that might be about right," Aunt Lucy offered. "After all, the Colson fellas were not highly thought of. Good riddance to bad rubbish. The law didn't care."

Grace said, "You know what? I might drop by the nursing home and talk to Sheriff Tate, see what he thinks. I'd sure like to clear Granny Lawson's name. It's so painful to think that she might have done that. I'd love to know that she didn't."

*****

The afternoon was spent quietly resting, Aunt Lucy napping and Grace stretched out on a lounge chair, listening to the birds sing in the yard. She couldn't believe how much she had missed the country life, hard as that existence had been at times. She knew in her heart she would be happy to live right there on Lawson Creek. She asked God for strength and for guidance. She promised Him to give it her best effort to stay off the bottle and stay focused on His will. She went to sleep and began to dream.

In her dream, Granny Lawson was beaming down at Grace's young self, patting her cheeks in a gesture of affection and approval. The dream didn't identify what it was that Grace had done, just Granny's absolute delight in the child. Grace woke up, but the feeling of being so loved and appreciated stayed with her for some time. She sat in the lounge, thinking, *Who was it in the Bible who said, "It has been good for me that I have been afflicted"? Maybe this is where I learn to walk in God's purpose. This is where God has brought me. I'm okay with everything He has revealed. In fact, I'm delighted, scared to death, but delighted. Maybe that's what Granny is trying to tell me: I'm on the right track. I'll have to take it one step at a time and one day at a time, try to not get ahead of God. The God Squad says to remember the acronym KISS: keep it simple, stupid.*

*****

The old piano had begun to dry out a bit, and Aunt Lucy was banging away on some old spirituals while Grace prepared their evening meal. The piano man, Charlie, had called to say he would be coming the following week with the repair parts to finish the restoration. Aunt Lucy was delighted; Grace simply hoped for more melodious tones and less noise. The dear aunt praised her Lord with that piano, never mind the praise was off-key and hard on the ears. Grace reminded herself that God listens to the heart. She said to herself, "Let's hope He listens and He's not as uptight about flaws and imperfections as we humans are. He understands our weakness and still looks out for us, like a good shepherd. Each little sheep is precious."

Somewhere Grace remembered Granny Lawson had said a similar thing. "He leads us beside the still waters. He restores our souls." Grace thought, *God has protected me all these years and has brought me to this place to find my son and granddaughters. He is about to restore us all, I believe that. I'm so grateful. Thank You, Lord.*

*****

The time was nearly midnight when Grace awoke to find Aunt Lucy pulling on her sleeve. "Grace, get up. There's too much traffic on this road," she said, "and I'm hearing helicopters. Get up and see what it is."

Grace stumbled to the front window, peeked out. Two huge Army-like trucks were passing by, going north toward the old farm. Grace could clearly hear the rotary sound of helicopters in the distance. Grace whispered, "Let's go back to bed, keep the lights off. I'll stay in your room with you. Come on, let's be quiet."

*****

The morning would break, and the whole community would be astir with speculation. The old farm had been raided from three different directions, a concerted effort by several law enforcement agencies. The media was out with cameras and questions. The sheriff called to warn Grace to stay quiet and say nothing. Her life could be in danger if someone thought she had ratted out the whole operation.

Grace learned that twenty-six people had been arrested and detained, evidence confiscated, and a temporary gate had been installed at the entrance to the farm; the place would be under guard until further notice. Grace would be expected to appear at the sheriff's office early on Monday. Lawyer Henderson had been arrested, and he would be in jail.

Grace took it all in, thanked the sheriff for calling, and promised to be there on Monday. Grace might get to confront Henderson. Would she tell him about their son? Would she tell her son about him? Grace would wrestle with the questions, her monkey brain chattering, sometimes screeching. The beloved church people would gather to pray and ask God to see her through, the very same church she had once resented and detested. God would hear the prayers. Grace's perspective had been long overdue for a reframing. God would see to it.

Identifying the Enemy

Peace did not come easy on Sunday. Grace made it through Sunday's Memorial Day celebration on automatic pilot; the flowers had been posted, the cemetery looked lovely, and the community turned out in a spirit of fellowship and goodwill. At the Sunday-night service, a large crowd gathered to pray for their community; they made sure Grace was loved and supported, some congratulating her for putting a stop to "the devil's work" that had gone on "far too long" on that old farm. Grace accepted their comments graciously, she hoped.

Back at home later in the evening, she asked Aunt Lucy, "Why am I feeling so antsy about this whole thing? I knew it was coming, but for some reason, I'm feeling nervous and jittery. I should feel relieved, but I feel dread and fear, not at all peaceful about it."

Aunt Lucy pondered a bit before she said, "It's not like you're used to dealing with this much stress without your usual medicine, Grace. My guess is, old Satan ain't a bit pleased with what's happened here, and he's gonna blame you, try to drag you down with fear and intimidation. The more fear you feel, the better he likes it. You'll have to turn it over to God, listen for His voice, don't give in to fear. God said He didn't give us a spirit of fear. Praise God in the face of fear and the devil will have to leave you alone. You're doing a good job, Grace, and it's the best thing you can do. Don't doubt yourself. Trust God and pray for your enemies. That's what I would do."

*****

Later, when Grace tried to sleep, she tossed and turned, her mind spinning. She could only think of one thing to soothe her emotions; she wanted a good, stiff drink. That would ease what ailed her; she just couldn't think of another thing that might work. After wrestling with her cravings for a couple of tortuous hours, she finally turned it over to God. She prayed, "You know, God, my heart is here with this community, and these cravings are not from You. They are all in my head. Please help me. I'm in trouble without Your help. What do I need to do?"

Two words floated through her consciousness. "Be still." The words were spoken softly, but clearly. Grace became very quiet, waiting, hoping, and listening. She heard the old barn owl hooting somewhere in the distance. She noticed how the moon was beaming across the valley and shining through her window. The monkey chatter had stopped in her head. A peaceful, comforting presence, something beyond her understanding, came over her, and she fell into a deep sleep.

*****

Monday morning found Grace reporting to the sheriff's office as instructed. Strangely enough, she wasn't feeling the dread and fear she had experienced the day before. She stopped in at the food store and bought some fresh pastries, a whole dozen, for the sheriff's men. The sheriff would have the coffee ready, of course.

The law enforcement team was gathering in the conference room when Grace appeared with her box of goodies. They brought the coffeepot, and between slurps and bites, they told Grace about their raid.

"We had 'em boxed in. They couldn't run. They were too shocked to move, complete roundup. Didn't see us coming. We got twenty-six people, including three women. We searched Henderson's office and his home. Evidence all over the place. He's locked up."

The sheriff interrupted the news. He said, "What we want to do, Ms. Grace, is get with your attorney and file the ownership papers. Get that done and we can turn the property over to you.

You'll need to think about putting up a permanent gate. Talk to the fence company about that. We don't want anybody going in there. These media folks aren't allowed to trespass, and you don't need to get involved with them. You can refer them to us. You don't know anything to tell the media, okay?"

Grace felt overwhelmed with all she had heard, so she simply nodded at the sheriff.

One of the sheriff's men, Drake, spoke up. "Ms. Grace, we're going to bring Henderson in here for questioning. We'd like you to hear what he wants to tell us, again, about renting that old farm. At some point, we'll bring you in to confront him about that. You'll need to refute his claim that the property was rented. He also claims he knew nothing about the activities. We already got that evidence on tape. We might have to remind him. You keep your cool, just like before. Henderson will hang himself. Let him do it, okay?"

Grace was shown to another room, where she waited with her coffee, welcoming a few minutes to herself. She prayed, "Please don't let me do any harm here. I know what Henderson's problem is. I've seen it in myself and my grandpa. Alcohol causes stupidity, loss of good judgment. Henderson doesn't have a clue what has happened to him over the years. As mad as I am about this thing, I still don't want to see him just totally destroyed. Help me, please, help me to know what I need to say."

After some deep, slow, and rhythmic breathing, Grace was beginning to relax when she was summoned back to the conference room. Upon entering the room, Grace took a good look at her old nemesis. His face was ashy gray, with red splotches along his neck and jaws. He didn't look at all healthy; he looked disheveled, hungover, and sick, with defiance and anger flashing in his eyes.

The sheriff asked, "Ms. Grace, Mr. Henderson tells us that he was renting the property. Is that true to your knowledge?"

Grace spoke clearly, no tremor in her voice. "Not exactly. He was paying cash, as I understand it, one hundred fifty dollars a month, to some of the family members who don't own the property. They believed he was riding horses and hunting on the property. It was not something they were watching. They simply needed the money."

"Who owns the property, Ms. Grace?" the sheriff asked.

"I believe that I do," Grace responded. "We've just recently located my grandpa Lawson's last will and testament, and it appears that the property falls to me. I hadn't known about that before now."

The sheriff prodded, apparently watching Henderson's reaction. "So there is no legitimate rental agreement with you or your extended family?"

"None," Grace said. "We would never have rented the property for illegal activities, and we certainly wouldn't have allowed the damage that's been done, or the embarrassment this whole thing is causing."

Henderson was clenching his teeth, but he remained quiet.

One of the investigators asked, "Mr. Henderson has decided he doesn't have to talk to us, and he can hold that position, but we'd like you, Ms. Grace, to tell us why you came back to town. Would you explain that?"

Grace was caught off guard by the question, but she collected herself and gave the best answer she could. "I came back simply to settle some personal problems that had hounded me for some forty years. The issue had to do with my family, some long dead and some hanging on to life, who wanted me to come home. I went to look at the old farm, and I realized something was going on that my aunt Lucy Bradford's family didn't know about. She had held on to the belief that her brother, my grandpa Lawson, had made out a last will and testament before he died, but it had never been located. She was not able to take care of the property, and it fell into neglect. I had no idea, until recently, that I might actually own it. I'm here because I'm aware of my responsibility to claim the property. I'm just sorry that it has become a criminal investigation. None of the family knew these things were going on."

"Who wrote the last will for your grandpa Lawson? What attorney? And where was it filed and recorded?" the investigator asked.

"The late Robert Henderson Sr.," Grace said. "The will was prepared a few months before Mr. Henderson died, and my grandpa died sometime later. The will came in an envelope addressed to my grandpa from the Henderson law office. A receipt was attached that indicated fees had been paid for recording, but there is no record of it ever being filed and recorded."

The investigator asked, "How do you think that happened? Any idea?"

Grace answered, "Well, it looks like sloppy work by the law office. I understand that Mr. Henderson was critically ill during that period, but the ball was dropped somewhere. I won't say it was deliberate, but why would they send the original paperwork to Grandpa Lawson? That's a good question."

Henderson decided to speak up. "I told you, Grace, there was no last will, at least none that I knew about, not even a copy. I never saw that will. I'm not lying about that."

Grace couldn't resist. She said, "But you were okay with that, thinking nobody would notice the property title had never been cleared, and if I never showed up again, you would just wait and steal the property from Aunt Lucy's relatives when she passed. You knew where I was all that time, and you didn't mention that to Aunt Lucy or her family, and certainly not to me. And all that time, you were making money on rent and catering, blah, blah, blah. What kind of person does a thing like that? What kind of person are you?"

Henderson lost his control. He yelled, "You stupid [expletive]! You come back here with your haughty butt in the air and accuse me! I never hurt that old ragged place. I didn't know about that will! I've worked by backside off. You never struck a lick, not in forty years. What gives you the right to come in now and stir up trouble for me?"

Henderson turned to the sheriff and continued, "Do you know that she came to town and tried to get me to go into business with her, split the profits, and when I didn't want her, she got mad? Maybe you ought to arrest her too. She caused this mess. We weren't bothering anybody, just entertaining some friends and making a little money on the side."

The sheriff cautioned Henderson to keep his voice down, and then he said, "Tell us about that conversation you had with Ms. Grace. What was it she offered you?"

Henderson proceeded to twist the whole conversation to his advantage and implicate Grace. She listened while he arrogantly hung himself, that conversation having been skillfully recorded. Henderson elaborated, thinking he was gaining ground, until the sheriff stopped him.

The sheriff put a tape player on the table, pushed the button, and said, "Here, let's listen to this tape and see if you are remembering that conversation correctly, okay?"

As the tape played, the blood drained from Henderson's face and his eyes began to blaze with fire. Grace watched his expression change as he realized that it had been a setup; she had trapped him. He glared at Grace, saying, "You couldn't just shut your mouth and go back to your fancy life…you couldn't mind your own business, could you? You'll regret this, lady."

The sheriff warned him, saying, "Threats can be added to the charges, Mr. Henderson. The lady did the right thing. You don't want to get in any deeper. Things are piling up fast and deep."

Henderson clamped his jaws and shut down; he knew he'd gone too far.

One of the investigators turned to Grace and asked, "Is there anything else you'd like to say, or any question you want to ask, before we get on with our day?"

The room grew quiet. Henderson looked like he might explode just any minute. Grace sat for a minute, silently asking God for help. Then, she made a choice.

"Sheriff," she said, "there's an old cold case in this area that goes back forty years. Three brothers, the Colson boys, grabbed me early one morning on the way to my bus stop, and they gang-raped me on the old east ridge of my property. Nobody was ever charged because somebody shot and killed the boys up there near their lumber camp. Nobody was charged with that either because the evidence was never found that pointed to anyone in particular. There are still questions about who avenged me, or was it someone who had lost a daughter in similar circumstances? I'm bringing this up to explain why I left the area and never looked back. I was shipped out, pregnant and humiliated, traumatized, seventeen years old. My baby boy was born in a girls' home and adopted there. It's always been my belief that my son belonged to the Colson boys, but in recent days, I believe he belongs to someone else."

Grace searched in her handbag until she found the packet of pictures of her son. She passed the photos of her son first, then the photo of Bob Henderson when he was young. She asked, "Who do all of you think my son looks like? Let Mr. Henderson have a good look. My son was born in October, not December, which means that I was pregnant before that rape."

The men all took a good look, and the sheriff responded, "Well, well, well, you might want to take a good look at these, Mr. Henderson." He pushed the pictures across the table.

Henderson looked back and forth at the two different young men. He stammered, "You can't blame me. I'm not responsible. It's coincidental. It can't be mine!" he was yelling.

Grace waited for the sheriff to warn him, and she said, "But I'm pretty sure that you and your dad helped my grandpa engineer my exile before any pregnancy could be blamed on you. You never even asked about me after that, did you?"

Grace had to take a couple of deep breaths, but she continued, "My family suspected this, but my grandpa and the late Mr. Henderson got me out of sight. It has turned out, years later, to be the best thing they could have done, considering how young and helpless I was at that time. I'm told this child has a respectable family and he turned out well, a hardworking, successful businessman. Now he wants to meet his original family." She looked directly at Henderson and asked, "What shall we tell him? Do you want this young man to know the truth, or shall we spin some bigger lies? This is your son, you know that, your only child. Do you have the guts to tell the truth, or do you want it to appear that you are a lazy, lying, greedy skunk? Do you want him to see what you have allowed yourself to become? What shall we say? What am I supposed to tell him when this all comes out in the media?"

The room grew very quiet. Henderson was staring at the pictures, his jaws clamped together, the muscles twitching in his face. He didn't answer the questions.

Grace wasn't through with him. She said, "You had three wives who tried to tell you about the drinking, what alcohol was doing to your head. I suspect other people have tried as well. I'm not here to judge you, Bob. I'm familiar with alcoholism and its subtle destruction.

"I've hidden in the bottle for years, and I nearly destroyed my life's work." Grace wiped the tears from her eyes before she could continue. "I'm telling you, here and now, prison won't be a place where recovery from alcoholism can take place. Recovery is too hard and extremely painful. If there's an ounce of self-respect left in you, stand up and tell the truth to these people and you might get a break. Come clean in front of God and this town. The people here aren't fooled. They've watched this for years. You can at least let our son know that his father had something of a conscience left underneath all that false arrogance. The disease of alcoholism can be understood, healed, and forgiven, evil deeds can be atoned, but an evil spirit... that's another matter. You need to think about this."

Henderson asked, "So you think I'm a washed-up old alcoholic and the whole town knows it?" His hands were trembling as he spoke.

Grace replied, glancing at his jerky, trembling condition, "Well, tell us, where along the line did you just decide to turn yourself into the least-respected attorney in this town? What is the payoff for that? Why did alcohol use take precedence over three marriages, and not long after the weddings? When did you make a conscious choice to steal land and property from poor people for a living? Did you not consider that God may be watching? I can ask these questions all day, Bob, and you can't find a sensible answer. Alcohol just subtly took over your brain and distorted any value system you were taught. You haven't noticed over forty years how much control you have lost. I didn't either. Desperation, somewhere along the line, had you grabbing at anything that even remotely smelled like money. Arrogance and greed are deadly vices. They sink ships, and yours has been on fire for a while. If I were you, I'd come clean, help the sheriff clean this mess up, let the town know that you haven't destroyed yourself completely. Then you can leave our son a legacy he can understand

THE ROAD TO HELL IS PAVED WITH... WHAT?

and admire. Just have the guts to tell the truth. Alcoholism is a disease, not a crime."

As she collected her pictures, Grace looked at the sheriff and said, "I'm available to help if there's anything else I can do. I'm retiring, and I'll be coming back to Lawson Creek permanently. You know where I'm found. Let me hear if there's anything I need to do around the old farm to help you further."

The sheriff stood to shake Grace's hand as she left the room. Drake followed Grace to the hallway with his arm draped around her shoulders. He said, "Ms. Grace, that took guts. Now, who did you say might be responsible for that old cold case? We could look into that for you." Grace repeated for him what she had learned in the cemetery.

*****

The piano repairs were underway when Grace made it home. Aunt Lucy was wrapped up in the tune-up; she and Charlie were happily improving the tones. Grace was happy to stay out of their way. The back porch with its lounge chair seemed inviting. Grace poured herself a glass of tea and sprawled out on the lounge, hoping she could hear the birds singing.

The monkey chatter was beginning to take over her thoughts until Grace remembered to focus her attention on her blessings, just how far she had come in a few short weeks. The progress far outweighed the losses; in fact, she couldn't think of any losses that had occurred. It seemed deliverance was happening, sometimes at an overwhelming pace, but deliverance nonetheless. Much work would be required, and a cool, level head, free of overreactive emotionalism, would be her best tool. Immediate gratification of emotional pain would not be helpful. In fact, that would abort the long-term purpose. Grace asked God for strength to keep her mind set on God's will and His purpose for the rest of her life.

*****

Tuesday morning brought the media out early. They rang the doorbell, but Grace spoke to them through the newly installed intercom system. She discouraged them by saying, "We don't know anything. We don't have any information yet. You can ask the sheriff's office about it. We can't help you. Sorry."

Aunt Lucy said, "The newspaper comes out on Wednesday, Grace. They'll be going after something else if we just ignore them long enough."

After lunch, the housekeeper came to stay with Aunt Lucy, and Grace left for the big city. On Wednesday, she would be facing the regulatory board to submit her request for retirement. Stella would be waiting, smiling from ear to ear, with an unexpected surprise. God had His mysterious ways, His wonders to coordinate.

A Dying Confession

Early on Tuesday morning, just after breakfast, Grace had taken an opportunity to make contact with her son. She dialed the number she had been given, hoping that a man's voice would answer. Instead, a female answered and introduced herself as the son's wife. When Grace explained her reason for calling, the woman said, "Oh my goodness, you just missed him! He left on a business trip this morning and won't be back until Saturday. He'll be so happy you called! He's been looking for you for years. When he calls, I'll tell him you have called. He'll be thrilled! It's something he's always wanted, to find you."

Grace held on to her composure as best as she could. She responded, "Tell him I'll definitely be in touch and we have to make plans to meet. I'm looking forward to that. I'm so excited about seeing him. Thank you so much. Have a blessed day. Bye!"

She wanted so badly to ask about the girls, what their names are, etc. But on second thought, she'd leave that to their father to disclose when he felt comfortable. Grace mused, *I don't want to be a pushy, nosy mother-in-law. That type is unpopular, I'm told.*

*****

It had been Grace's intention to drive straight through for a couple of hours to introduce herself to her son, but she was forced to put that impulsive behavior aside and deal with a more reasonable approach. A more-thought-out plan, a special celebration might be the better thing. A forty-year reunion with a family member one had never met might call for a special occasion, not a casual, drive-by introduction.

Grace thought she might plan a welcome party at some point and invite the family as honorary guests.

Grace put the plan to meet her son on hold and focused on finding the veterans hospital, just an hour's drive out of her way to the big city. As she left town, headed south, she stopped to fill her tank and purchased a road map. After carefully tracing the route to her intended destination, she headed in a more westerly direction, toward the veterans' home, where she wanted to find Brandon O'Neil, the man who some thought had murdered the Colson brothers on the old east ridge. Grace had a few questions to ask Mr. O'Neil.

After speaking with the home by phone, Grace had been told that Mr. O'Neil, indeed, was a long-term resident and he welcomed company, especially those who brought gifts. When Grace asked what gifts he preferred, she was told, "He doesn't eat anything by mouth. He's fed intravenously. But he loves fresh flowers and cards, just to know someone cares."

Armed with lovely flowers and a nice card featuring a trio of beautiful puppies, Grace arrived at the veterans' home. She was directed to a room occupied by a disabled man lying propped on pillows and hooked to an IV, with several medical monitors and machines all around his bed. Obviously, Mr. O'Neil was not in the best of conditions and looked to be pretty elderly.

Grace spoke to Mr. O'Neil as she showed him the flowers and the card. His eyes brightened, and he appeared to be comprehending, but he never moved his hands to receive his gifts. In a weak, raspy voice, he said, "Thank you, lady. This is nice. Put the flowers in the window, please, where I can see them."

Grace placed the flowers as she was told, and as she turned back to the bed, Mr. O'Neil asked, "Who sent the card and flowers?"

Realizing that Mr. O'Neil thought she was a delivery lady, Grace stepped to the bed to introduce herself. She leaned down and said to him, "Mr. O'Neil, my name is Grace Lawson, and I'm from way back in time, nearly forty years ago. As a young girl, I was a resident of Lawson Creek, and the Colson brothers raped me up on the old east ridge of my grandpa Lawson's farm. I've been away from that community for a long time, but I've been wondering if you might remember that period. Do you recall anything about that incident or that crime?"

The old man's eyes widened as he stared at Grace. With his weak and raspy, almost-breathless voice, he said, "You were the little girl that got away, ran before they could burn you. Yeah, I remember that. They burnt my little angel. It haunts me to this day. My little girl couldn't get away. It's painful to think about…even now."

Grace apologized. "I'm sorry that this upsets you. My family on Lawson Creek believes that my grandma Lawson killed the Colson brothers to avenge me, and I just can't accept that she would do that. She was capable of using a firearm pretty well, but I doubt that she would have done such a thing. She was a gentle soul. I was hoping you could help me settle my doubts. Do you remember anything about that old crime that would point to anybody else?"

Mr. O'Neil hesitated, as if in deep thought. After a bit, he nodded, patting a place on the bed for Grace to sit close to his side. He took a few breaths, and with a quiet voice, he said, "You listen…carefully. Your grandma didn't have the skills to take down three strong men with four bullets. She didn't have the training to do that job and get away. You tell your family that she did not do that." The old veteran leaned back on his pillow to rest and breathe.

Grace could see the old man was tiring, so she asked, "Would you like to hear a story?"

Mr. O'Neil nodded, and Grace began. "I've been away for almost forty years, and I've recently learned that I own the old farm there on Lawson Creek, where I was raised. I was sent away to a girls' home to have my baby after that incident on the ridge. I was seventeen years old at that time, and now I'm fifty-seven, and I'm trying to deal with that background. There seems to be more questions than answers, and I'm confused. If you know anything that would help me to find some peace with my heritage, I would very much appreciate your help."

Mr. O'Neil nodded. He said, "I can help a little, I think. What do you need to know?"

Grace continued, "My son, who is now almost forty years old, has been trying to meet me, and I'm excited about that, but I'd like to know more about my family before I have to share with him a background, I can't tell the truth about. My poor granny Lawson stands accused of committing murder, my grandpa Lawson, a preacher, couldn't live up to what he tried to teach, and I've apparently inherited his tendency for alcohol abuse. I'm prone to hide behind the bottle myself to escape pain that I can't identify in myself. I've been trying to keep a clear head and deal with the truth in my life, but this old story about my young years haunts me. Why did my grandpa just send me away? Why didn't anyone support me? Why did they try to forget about me? Now, I find that Grandpa Lawson turned around and left the old farm to me but never told me, or anyone else. I'm confused. Was he trying to make amends, or was he compelled by legal counsel to cover something up, save the farm at the same time? It's a mystery that I'm trying to piece together like a puzzle, one piece at a time, but I don't know what the bigger picture looks like. Do you understand where I'm coming from, Mr. O'Neil?"

Mr. O'Neil had been listening quietly, often nodding as she spoke. He inhaled deeply for a few stronger breaths, and he reached for Grace's hand. With his weak, raspy voice but a determined effort, he said, "I can help you with two things, two puzzle pieces. First, you will never clear your head with alcohol. It's done me lots of damage before I got out of 'Nam, that and heroin. That's how we got out of that war—we just drank our way through it."

The old veteran rested for a minute, breathing deep and slow, but he held on to Grace's hand. After a brief rest, he continued, "You look here over my bed and around these walls and tell me what you see, Grace." He turned loose of her hand and pointed to the framed pictures and plaques that decorated his room. With his index figure, he motioned for Grace to take a closer look around the room.

Grace stood and began to scan the military pictures and plaques hanging around the walls. She looked at more than a dozen plaques, awards, citations, and certificates of achievement bestowed upon Mr. O'Neil for his service to his country. His medals were displayed in a glass case, locked for security, but available for guests to admire. As she walked around the room, scanning the military paraphernalia, she wondered what he might expect her to say. What did he mean by "Tell me what you see"?

Grace made an effort. She said, "You certainly served your country well, Mr. O'Neil. You can be proud of this legacy. I'm so honored to have met you." She took the old man's hand, thinking he might be too weak to respond, but he rallied. With an unexpected strength in his voice, he said, "When I was young, during the time you speak about, I was drinking a lot, didn't know then what I know now about that old devil, moonshine. Our family drank it for medicine and pleasure. When my little girl went missing, I wasn't able to think about anything but how to find somebody to blame. I was a mad man, you understand?"

Grace responded, "I surely do. Please don't wear yourself out. I'm listening. You take your time."

The old man continued, "The sheriff couldn't figure out how to prove what my family tried to tell him about the Colson boys. We knew the Colson boys were messing up the girls all around our community, but the girls wouldn't talk—scared, you know." He motioned for Grace to wait while he caught his breath. He pointed toward the pictures and plaques. "You can see that I'm a munitions expert, a firearm specialist, a skilled marksman. I was one of the best frontline scouts in our troop, in the whole unit. We found and eliminated the enemy before the troops moved in. You following me here, Grace?"

Grace nodded, holding on to his hand, waiting for him to regain his breath. The heart monitor at the side of his bed caught her eye. She didn't know much about heart monitors, but she felt concerned, hoping she wasn't pushing him beyond his capacity.

The old veteran rested for a few minutes, and opening his eyes, he continued. "Your grandma was a tiny little woman—Cherokee, I think. She gave me some of her cold milk out of that springhouse and brought me some food. I think she heard the shots from the ridge, but she never asked me. I was in my fatigues, and she thought I was a soldier just walking across the ridge toward home. She gave me some biscuits and sausage, some boiled eggs, and a bag of homemade cookies. She told me how to take the west ridge and cross the mountain. I left before anybody knew I was there. I made it across that ridge, went home, and was off to 'Nam before anybody could ask. I reckon she never told anybody I was there."

Grace spoke up, trying to allow some time for him to rest. "She never said a word to anybody, apparently, and she took the blame. I'm so grateful that you have told me. You had an amazing career, and your legacy stands as a witness. I can follow Granny's example. I won't talk about it. You've given me a great gift. I thank you so much for this."

As Grace wiped her tears, the old veteran spoke again. "Yes, let my family believe the best of me when I'm gone. You can go tell old Sheriff Tate that he was right, that I'm grateful he didn't come after me. I got off the alcohol and heroin and tried to make amends. God gives me peace about it. Who knows how many little girls were saved? How many would have been sacrificed if I had been a coward? Law enforcement is just too slow, the wheels of justice too late. Victims pile up. You were saved, Grace. You thank God for that, and listen for His guidance. God has a purpose in all this, bringing you back. But you can't drown His voice with alcohol. That will cause you to destroy your own work, cause early death. You promise me, no more drinking. Today, make me that promise."

Grace responded, "I promise I will not go back to that. I want to leave my family a legacy. I will listen to God's voice for guidance on that. Thank you for helping me today. Your courage and valor inspire me. You've given me a precious gift, Mr. O'Neil." She bent to kiss the old veteran's brow.

He smiled as he responded, "Thank you for the flowers. I like little puppies." Grace thought she was being dismissed, but he tugged at her hand, motioning for her to lean in and listen.

"I forget," he said. "There's a rock crevice behind that rock wall that was built around the old waterfall coming out of the cliffs at your grandma's spring. Sometime after I'm gone, you have a look between the rock wall and the cliffs behind, on the western end of the structure. If time hasn't destroyed it, you'll find my weapon. When your grandma went to fix the sack of food, I dropped the rifle down between the stacked stone wall and the cliffs, propped it between crevices in the mountain rock, and left it there. I thought one day I'd get it, but I never went back. You understand, I couldn't be caught with that weapon. Too risky. If you find what's left of that, just keep it to remind yourself of your promise to me, okay?"

Grace bowed her head and said a prayer for Brandon O'Neil, an exceptional servant of God's purpose. He was smiling, eyes closed and breathing evenly, as she gathered herself to leave. The heart monitor was slowly moving along. Grace knew God had been listening. She quietly left the room.

On her way out of the hospital, Grace stopped at the nurse's station. An attendant, monitoring the data screen, looked up and asked, "Did you have a good visit with Brandon?"

Grace replied, "I did. He's weak, but he's holding his own."

The lady laughed. "Yes, he always does. He makes the most of his time. He is quite the hero around here."

Grace asked, "If I leave my phone number, would you be able to call me if he ever needs anything? I want to help him, anything he wants or needs."

The lady smiled but sadly shook her head. She said, "All of us would help him if we could, but he's in God's hands now. He'll only be with us another week or so, maybe not even that long. He's ready to go. He won't be needing anything for himself. If you would like to help his family, you can call the main office and they will connect you with the family. I'm not allowed to share that information here."

Grace made it to the parking lot and into her car before the dam broke. The pain was overwhelming, and the tears poured. She sat behind her shaded windows and let the pain express itself; she had a heart-wrenching cry. When the pain began to subside, she cleaned her face, cranked her car, and left the parking lot, headed south toward her home.

*****

During the next hour, Grace focused on following her map to the edge of the city, where she made a turn toward her condo. The traffic was heavy, and she became stressed, but she gave no thought to stopping for a drink. She felt the craving, but she remembered her promise to that old hero. Grace had been taught that physical and psychological cravings would be a challenge for the rest of her life, but she knew she could prevail. She would simply thank God for His protection and His love every time she felt tempted, and the monkey chatter would stop. A miracle she couldn't adequately comprehend, but she'd believe and receive. She'd prevail.

*****

At the condo, Stella was busy cooking Grace's favorite dinner, grilled fish with hush puppies and a wonderful fresh garden salad. Stella said, "Heh, I knew you'd be in here tonight. Look at this food. Needs about ten minutes. Get washed up and we can talk."

Grace hurried right along. The smell of the fish made her mouth water, and Stella was eager to talk. She was hardly seated before Stella asked, "You want to hear some terrific news? I'm dying to tell you—I can't wait any longer!"

As soon as quick prayers were said, Stella started rambling. "My boss gave me a whopper bonus for that convention we hosted, and he's gonna help me finance this condo, Grace. He says I deserve it. You haven't changed your mind, have you? You didn't, did you?

"My sister is coming to live with me and attend the college. She can walk to school from here. We're so excited! Nobody in our family has ever been to college. She can do it, Grace. Everything is falling into place. Please tell me you haven't changed your mind."

Grace had her mouth full, but she shook her head as she tried to swallow. She was staring at Stella as she managed to say, "No, I haven't. My mind is firmly made up, but please slow down and tell me again, what exactly is going on? How's it coming together? Slow down."

Stella explained how her boss had arranged the financing through his business connections and how the sister would move in with Stella, pay rent, but be able to work and attend college. Stella was so excited to be able to help her younger sister move on up.

THE ROAD TO HELL IS PAVED WITH... WHAT?

When Stella ran out of steam, Grace got a word in. "So...let me catch up. I'll have to clear out right away, move out. How long before I have to be out?"

Stella laughed and said, "You stay as long as you want to, Grace. It can't happen overnight. There's still paperwork, the slow grind of the paper mill. It'll be a while, and my sister won't start college until this fall. You've got all summer, even if we close the deal. You know you can stay with me. Don't sweat it. We'll take care of you, Grace."

*****

After dinner, the girls were making plans. They decided to celebrate with a late-night swim, a cup of hot chamomile tea to warm up, and a prayer of thanksgiving before bedtime.

Life had taken them down a most unexpected road, a joyful and exciting time for both of them. Grace slept through the night without interruption. Early in the morning, she woke up to remember her appointment with the regulatory board. Strangely, she felt no apprehension about it. She said to herself, "This will all work out. I'll simply speak my truth and let God handle the board and its reaction."

Grace would be right; things would work out, but things would not work quite like Grace might have anticipated. Surprises were coming that would blow Grace's fragile mind.

One Door Closes, Another Opens

Stella left the condo early, and Grace had time for a quiet coffee by herself. She took time to reflect on how far she had come in just a few weeks; her emotional and spiritual outlook had certainly changed for the better. The recovery group, her old trusty God Squad, had pushed and shoved her, with love and compassion, into an examination of her life beyond what she had wanted, but her perspective had radically changed. Inside her heart, she felt gleeful, joyous, and excited. Her human side, however, screamed out for staunch control, immediate relief of emotional discomfort, and her beloved old friend, alcohol.

Grace marveled at how alcohol abuse simply buried its victims in denial, total lack of mindfulness, all awareness obscured and obliterated, the subtle erosion of willpower and self-discipline, over time, creating a false and warped perception of reality. As the alcohol abuse continued, the alcoholic drifted further and further away from sanity and simply became self-destructive.

The path of self-destruction that her grandpa had taken bore witness to Grace as she realized she, herself, had taken the same path. Even her old beau, Bobby Henderson, had taken that route to his own destruction, now facing what might be his total ruin, all because he had no idea what was causing the damage.

Grace remembered the three facets of the human being: body, mind, and spirit. She tried to understand how the body, controlled by alcohol and drugs, dominated the mind. That left the spiritual aspect of man suppressed, dormant, and waiting for the mind to humble itself enough to cry out for help. That humbling, unfortunately, required a breakdown of denial, a beating down of ego and pride—perhaps total loss and humiliation.

Maybe the long years of suffering had been the message all the time, Grace was thinking, but the alcohol served to deaden the pain and deafen the message it brought. Did Grandpa Lawson, the preacher man, escape death's hold just long enough to repent, make some amends, and ask God for help? Had Grace been given the same opportunity? And how did it all come together for the higher purpose of God? Grace was full of questions; she wanted God to send some easy format to study, or something similar to an agenda to follow. Apparently, God was teaching her to walk in faith—not an easy task for advancing alcoholism.

Grace was caught up in amazement at the unfolding of her life when the phone rang. She snapped out of her thoughts as she picked up the phone. The college was calling to inform her that she should appear before the board at eleven thirty this morning instead of the usual schedule. Grace glanced at the clock; it was already nine thirty, and she hadn't dressed. She jumped up and hurried to her room, thinking, *Funny how time flies when I'm trying to wrap my head around all these things. Why haven't I thought of these things before? I was simply too busy with my old bottle. I shut it all down—that's the truth.*

Looking through her closet, Grace selected what she thought was her most attractive and professional outfit. She was determined to appear professional and poised, exhibit grace and dignity no matter what the board might have to say to her. She remembered how the sheriff's men had taught her the value of "stay calm and carry on." She intended to relate her ugly truth with humility and total honesty without losing self-respect; she would not react to comments and criticisms. She wanted to walk away from a long, hard profession that she had never enjoyed. It was simply a means to a paycheck most of the time. She could hardly remember a day when she actually looked forward to going to work.

Grace now believed that God had called her out of that role and had given her a greater purpose. She would not shout about that in front of the board, but at home she could turn into Aunt Lucy, dance and praise the Lord. Grace smiled as she recalled just how free and unrestrained dear old Aunt Lucy could be when prayers were answered; even the simplest blessing brought out her gratitude and praise. Grace had learned a lot from that example, and her dear old aunt had taught her God hears the heart.

Looking herself over in a three-way mirror, Grace decided she had done well. She appeared well dressed and groomed, demonstrating self-respect and self-assurance. There would be no evidence of the effects of alcohol abuse, no neglect of the self, no attitude of resistance, no denial, no worn-out excuses, no cover-ups, no argumentation—the plain and simple truth would be sufficient.

*****

After a quick prayer, Grace left for her appointment. As she left the driveway, she spotted Professor John walking along the sidewalk. She rolled the window down and gestured for him to hop in. He seemed happy to have a ride. "How are you, Grace?" he asked. "I've been wondering how things are going with you."

Grace started chattering away, happy to share her adventures with her friend. She was still chattering when they arrived at the boardroom, and John opened the door to allow her to enter. Grace stopped dead still, staring at the room. A celebration was prepped; the tables were covered with tablecloths, dishes, and flowers. Balloons decorated the entire room. While Grace was staring, stunned, at a loss as to what she had interrupted, the whole room exploded with applause.

"Come in, come in, Professors Larkin and Lawson. You two can sit with Professors Lee and Adams. All four of you are retiring. This is your party. Get comfortable and enjoy it." The speaker escorted them to an honorary table in front of the room.

Grace was speechless. She looked at Professor John quizzically, mouthing a question, "Did you know about this?"

The professor merely shrugged. Grace gave him a quick gesture; she swiped her finger across her own throat while she glared at him. He didn't flinch, just smiled at her.

One of the college administrators brought the group to attention. He said, "We are retiring some of our most dedicated and talented teachers today, and we want to recognize their contribution to this department, and we want to express how much we have benefited from their presence here at the school."

They introduced each of the retirees, beginning with the youngest. Professor Lee had served twenty-two years and was retiring to take care of her elderly parents. Professor Adams was retiring, after twenty-five years, to serve as a missionary to a foreign country. Professor Lawson was retiring, after twenty-eight years, to serve the underprivileged communities of Appalachia. Professor John Larkin was retiring, after thirty years, to—the speaker paused, staring at his notes—retiring to fish. That comment brought laughter and applause; some people cheered.

After the laughter subsided, the double doors opened and carts of food began to arrive. The chairman said, "Eat and enjoy. You have a lot to celebrate."

The meal was almost over and the dessert cart had arrived when a comedian from the drama department arrived. He was dressed as an elderly, long-retired, shaky, rambling, nerdy old professor, decked out in baggy pants held up by suspenders, with a big ugly bow tie hanging lopsided at the neckline of his checkered shirt. He said he was asked to give some pointers, from his long experience, on how to survive retirement. He started with "How to avoid the pitfalls of leisure time."

The nerdy old professor made a point about how to evade the "muck and mire of the money-grabbing marriages"—no fourth and fifth marriages recommended, he said. His jokes were hilarious, the crowd delighted. He warned his audience about the "crazies" that beset the retired folks who have no focus or purpose in life except "to hold down the comfy old sofa." He went on to explain how that leads to the "old folks' home." He elaborated with wit and humor how to avoid and evade that destination. The audience was rolling with laughter. Before he left, he hit a serious note with, "Don't let retirement scare you. It's just that time in life to make up for all the mistakes of your youth. Do what you can to help your communities, and spread God's Word, peace, and love all around." The man was a hit; he got a standing ovation.

Plaques denoting years of service were presented to the retirees. Grace received two matching plaques, one for her years of service and one for her dedication and selfless focus. Grace would later dub the second plaque "an award for workaholism."

As Grace stepped forward to receive her awards, she held herself upright, squared her shoulders, took a deep breath, and thanked the college administration and all her peers for being so kind. She gave a brief rundown of her struggle with alcohol, her denial and her resistance to seeking help for herself. She gave the board a sincere apology for the difficulty she had caused, and she thanked the board for helping to save her life. She asked for forgiveness. She also asked the administrators to please make twelve-step programs available for the staff and students as soon as possible. She made herself an example of why programs to address addiction were needed. She thanked everyone, said "I love all of you," and stepped down. The room stood in applause.

As the gathering ended, Grace received hugs and handshakes, words of encouragement, and promises of prayer. She had never felt so appreciated, or even recognized, in all her years of employment at the college. She cried through much of the attention.

*****

Professor John was waiting at the car when Grace got to the parking space. He asked, "Are you okay, Grace?"

Grace mumbled, "I think so. Just a bit stunned, to say the least. This was unexpected."

"Yeah, I know," he said. "You were expecting the firing squad. You deserved this, Grace. You just soak it up as merited. Nobody knows that better than me, you know that."

As Grace backed out of the parking space, she noticed that her name had been removed from the "Reserved for" sign. She had removed her personal items from her office last week. She was free to go—no reason to look back—but somehow, she felt a certain sadness. After a deep breath, she asked, "John, do you have any plans for this afternoon? I simply can't be alone right now. Could I help you paint your condo or something? I have to be busy, not alone."

After glancing at the tears in Grace's eyes, he said, "How about helping me stage my furniture and make photos for the real estate market? I'm posting my condo for sale this week, and I need help with that. Would that keep you busy?" Grace nodded, wiping tears from her eyes.

She dropped John off at his condo and said, "I'll be right back. A change of clothes and some work gloves and I am free labor. Thank you, John, for understanding where I am right now."

*****

Together, Grace and John worked at clearing the unnecessary clutter from the floor space in his condo. They arranged the furniture and tried to display a "neutral" appearance for any prospective buyers. They had to make a few trips to the college to dispose of the professor's huge collection of scholarly books. Grace asked, "What do you intend to do with your furniture, John? The furniture won't fit in your motorhome, you know."

John answered, "Sell the furniture with the condo. It won't travel with me, and I'm all about traveling light these days. Buyers usually like convenience, anyway. They like to move right in—no lugging furniture these days."

Grace gave some thought to that idea. She decided she'd ask Stella about that; after all, where would she store furniture? And why would she need it, anyway? Aunt Lucy's place was sufficiently stuffed already, and the old farmhouse would need to be renovated. She shared her thoughts with John. He simply said, "Travel light, Grace. With moving and storage costs, you will lose more money than you'll save. I've seen the elegant style of your furnishings. Do you think that style fits your old farmhouse setting?"

Grace cracked up, laughing. "No," she said. "That elegant style won't go with horse manure and copperheads. I'll need something a bit more durable and rugged than that. I'll ask Stella if she can swing it. Otherwise, a yard sale will be happening."

Sometime later, John suggested they stop for a break, have a sandwich and some tea. They sat on the patio at the rear of the building. Grace asked a question she'd wanted to ask all afternoon. "John, do you think the board just simply retired me because they were glad to be rid of me, glad to see me go? Do you think they took the easy way out, made it look good for the college?"

John was quick to say, "Grace, I know you have some difficulty believing in yourself, being the perfectionist that you are, but that whole group agreed to do something to show love and respect for you. They agreed that to encourage your retirement would be an act of love and support. You could learn to love yourself, Grace, respect yourself as much as we all do. Will you look at yourself from that perspective?"

"You didn't engineer that whole thing, did you, John? Twisting arms and pulling strings seems to be a specialty of yours."

"Grace," he said, "my influence wouldn't have mattered. I handed in my retirement request last month. Who would have cared what I thought?"

Grace responded, "Somehow, I just can't believe that wonderful send-off they gave us and how they awarded me. It's unbelievable."

John responded with, "Grace, have you ever heard of forgiveness? Good people know the importance of forgiveness, granting second chances. You might consider being as generous with yourself."

He went on to say, "You're too hard on yourself. God can't work with you if you don't think enough of yourself. Try to see the better side of yourself. God does. The rest of us do too. You might get off your own back and appreciate what and who you actually are. God is on your side, and so are the rest of us. All you friends."

Grace said, "If it's all in my head, I can reject the negativity and just be grateful. That seems to quell the monkey chatter of doubt in my thoughts. Thank you, John. You're a good man."

"Oh, I agree. I'm well worth knowing," he said boastfully. "Now, if I can just collect on that hug you owe me, I'll be a happy man. You do remember that we're retired now? No rules about fraternizing. And you owe me a good hug, or two…or three…or more." He smiled broadly at Grace.

Grace quietly asked, "Are you coming on to me, John, or am I missing something?"

In an exasperated tone, John said, "Well, lady, I've been standing around for years, admiring you from afar, hoping you would stop looking right past me. Would it kill you to catch on? I'm harmless. Give me a break, would you?"

Grace defended herself. She said, "I'm just beginning to accept you as my friend and not my director. You make me nervous. But I can work on that. You give some time to get used to our new way of communicating and I'll catch up. Right now, my head is spinning with all the changes in my life. I feel that relapse is at the door. I'm scared. You ask yourself if you really want to be involved with a recovering alcoholic, prone to struggle with relapse, okay?"

John pulled his chair close to Grace's side and reached for her hand. "As long as you need me or want me, Grace, I'll be here for you. I'll help you fight, just like today. All you had to do was ask. We have a good relationship. We don't have to let a disease come between us. I'm not a perfect man, but I'm trustworthy and on your side. You are my version, in fact my dream, of a lovely woman. I've admired you for years. Let's give our relationship a chance. In the end, if it isn't working out, we will still be friends, help each other, just like we do now. What do you think?"

Grace didn't run, like she so wanted to do. She nodded, wiping away the tears. She said, "I cry a lot these days. Can you handle it? I'm hoping that symptom goes away. My feelings are so intense right now. But at least I'm not frozen up anymore. I can feel something without running to a bottle." To emphasize her point, she leaned over and kissed his cheek.

John returned the kiss as he said, "I understand, and I won't push. Just trust me and I'll prove myself worthy. You'll see."

*****

THE ROAD TO HELL IS PAVED WITH... WHAT?

Stella was driving in from Wednesday night's prayer service when she passed Grace on the street, walking back to the condo. Not accustomed to seeing Grace out at night, she asked, "Where have you been?"

Grace just had to tell. "On a romantic rendezvous with my pal John."

Stella looked at the work gloves, the dirty jeans and baggy shirt, the messy hair and tearstained face, the general sloppy appearance, and she said, "Listen, girl, you might want me to give you some pointers on romantic rendezvous. Men like a little more class than this. Let's get you in off the street, com'on."

The two friends talked until midnight. Stella was extremely excited to hear about Grace's furniture offer. Grace was eager to hear that paperwork for the purchase of the condo was being processed. Both of the ladies were happy; they held hands at their makeshift altar, in front of the fireplace, and gave God praise for everything.

Later, just before she collapsed in bed, Grace asked God to please help her sort out her feelings for her beloved friend John.

Restoration was happening faster than Grace could keep up with. Her feelings were bouncing from extreme gratitude and joyfulness to doubt and terror. Would she make it with sobriety and hang on, or would her body and mind betray her? Grace fell asleep, leaving her concerns with God.

An Unexpected Turn of Events

Early on Friday morning, long before daybreak, Grace left the city headed toward her beloved Lawson Creek. She had spent most of the previous day decluttering the condo and packing boxes of her personal items to transport. Her car was loaded with boxes and bags. Stella had been delighted with the idea that she could keep the furnishings in the condo. She said, "I was worried about bringing my old stuff. It's so old and tattered. This is an answer to prayer, Grace. You can't imagine how much this means. You make a good price, and I'll find a way to handle paying you. God will help me."

Grace had arranged to borrow Professor John's appraiser. That appraiser would be coming to appraise John's furnishings along with the condo; he'd simply take a look at Grace's furnishings as well. John had volunteered to handle that piece of business for Grace.

When Grace said goodbye to John, he said, "Don't worry about a thing. I'll be right behind you in a week or so. As soon as I get a good offer and contract on my condo, I'll be coming, Grace."

The reliable old God Squad, the Thursday-night group, had held a special prayer for Grace. She said to the group, "I feel like I'm taking that proverbial old 'midnight train to Georgia,' back to my roots, looking for myself. I'm scared to death, but I know God has called me. I'll be back to visit on occasion, and I want all of you to come see what God is doing with me and my life. I'm excited and petrified at the same time."

The God Squad had some questions. "Grace, are you feeling your feelings without running to the bottle? Are your cravings beginning to diminish? How is the nausea and shakiness? Are you sleeping well, resting enough, trusting and praying, asking God for guidance?"

She looked around the table, noting the sincere love and concern, and she said, "To be honest, my craving is almost uncontrollable at times, but I have learned to start reciting my gratitude list, and that helps. My emotions chatter away, but I know they cannot be trusted. I distract myself with praise, and the monkey chatter quietens down. I'm resting and sleeping pretty well. I just surrender everything to God. My nausea has mostly stopped, and I shake rarely, except in the dense city traffic. I think that's not uncommon. I certainly won't have that problem where I'm going. Rattlesnakes and black bears might provoke it, but not traffic."

Everyone laughed as they hugged Grace and sent her on her way, promising to keep her in their prayers. Grace did her grieving at home with her dear sister Stella. After they had a good cry, the two girls grabbed their swimsuits and headed to the pool for a late-night swim. Soon peace and joy took over.

*****

Early the next morning, Grace was on her way. The dawn was beginning to brighten, and the mountains were appearing in the distance. Grace found herself singing, her voice sounding off-key and crackly, similar to the old piano. Grace didn't let that stop her; she sang anyway. She ignored the usual neon signs signifying spots to find alcohol. When her voice grew tired, she started thinking about her friend John. Had God given her a lifetime companion to walk with her on this incredible journey? John had not backed away from her troubled past or her present struggles. Grace had to admit, she had not trusted anyone in the past and had avoided relationships; she trusted her old bottle of medicine. John had never betrayed her on any level.

Maybe she'd been too insecure. Maybe she could relax and see what God had in mind. While she was musing over these things, the time passed and she found herself in the parking lot of the grocery store in her little hometown. She had arrived just as the sheriff was leaving with his box of doughnuts. Grace said, "Good morning, Sheriff. I see you beat me to the goodies this morning."

"Why, good morning, Ms. Grace," the sheriff responded. "I've been wondering if you might get here this weekend. Your old pal Henderson is in the hospital, under guard. He's had a massive heart attack. He'll be undergoing surgery, and he's asking for you. His sister came by to tell us. I meant to call you this morning."

Grace asked, "When did this happen? Where is he now? What hospital?"

The sheriff replied, "He's here at our hospital right now, but his sister is having him moved to a bigger facility where there's a special cardiac team. I think his surgery is scheduled for Monday. He collapsed yesterday morning. If you want to see him, go as soon as you can. His sister says he's helpless, can't harm you. He's under guard."

"I'll check on Aunt Lucy, and I'll come back to see what Henderson wants. I'll keep you posted," Grace said as she hurried along. In the store, she couldn't remember why she had said that. Was Henderson trying to control her again? She'd have to go and see.

*****

At Aunt Lucy's, over breakfast, Grace related the news. Aunt Lucy said, "Regardless of what he says, Grace, you forgive him and let him die in peace if God is calling him. He's the father of your son. You release him. God will hear and bless you for that."

Grace made fast work of unloading her car. She showered and dressed. She had no idea of what, or who, she might be facing, but she felt compelled to hurry. Something was happening.

Aunt Lucy was playing away at the old piano when Grace came through to leave. She said, "Gosh, Aunt Lucy, that piano sounds beautiful! The tones are clear and in harmony."

"Take a look, Grace, and tell me about the finish. Did we do a good job with the wood?"

Grace was amazed as she looked at the old wood. "This is remarkable! That old wood looks new. That Charlie knows his antiques, for sure," she said.

Aunt Lucy laughed and replied, "I knew it, I knew it! It hasn't sounded like this in years. I'm so proud! Thank you, Grace. God will reward you, you'll see."

Tears were falling from Grace's eyes as she made her way out the door. She was thinking that dear old Aunt Lucy deserved every dollar spent, and then some.

*****

At the hospital, Grace was shown to a secluded ward. The nurse in charge told Grace that Henderson's condition was critical—only one visitor at a time and only for ten minutes, maximum. Grace would be allowed a quick visit, only because Henderson asked. Grace was dressed in a gown and mask and shown to the room. A guard was posted at the door. The guard took note of the time and scanned Grace's ID. He said, "Henderson has been asking for you. Yell if you need any help."

Henderson was almost unrecognizable, his face covered with a mask, his forehead pale, medical assist machines all around. He looked like a man already dead, being artificially sustained. Grace leaned over the bed near his face and asked, "Bob, can you hear me? This is Grace. You wanted me to come?"

He opened his eyes, smiled weakly, and held out his hand. Grace took his hand but lowered his arm back to a resting position. His grip was weak, and his breathing raspy and strained. With a whispering voice, he said, "Thank you for coming, Grace. You're the only one who makes sense to me. I've messed up. The drinking has destroyed me. You got it right. I want to ask your forgiveness. We suspected the baby you had was mine. Me and Dad talked your grandpa into getting you out of town. Your old grandpa didn't argue. He wanted to keep his contract on the lumber, keep the farm. When Dad died, I was drinking too much to care. I burnt your grandpa's file, hoping I'd never hear from you again. It was wrong, Grace. We were all wrong. I want you to forgive me."

Grace responded, "Bob, I'm not holding anything against you now. We're not going to rehash that old story. It's in the past. Let's focus on where we are today. What do you want me to do to help? God has brought us to this point. What else can we do but be grateful, learn what we need to know, and keep walking? We have a son—remember that? We can ask God to help you get well and meet him. I'm eager to meet him. Aren't you?"

With surprising strength, Henderson gripped Grace's hand and said, "Yes, that's what you can do for me. Bring our son to see me before I'm gone. At this point, there's no guarantee I'll survive much longer. You pray, Grace. I want to be able to see our son."

Grace kissed Henderson's hand before she let go. She said, "Bye for now, Bob, but we'll be seeing you."

He never responded.

The nurse opened the door and beckoned Grace to leave. She whispered, "Let him rest. He can't take much excitement right now. You can come back another time, later."

On her way out, Grace was stopped by the guard. He said, "Ma'am, you need to stop at the waiting room. Henderson's sister wants to speak with you." He pointed Grace to the waiting room at the end of the hall.

In the waiting room, Grace introduced herself to a middle-aged woman who was barely holding on to her composure. Grace offered the grieving woman some fresh tissues as she said, "I know this must be painful for you. Bob is talking to me, but he's weak and runs out of breath. How can I help you?"

The lady dried her eyes, caught a deep breath, and introduced herself as Margie. She said, "I'm Bob's sister. We begged him to stop his alcohol abuse, for years, and now it has come to this. He may not survive the surgery. I'm talking to the best doctors I can find, but it may not make any difference. Even if he survives, it will be a long, drawn-out recovery. He's a difficult man. I don't know how we can handle him. I live in Houston. He may have to come there."

Grace said, "I just talked with him. He's stronger than he looks, especially when I mentioned our son. Did he tell you that we have a son, nearly forty years old now?"

"Yes, he did," Margie said. "He told me about that, and he said he is going to do the right thing for you and your son. He asked to have his attorney and witnesses this afternoon. They're coming. He wants to declare his last wishes before he goes into surgery. I told him to do whatever he feels is right to do, whatever he feels good about. I don't have a problem with that. I've been away too long. I'm not attached to the old homeplace anymore."

"You know, Margie," Grace said, "God may not be finished with him. I know he is scared to death. He's facing something that he is powerless over. It's beyond his ability to fix. Maybe God has brought him to a turning point. We can pray for that. God may give him another chance. Let's see how the surgery goes, okay?"

Margie responded, "Even if he can survive, there are criminal charges hanging over his head. He's in deep trouble. He knows it. I'm afraid he won't fight to live."

"I'm not going to prosecute him," Grace said. "He has taken advantage of my family, but he hasn't done any damage to me. My old farm would have rotted down, anyway. I didn't have a clue that I owned it until recently. I doubt if the law will throw the book at a sick man. They might just fine him or something. We can hope for mercy."

Margie asked, "When you meet your son, could you let me meet him too? I'll be staying here in Bob's place for a while, to see where this goes, and I'd like to meet my nephew before I have to leave."

"I'll do that," Grace said. She moved to leave, and the woman stood to give Grace a hug. She said, "Bob is right, you are a good person. Thank you for coming to see him. You didn't have to do that. Thank you for stopping to see me. I need the support. You take my phone number and let me know when your son comes. He is welcome to come and visit with me."

On her way to the car, Grace marveled at the contrast between the arrogant and pushy brother and the meek, loving, and gracious sister—strikingly different personalities. She had often heard the recovery group say, "No matter how many kids, or how few, they all come out of the genetic pool with scrambled eggs for genetics. Sometimes they win the lottery, and sometimes they don't. The secret lies in recognizing and capitalizing on the unique gifts of each one.

That becomes an inner challenge, bringing the unique gifts of God to His plan and purpose."

Grace mused, *Henderson and me, we got some genes that threw us under the bus. I tripped up on anger, resentment, and self-pity. He puffed up on arrogance and entitlement. The devil must have had a good laugh, but he won't win. God will call us out of that bondage, and I'm ready to go. God will take care of Bob Henderson. That's His little child too.*

*****

Before leaving town, headed toward Lawson Creek, Grace stopped by her lawyer's office to check on the progress of her claim to the old Lawson farm. Everything had been filed, and the surveyor had almost finished his job. No problem had arisen about ownership. By Monday or Tuesday of the following week, all legal tangles would be resolved, the property lines clearly defined; Grace could take over. The attorney shook Grace's hand as he said, "Lady, you have done this town a favor. We're proud of you. You can turn that old farm into something profitable for yourself, maybe grow some apples and grapes. People pay good money for grape vineyards these days. You can also put that old property on the State's Registry of Historic Lands, if you want to—no development allowed. You think about that."

On her way home, Grace made a brief stop at the sheriff's office to report. As Sheriff Cosby listened to the recount of her visit with Henderson, he asked, "Do you think he has any chance of making it, Ms. Grace? I hear from his sister that it's doubtful. Chances are slim."

Grace replied, "Well, right now it looks bad. He's too weak. After surgery, he might gain some ground, if he survives. His sister thinks that might take a long time. She's not holding out much hope. She worried about the charges against him, what that will do to his attitude."

"You know," the sheriff said, "we found the sales contract where he offered you a million and a half for that old farm. We also found another contract where he was selling the same property to his Columbian friends for three and a half million. His co-conspirators thought he owned the property, that he was giving them a great deal. They had all kinds of plans for a helicopter pad and all that. When you threw a wrench in his plan, he went off ballistic. He could have made a cool two million dollars where you had no idea. He was betting you wouldn't look."

Grace was stunned, but the sheriff continued, "He's lost his bet. Now his butt is in a very big crack. These people he was dealing with are criminals. If they can get to him, he's a dead man. I don't expect him to last long. When you cause trouble for people like that, they find a way to repay. Henderson knows that."

Shivering, Grace asked, "Do you think they'll come after me? I stirred this mess up, and Henderson might be the first to tell them I did. He may shift the blame to me."

The sheriff was quick to answer, "I can't say for sure, but we have all made it quite clear that you don't live here, had no idea that the property belonged to you, and had nothing to do with the raid. We told them that neighborhood complaints and phone calls tipped us off. We called you in to lay claim to an abandoned property. You stick to that story, Ms. Grace, because you didn't actually tell us anything. You're just here to claim your property." He winked at Grace and gave her a warm hug.

*****

On the way home, her emotions chattering away like crazy monkeys, Grace simply had to let it all go—the stress, the grief, the fear, the uncertainty, the human reactionary stuff, and the mind-boggling confusion. She started singing, "His eye is on the Sparrow, and I know He watches me…"

Over lunch, Grace asked Aunt Lucy, "Do you know how to play that old hymn 'His Eye Is on the Sparrow'?"

Aunt Lucy hummed a bit, then she began to sing, "I sing because I'm happy… I sing because I'm free… His eye is on the Sparrow… and I know He watches me." After a bit, she said, "Grace, that old song is in my piano music somewhere. You can find it and we can sing. You can still sing, you just need to practice."

So practice Grace did. She sang her heart out, tuning her pitch to the melodious old piano with her aunt's help. She gave her voice a good workout, not because she was particularly interested in performing anywhere, but because she merely wanted to express her joy and praise to God for her deliverance. Aunt Lucy had taught her how to do that, with God as the only listener, hearing praise from her heart.

Blessings were about to abound. Saturday would turn out to be one of the happiest days of Grace's life; gifts of abundance were coming.

And I Will Restore unto You

In the early-morning hours of Saturday, the old red rooster was just beginning to announce the dawn when Grace was awakened by a dream. Granny Lawson, who had not appeared in dreams for several nights, was dancing with young Grace, hand in hand, around and around, laughing joyously about something unidentified. Grace was caught up in the gaiety and laughter, but the vision vanished when she heard the rooster crow. She lay perfectly still, hoping for a rerun, but reality and old Rooster interfered. Grace thought, *My mother hasn't appeared in dreams for some time, but Granny comes to celebrate. It's not my subconscious. She's delighted with me about something. I'm not making these dreams up. I know it's a message of some kind.*

The crackle and smell of the frying bacon got Aunt Lucy's attention, and she came tapping her cane down the hallway, asking, "Are we going somewhere? You got that old rooster beat this morning, and the coffee brewing away. What's up?"

Grace laughed. "No," she said. "I think it might rain today. We aren't going anywhere. I wanted to walk over the old farm, but I might have to wait. Do you want to go somewhere today? You've hardly been out of this house. Do you want to ride somewhere? How about family? Anybody you want to visit?"

Aunt Lucy responded, "No, I already visited with John and Helen, just the other day. They are both happy with my plan to let you take over this old place when I go to the nursing home. They can't afford to help me, and they're relieved to hear that you will. They don't want the upkeep involved with my place, and they don't want to worry about me. They're on board with our plan, Grace. When you get the money sorted out, I'm ready."

Grace was slow to respond. Finally, she said, "We could get your clothes and personal items together today while it rains, Aunt Lucy, and you'll be ready to go. We can try this for a month or two, and at any time you're unhappy, you're coming back, okay?"

"Oh, I'm looking forward to having some friends around every day," Aunt Lucy said. "It gets mighty lonesome around here. Even my old piano can't replace good friends and fellowship. You gonna be busy as a mad hornet when you get things rolling on the farm. You don't need to worry about me. I want to enjoy myself. My friends will be glad I'm coming. I can come back and visit from time to time. You'll see."

*****

Grace cleared the kitchen, straightened and dusted the living area, vacuumed the floors, and headed for the shower. She dressed herself for a ride somewhere, anywhere. The emotional monkeys were screeching, trying to take over her mind. How could she take beloved Aunt Lucy out of her old home, stick her in a nursing home, and take over, without falling completely apart?

She was on her knees, asking God to give her enough strength, when they heard the old aunt calling from the front door, "Grace… Grace…come here."

At the front door, Grace could see a tall man waiting. He was dressed in jeans and a casual shirt, holding a white bakery box in his hand. Grace thought he might be delivering something; she opened the door. As she pushed the screen door aside, to her left, just out of range of her vision, two young girls yelled, "Surprise!"

These girls jumped around, throwing confetti all over the open-mouthed Grace. They tooted their little whistles and danced with their balloons. Grace was totally at a loss; she thought they must have the wrong house. She turned to inform the man, and as she looked closely at him, she couldn't believe her eyes. The man was just smiling, laughing with the girls. He said, "Good morning, Ms. Grace. Sorry we're a little messy with our surprise. This is Jill and Jodie, and I'm Greg. We've been looking for you for a long time."

Grace was speechless. Greg put the box down in the old porch rocker and gave his speechless mother a warm, affectionate hug. The girls tied their balloons to the porch railing and gave their new grandmother a happy, joyful embrace. Grace was sobbing by that time; she couldn't find her voice. Aunt Lucy, who had been standing just inside the door, intervened. "Come in, come in. Welcome! We're so glad you're here."

The girls stepped in to meet and hug the elderly aunt. Grace was so overcome she couldn't turn loose of Greg; he was practically holding her up. He wiped at his own face as he helped her through the door. He said, "Let's get this box inside before the cake melts. We brought cake and goodies for this special occasion."

The girls were busy looking at the gallery of pictures on the walls. They soon discovered the antique piano. Soon Aunt Lucy was playing away, the girls fascinated with how a totally blind person could play so well. While Aunt Lucy entertained the girls, Greg and Grace had a reunion in the kitchen. They laid out the cake and cookies. Mostly they just stared at each other, laughing and crying at the same time.

Grace was excited to hear the girls singing hymns along with the piano. Greg said, "Oh, they take piano lessons. That's one of their things, along with sports and boys. It takes a village to keep them busy."

"How did you find me, Greg?" Grace had to ask.

"Simple," Greg said. "I traced the phone number you called from, came into town, and asked around. Seems like everybody knows Grace Lawson. You're quite the celebrity around here. The girls planned the surprise. Otherwise, I'd have called first. These girls like surprises. You can thank them—they love new adventures. It's their kind of thing."

Hot chocolate and cookies were shared all around, the cake reserved for a later treat. The girls swept the confetti off the porch while Grace and Greg packed a cooler; they were headed for the old farm. If the girls liked adventures, they would be thrilled with a rustic old farm.

When asked if she'd like to come along, Aunt Lucy said, "Heavens, no. I've had all the excitement I can do already. I'm stuffed with cookies, and I have to rest. You go and enjoy yourselves. I'll expect you back sometime later to eat that cake. I'm off to take a long nap."

*****

Grace took one look at Greg's fancy car and said, "Let's take my SUV. The roads get rough where we're going, and that car won't like the terrain."

The girls happily jumped in the back seat, all excited about the adventure. As Grace opened the gate to the old ragged road to the farm, the girls squealed with excitement and hung their upper bodies out of the rear windows. Even the rocky road didn't subdue their enthusiasm. At the creek, Grace warned them, "We have to ford this creek. Roll up your windows and sit still. I'm not good at this. Hold on, everybody."

Grace geared the car down, as she had seen the sheriff do, and crawled into the water. She made it to the opposite side without a glitch. She heard Greg let out a sigh of relief.

The girls went back to their sightseeing. Grace said, "Don't get uptight, Greg, not yet. This is just a preview of adventures to come."

His reply was encouraging. He said, "I'm glad you're driving. So this is your old homeplace, where you were raised?"

As Grace related the history and her role in the story, the girls moved up beside their new Grammy Grace to listen. Earlier, they had decided to call her Grammy, not some "old" name they said didn't fit. Grace accepted the new title with grace and gratitude. Grammy Grace would be her title for the rest of her life, as far as she was concerned.

Grammy Grace took them on a tour of the old farm, walking them through the old buildings and grounds, explaining as she went how she had experienced the times. Greg became fascinated with the waterfall pouring out of the mountain at the old spring. The girls were awed by the old barn and its upper floor. Greg, the structural engineer, inspected everything he saw. He said, "Boy, oh boy, I like to see what held these old structures together for so many years. This is amazing!" He brought out his camera and started making pictures. His girls did their posing, and Grace was persuaded to sit in a beautiful frame with the old house in the background.

The girls waded in the creek with their pants rolled up, squealing with laughter. While they were busy being entertained, Grace told her son about the raid on the property and why it had been so long in coming. When she got to the hard part about Henderson and his role, she simply told him the truth. "Greg, this man is your father. I want you to hear that from me. He and I had a high school affair. I was already pregnant when the rape happened to me. Your father suspected but didn't know for sure until lately. I didn't know myself until I saw your pictures. You and your father look like twins in your high school days. I'll show you later."

Greg took the news without a flinch. He encouraged Grace to keep talking.

Grace continued, "Your father is Bob Henderson, a local attorney, from a very well-respected family. He used to be very athletic, very intelligent, and had every advantage. However, his alcohol use took over somewhere along the way, and he wasn't suited for the practice of law. He started cheating people out of their real estate. He ignored the law practice that his dad had built, and he deteriorated into easy money…and crime. He has used this old farm for illegal purposes for almost ten years. When I came back, for reasons I'll explain to you later, he thought he could make a profit from my ignorance before I caught on. He lost the gamble, and the sheriff had the appropriate law enforcement agencies come in. They shut him down. I intend to clean this place up and restore what I can. There's about three hundred acres of this beautiful old place, and I intend to keep it, bring it back to life."

Greg asked, "Is this man in jail now?"

"No," Grace answered. "He's in the hospital, at death's door, if I'm not wrong." She went on to explain what had happened. "He wants to meet you, Greg, before he has his surgery on Monday. If you want to see him, I suggest you go. I can get you in. You'll only get ten minutes at the most. He's critical. He apologized to me and admitted he had a hand in getting me sent away when I was pregnant with you. He never tried to contact me after that, but I don't hold anything against him now. God worked it out. I've done well, and you've done extremely well. You can be grateful that we didn't have to raise you here. As you can see, life would have been hard. If you want to go see him, today may be your only chance. You decide and I'll go with you if you want to do that."

Greg didn't stammer as he said, "Let's go. I want to know the truth, and I appreciate you telling me. You didn't have to do that. But this is good. It's torture growing up and wondering who exactly gave you away and why. My adoptive parents were very good to me, but they're gone now, and I would like to know about my roots. I want my kids to know. You can help us understand that part of my heritage. Let's go meet Mr. Henderson."

He motioned for the girls to get out of the creek. He said, "Girls, come on, we have a mission to run."

The girls found their shoes, pulled their pant legs into place, and hopped into the car. Grace glanced at the time. Aunt Lucy would be sleeping, there would be plenty of time, and Greg seemed anxious to find another piece of his history puzzle. Grace was determined to help him.

On the way into town, Grace asked Greg about his life as a child. He told of being adopted by an older couple who spoiled him but had required a lot from him. He had to study hard and finish an extended education. He helped his dad in a trucking company on weekends and holidays. After his mom died of cancer, his dad didn't have the heart to go much further without her; he died within two years. Greg had inherited the trucking business, and he now worked for an engineering firm. The engineering firm sent him out to evaluate old bridges and buildings for reconstruction and repurposing. Greg said, "I travel all over, inspecting old bridges and structures. It's a good life, but I have to be away from the girls more than I like."

At the hospital, Grace spoke to the front desk, explained what she needed, and waited for instructions. She was told to keep the children in the front waiting area, and Greg would be admitted to the critical ward to see his father. As Greg walked to the elevators, Grace would have sworn she was looking at the original Bobby Henderson.

The girls were entertaining Grace with their stories of baseball games and soccer. She kept the questions coming, and they kept chattering. Forty-five minutes later, Greg still had not appeared. Grace became concerned; the visits were strictly limited to ten minutes. Where was Greg?

At last, the elevator door opened and Greg stepped out, accompanied by Margie. She came straight to the girls, saying, "Hello, my name is Margie, and I'm your new aunt. Your dad tells me you are Jill and Jodie. Now, which one is Jill and who is Jodie?"

While the girls were meeting their new aunt, Greg said to Grace, "Sorry that took so long. We got carried away."

Grace asked, "No problem. Did you get to speak with Bob?"

"I did," Greg answered. "He wants to meet the girls, but his nurse said to give it a couple of hours and let him rest. Margie wants us to ride out and see the old Henderson place. Would your aunt be okay?"

"Aunt Lucy will sleep until about four o'clock. We've got plenty of time, and she'll understand if we're a little late," Grace answered.

*****

With Greg and Grace up front and Margie with the girls in back, they toured the old Henderson property. A mere three miles out of town, on a ridge overlooking pastures and a fishpond, sat an older, colonial-style house with white fencing all around. Horses were grazing around the fields, and ducks were on the pond. Margie explained that there used to be more than two hundred acres, but her brother had sold most of it to development, keeping the house with about ten acres. The house had deteriorated, needing lots of upgrades and repairs before it could be sold. Her brother, Margie said, sold out her interest in the property, promising to keep everything up-to-date, but he had failed to keep his promise. She said, in so many words, that her own brother had cheated her out of her part and spent the money.

Grace and Greg didn't ask many questions. Margie went on to say, "I know he didn't have a conscience toward anybody but himself, and that has brought him to this. We all need to just forgive him. He's not a bad man. He got himself in a bad trap, trapped with wrong motives. We can just love him through this and pray God will give him another chance. I've encouraged him to leave this old place to you, Grace, for the shameful way he treated you, atone for that. It's the least he can do."

*****

Back at the hospital, the girls were taken to the ward to see their grandfather. Greg would go in with them. Grace and Margie waited. Margie said to Grace, "If I understand it right, the old homeplace and barn, and Bob's office lot, will go to you and your son. That's what I heard Bob say to the attorneys. Of course, we have to settle all the debts and claims against the estate, medical bills, and all that. I'm going to sign away my rights when the time comes. I can't afford to fix up that place or the office. They both need to be sold as is. If there's anything left, I told Bob he should leave it to you and the son he failed to recognize. I told him that. I think he might have listened."

Grace asked, "Don't you want to come back someday, bring family?"

Margie was quick to say no. She hesitated a minute before she continued. She said, "I saw my brother nearly break my mom and dad when they did all they could to help him, stop him from drinking. He lied and manipulated them. He wasted three good marriages, lost his job at the law firm that hired him right out of law school, and just generally fell into ruin. My dad always said alcohol would finish him, and here we are, at death's door." She was crying.

Grace hugged Margie and let her cry. She said, "Margie, we'll help you. You don't have to face this alone. Let's see where we stand after surgery."

The elevator doors opened, and the girls popped out. Their dad, they said, had stopped to talk with a doctor. They made plans with Grammy Grace to find some pizza for supper. Margie approved their plan, and she gave them a warm hug as they were leaving.

On the way out of town, Grace asked no questions. She secured the pizza for the girls and left Greg with his own thoughts. Later, when the girls dashed into Aunt Lucy's house with the pizza, Grace asked Greg, "Are you all right?"

He answered, "Yeah. I'm more stunned than anything. I'll have to work on sorting it all out. Don't worry, I'll manage it." He gave Grace a warm hug, saying, "Grammy Grace, you are a treasure. The girls and I have won the lottery."

Grace laughed, saying, "Hold your appraisal until you've seen the foundation. I'm feeling a lot like the old buildings you have to renovate and restore. I'm a bit wobbly."

Mother and son joined the girls and Aunt Lucy for pizza and delicious cake. Grace marveled at her instant family. Later, as she watched them drive away, she kept her composure until the car was out of sight, then she and Aunt Lucy danced, hand in hand, around and around, praising God, laughing and crying at the same time. It was bedtime before Grace remembered that same dance in the dream with Granny Lawson. Granny was apparently beyond the veil, but she had seen this coming; she had shown Grace. God had sent a miracle, and Grace's life had taken on a whole new reality.

A Tragedy and a Gift

The following week went by in a blur; Grace had no time for emotional reaction. She put herself on automatic pilot; a reboot of her perspective was coming hard and fast. It all started with Aunt Lucy's insistence on having herself installed at the nursing home. Grace resisted, saying, "I simply can't take you out of your home and just take it for myself. I know how that feels. I can't do that to you, Aunt Lucy. You have to understand how that feels, how painful that is for me to even think about."

Aunt Lucy replied, somewhat sternly, "Grace, I know you got ripped out of your home and family years ago, and that damaged you, but this is different. I'm an old lady, tired of being by myself, and this is the best thing for me to do." She softened her tone as she continued, "You let me have some peace here. I don't want to be a burden to nobody, and I can enjoy some fellowship with my friends. You have got your hands full, and John and Helen can hardly help themselves. Grace, you are a godsend to all of us. Just ask John. He's relieved, and the boys need your help. I want you to focus on them, not be burdened down with me. You need to invest your time where it matters. God will take care of me. Let's go and make good of the time we still got, okay?"

Grace wiped at the tears as she answered, "I hear you, Aunt Lucy, and on some deep level, I agree, but I feel sick about it."

Aunt Lucy replied, "That's your old wounds blocking your common sense, chile. The devil is trying to interfere in God's plan for your life. If that devil can keep your wounds festering, he can stop you, Grace. You've been licking at your old wounds long enough, haven't you? I'm being hard here, chile, but this is a whole new day the Lord has made. Let us rejoice and be glad in it, okay?"

Grace was crying, but she managed to say, "You're right. I'm falling back into old emotional reactions before I think, a habit that fueled my addiction for years. I don't want to go back to that. My life is so blessed. I've got purpose like I've never had before. Despite the challenge, I find peace and joy in my heart. If you want to move into that facility, I'll get that going tomorrow, Aunt Lucy. You can go."

Aunt Lucy happily nodded and said, "Let's get me packed. I'm so excited!"

The appropriate "day clothes" and "night clothes" were sorted and packed for Aunt Lucy's new residency. The old dear was so excited Grace had to join the mood. Grace tried to mimic the dear old soul, thinking she might get past her grief and accept the situation. She squared her shoulders and resolved to give up her hold on the "festering wounds" and just let God's plan for Aunt Lucy materialize.

*****

Early on Monday morning, Grace called to make arrangements with the nursing home. She was asked to bring her aunt at 4:00 p.m.; a room would be waiting. Grace breathed a sigh of relief. That left time to speak with John and settle any disputes that might arise with family.

The phone rang around 9:00 a.m., and Aunt Lucy handed the phone to Grace. The female voice said, "Grace, this is Margie. Bob passed away early this morning. I thought you'd want to know."

"Oh, I'm so sorry, Margie," Grace said. "I thought he would hold on. I prayed that he could."

Margie answered, "I prayed for that, too, but last evening, when I went to see him, he just looked at me and said, 'You take care of yourself, sis. Don't worry about me.' I think he knew he couldn't go any further. The doctors didn't hold out much hope. They thought he had too many other problems. His liver was gone. He was much too weak."

THE ROAD TO HELL IS PAVED WITH... WHAT?

"Margie, what do you need me to do to help you?" Grace asked. "I'll come and help. I'm ready to do whatever you need."

Margie answered, "There's nothing to do as far as a funeral, just cremation and a spot for his ashes with Mom and Dad. I'm going to arrange that, and tomorrow I'll be cleaning out the old house. His office will be handled by the attorneys, and we'll wait on probate from there. He didn't want a traditional viewing or anything. He made that clear in his last will."

Grace said, "I'll be more than glad to help you tomorrow. You don't need to be alone, and neither do I. Aunt Lucy is moving to a nursing facility today, and being by myself might be awful. Can I come and help you, just keep you company? I'm good free labor."

"Grace, to be honest, I do need help hauling his personal stuff out, and I want to sort through Mom and Dad's old things. I could use the help, and if you could let us use your car—mine is a small rental—we could make some good progress. I want to go back to Houston as soon as I can. You would be a lifesaver if you could come and help tomorrow."

With arrangements made, Grace put the phone down and sat dumfounded for a few minutes. Aunt Lucy broke the silence with, "Grace, God sent you back to us before the same thing happened to you. As sad as this is, we have to see it as a lesson we can all learn. We'll lean into God's strength here. You go help the man's sister, and you won't have time to be upset about what I'm doing. God will bless you for that."

*****

Later that afternoon, Grace loaded her aunt in the car, picked up John and his wheelchair, and headed toward town for their appointment. The enormous pile of paperwork was soon completed, the money deposited, and Aunt Lucy was admitted to the facility where she could be with her old friends. The dear old soul couldn't wait. Grace held back the tears, but she marched right on.

With the admittance completed, an attendant came for the new resident. He wheeled Aunt Lucy into the dining area, motioning for

Grace and John to follow. The residents were gathered for their evening meal, and they cheered and whistled when Aunt Lucy came in. A speaker said, "Welcome, Lucy Bradford. Come and join us. We've been expecting you. Come in and meet some new friends and say hello to your old pals." A "Welcome, Lucy" banner had been strung across the top of the food bar. Grace bent to describe the balloons and decor to her dear aunt. The old one wiped at tears as she said, "See, Grace, I got lots of friends. This is wonderful!"

While Aunt Lucy was caught up in the excitement, John and Grace toured the room where she would be living. They found the same festive atmosphere in her room—flowers and balloons. Her roommate would be capable of helping the blind one to navigate the room. Grace installed the clothes and personal supplies, ordered a phone for the bedside, and placed Aunt Lucy's favorite covers on the bed. The social worker suggested that John and Grace say, "See you in the morning," and leave when the aides put their new resident to bed. "Keep it cheerful. That works best," she said.

John tried to make a joke as they were leaving. "Now, Granny, you can't be running around without your clothes like you do at home. Try to remember that, okay?"

His granny waved him off with, "I'll dance naked on a pole if I want to. You get yourself on home. I got this."

On the way home, Grace said, "John, I feel just awful about this, but she insisted."

John answered, "Honestly, Grace, I feel better than I have in years. This is a big burden lifted. Granny was coming to her end, and we didn't know what to do or how to handle it. My wife has all she can do with me in the house, and the boys aren't capable. You don't know how much weight has been lifted, Grace. You're more than welcome to that old house. It needs lots of work, and we can't afford even the taxes. You can handle that—we can't. Don't let this thing trouble you. We're happy with it. And you can see, Granny loves it."

*****

THE ROAD TO HELL IS PAVED WITH… WHAT?

Later in the evening, Grace remembered to call Greg. She said, "I'm sorry, I've had a long, hard day." She related the news about his father and what she had been told about the arrangements for his funeral.

Greg said, "I stopped in to see him again before I left on Saturday, and he said, 'Take care of your mother, son, and I'll do what I can for you.' I got the impression he was saying goodbye at that point. I'm not surprised. I talked with one of his doctors, and he said the whole body had been compromised. There wasn't much hope. I'll take some time and drive in later in the week, see what I can do to help."

*****

The next three days, Grace spent with Margie at the old Henderson home, attempting to clear and clean trash, garbage, and litter left by a very sick alcoholic who had slowly deteriorated without awareness of how sick he had become. There must have been at least three dozen bottles of vodka, bourbon, and whiskey scattered about the premises. Hugh boxes of empty bottles could be found in all the storage areas. Cobwebs and roach infestation were everywhere; the whole place smelled of filth and rot. Apparently, nothing resembling house cleaning had been done in a long while.

The two ladies got busy hauling large bags of trash to the county dump and glass bottles to recycle. The man's bed smelled to high heaven—the sheets hadn't been changed in months. They decided to drag the whole thing out to a burn pile and set fire to it. While the fire was blazing, they dumped a huge pile of unwashed laundry and his personal clothing on it. Margie was determined; she said she couldn't leave a mess like that for anybody to see. She apologized to Grace, saying, "I'm sorry you have to see this."

Grace replied, "Don't apologize. Alcoholism is a disease, not a moral failure. The loss of self-respect and awareness is the outcome. It was not intentional on his part. Skid row happens between the ears, especially with long-term abusers. His life was controlled by his disease. God has him now. We can be grateful for that relief, can't we?"

The two girls cried and worked, then cried some more, relieved to know that God had taken Bob Henderson to his rest.

*****

Grace had been stopping by the nursing home each morning to check on Aunt Lucy. The old dear was enjoying herself, holding her own at the piano and chattering with her friends. She seemed quite content with her new surroundings, and her roommate was a perfect fit, she said.

*****

By Thursday evening, the ladies had the old Henderson home looking and smelling much better. The dead roaches were still showing up, but the place appeared to be livable. All of Henderson's clothing had been removed, either burnt or donated. The car, the mower, and all the tools had to be left in the garage. Margie and Grace had covered the basic cleanup; it was all they could do until the estate was settled.

Grace hugged Margie and bade her goodbye. The plane would be leaving for Houston early the next day. Margie was ready to go home. She left keys to the old Henderson place with Grace, saying, "You and your son may inherit this place. I wish you the best. If you are ever in Houston, come and visit with me."

*****

Back at home, Grace helped herself to a long hot shower. She made a mental note to call the satellite company and get set up for a TV. Aunt Lucy had said, "No need for a blind person to spend good money on something that can't be seen." Grace had a different thought; a TV could keep her good company. That rooster and his hens just didn't suffice.

After spending the past few evenings by herself in the little house, listening to crickets and night owls, Grace came to the conclusion that the old blind aunt was right; a cheerful place with fellowship and a roommate to chat with might be good medicine. A good TV hanging on the wall could certainly improve the atmosphere and keep the emotional monkeys from chattering. She put that satellite company on the top of the list, "first thing tomorrow," and went to sleep.

*****

On Friday after breakfast, Grace was dressed to soldier on and do business. She had to get the cottage in her name, get her new address established, and find contractors for the roadwork and electricity needed at the old farm. Her ownership had been clearly established, and the work had to begin. Her attorney had said, "Go for it. You're the boss."

Grace felt weak and squeamish after she realized that she had the authority but not a clue where she needed to start. She made a list of items she wanted to cross off, and she picked up the phone book to make some contacts. Before she could dial anyone, she heard a noise in the front yard. She looked out to see Greg come bouncing to the front door.

"Good morning, Grammy Grace," he said. "I'm here for a cup of coffee, and you got free labor the rest of the week. How's that for a deal?"

Needless to say, Grace was delighted to let him in. After some discussion, Greg took over the task of consulting road construction experts, and he would also oversee the power and light company as they strung power lines across the property. Grace could take John to sign over his interest in Aunt Lucy's cottage, avoiding a potential legal entanglement at some point. The satellite company would be scheduled, and a new TV could be located. Things started looking up for Grace. She marveled how God had sent Greg to help at the point of her despair. God was definitely on her side; she didn't doubt it.

By Sunday morning, both Greg and Grace were tired out. Much progress had been made, or at least scheduled. They left for a ride to the scenic vista on the old west ridge. After Greg took some time to gaze over the valley below, he said, "You know, we could ask the telephone company if they could install a cell tower over on that east ridge. They could come in from the back of the ridge, and we'd only see the tower. Wouldn't that be nice, wireless service?"

Grace asked, "How much land would they take to do that?"

Greg answered, "They lease the space and pay for the structure. You still own the land. Let me inquire about that. We sure need wireless service around here."

Later, Greg reminded Grace, "You'll need to have some funds in place when the road construction begins. That road is going to cost a bit, and if you want a bridge across the creek, that will be an added expense. Do you think you can handle that?"

After giving him a friendly hug, she said, "My funds are coming this week. My friend who bought my condo has assured me we'll close next week. I want that money budgeted for the farm. I'm paying the nursing home bill with what I have in my savings account. My retirement pension will be coming. I'm not strapped just yet. You pop in anytime, Greg. You can see I'm in over my head. I do appreciate your help. It means the world to me. I feel much more secure."

Greg had meant to leave right after lunch, but he and Grace had a long conversation about what had actually happened to his father. Grace explained, "Sometimes alcoholism is simply acquired by habitual use. It is my guess that his condition was one of long-term abuse. On the other hand, my heritage came from a Cherokee bloodline. Native Americans are all susceptible to alcohol's impact. Most of the men in my grandpa's bloodline died early. My dad died transporting moonshine, and most of my cousins died except John, and it was a drunken car accident that crippled him. We're all at the mercy of the genetic pool. Awareness and abstinence, along with a strong faith in God, is the only answer. That's my experience."

Greg gave his mother a warm hug. He said, "You teach this to my girls, tell them about this risk, share your wisdom with them.

That's all I ask. My girls are smart, and they'll learn to deal with their heritage. You may save their lives, you know."

*****

After Greg left for his home, Grace took some time to breathe and relax; she'd hardly had time to relax all week. The chores ahead might be daunting, but the process had begun. Greg would be coming to help, the old God Squad would be available for counsel, and Aunt Lucy was happily enjoying her friends. Grace humbly thanked her Lord and fell asleep.

She slept without interruption until Red Rooster started crowing at the crack of dawn. God had made a whole new day. Grace would be glad in it.

Blessings Abound

The following week, Grace trailed around with people from the local power and light company, the road construction crew, and the telephone company. Measurements and estimates, possibilities and preferences, complications and cost—Grace's head was swirling. She called her son every evening with an update, asking his opinion on some of the issues. She had to take copious notes. To keep her focus intense, she stayed away from fear and negativity. She held on to her faith, constantly asking God to simply strengthen her. Only once did she feel nausea and stomach-churning fear; the road crew had given her a guesstimate of what the old road might cost, including the bridge. Her funds from the sale of her condo would be reduced considerably. She told herself, "Grace, you can't do anything with the old farm without a good road and electricity, and the bridge is essential. Get over it. God will provide."

*****

Early on Friday, Grace left for the city. The real estate closing on the condo was scheduled for 2:00 p.m., and Grace was nervous to get her money; the emotional monkeys were screaming. She ignored the road side stops where alcohol might be found and drove straight through to her condo.

Stella grabbed Grace at the door, rattling on about how she loved the condo lifestyle; she'd never felt so blessed in her entire life. Grace mused to herself how perspectives varied—Stella in the condo, and Aunt Lucy in the nursing home, both of them enjoying life. Grace considered the lesson worth learning.

The real estate closing went over with only one hitch; Stella did not want to afford the big expensive TV that hung in the living area. "Can we sell it, Grace?" she asked.

Grace had to laugh. She said, "No, I'll put that in my cottage and have my own personal theater. Lord knows I need some distraction. The night noises are killing me, and then there's a certain rooster. He thinks he owns the place."

*****

Late on Saturday afternoon, Grace returned to Lawson Creek loaded with the gigantic TV and a few of her remaining possessions. Professor John, her beloved friend, trailed Grace with his motorhome, his old Jeep, and his determination to capture the love of his life. With his condo sold, he was a happy man. Grace wondered just how long it might take him to grasp the challenging situation ahead and change his mind. If John had retired "to fish," he would be sorely disappointed.

But John didn't get ruffled until the old red rooster decided to perch on top of his motorhome. The motorhome had been beautifully waxed and shined prior to its placement under the tree where the rooster and his hens roosted. That early-morning crowing didn't go over very well either. The territorial fight had begun.

Grace said, "Well, you have a choice, John. You can park where we have water and electricity available, or you can rent a space about eight miles south. Red Rooster owns the yard, and I'm sorry. He was here first, and he's a good alarm system. We can find another place for you."

John simply draped his lovely motorhome with a huge tarp and spent his time in the cottage with Grace. He made himself useful hanging the TV and cooking some delightful meals. But Grace made arrangements with John and Helen to allow the motorhome to take up residence at the north end of their property, on a small lot near the creek. The lot had been home to a single wide trailer when the couple first started their family. The concrete pad was already in place, with electricity and water at the door.

THE ROAD TO HELL IS PAVED WITH... WHAT?

So her dear friend John found himself on the creek; he could fish from his front door. Also, he could walk across the property and visit with Grace; he didn't have to listen to that annoying rooster. Grace had to make him aware of the conservative nature of the community. She was committed to teach at the local church; fraternizing with or living with an unmarried male would reflect badly on her. She asked John to please keep their relationship appropriate.

John agreed except to say, "If you would consider marrying me, problem solved."

Grace chirped, "And if I do that, you're saddled with a bunch of work you didn't sign up for. How long would it take us to be at each other's throats? That's my concern."

"Okay," John responded, "if I'm hearing you right, you're afraid I'll run from the work and leave you? Grace, I'm here because I want to help you. Give yourself some credit. You are worth whatever it takes. I don't want to lose you, certainly not over a little hard work."

*****

They planned their wedding for the end of summer, followed by a trip across the country in the motorhome. They agreed to keep the secret until Grace's family came to visit over the Fourth of July holiday. With their quiet wedding plans made, they got busy with the pressing work.

The electric company was replacing the power poles and lines along the old road. The construction crew was bringing in the gravel for the road, and the telephone company was evaluating the old east ridge for a new cell tower. Progress was afoot.

When the Fourth of July weekend came, Greg and his family came to visit. Grace invited John, Helen, and the boys; they brought Aunt Lucy for a visit. Over dessert, John and Grace made their announcement. The occasion turned into a celebration. The whole family had noticed John's complete devotion to Grace. Greg was especially relieved to know his mother would have a trusted full-time companion. It was decided by the kids to call them Papa John and Grammy Grace. Papa John was thrilled; he had no living family of his own.

*****

A seminar was scheduled for mid-July, and Grace prepared for her role as educator for the Baptist church. She would be teaching about alcoholism and its related disorders. She had the boys, Al and Ronnie, dress up as drunken derelicts and do some hilarious skits to kick off the session. The boys got into their role, and after the crowd laughed and relaxed, Grace began to speak about the serious effects of alcohol and its dangerous potential. She used a large screen and projector to display pictures of the alcoholic's brain, compared to a normal brain. The crowd became quiet and serious as she made her points clear and simple: alcohol and drugs destroy the human brain and ruin lives. She finished her presentation with the story of her own struggles, making the point that no matter how educated, how successful, how wealthy one might be, alcohol will not discriminate. She pointed at the "drunken bums," Al and Ronnie, and asked, "Could this happen to your family? Think about it."

Within the week, the local newspaper featured a story about Dr. Grace Lawson and her next appearance, coming up at the local library, free to the public and "well worth attending."

Grace thought the local library would not produce a big crowd, but she was surprised. The library had a large collection of books on alcoholism and addiction, written by some of the most prominent, well-known authors, on display for everyone to see. Grace's entire presentation was taped, and the tapes could be bought, along with the books. Not only had Grace helped the local library, but she had also educated quite a number of people. She walked away thinking, *What more could I ask? God is showing me. Thank You, Lord! I can do this. I can and I will.*

*****

The mail was being forwarded, and Grace received her official notification of retirement and the benefits she would receive from her pension. In the packet from the college, she also received an old accounting of the last draw she had made on her educational trust established by her mother in 1949, when she was six years old. The trust had paid for tuition, books, and housing as long as she stayed in school, but in the last year of her doctoral studies, she had been told that the trust had run out. For years she had not looked at the trust; the college maintained the records.

When Grace asked John if there might be any reason to look at that old trust, he said, "Let me inquire about it. You might have accrued a little interest on what was left."

Within the next week, a letter arrived showing a history of Grace's withdrawals, plus almost thirty years of growth and accumulated value since the withdrawals stopped. Grace had understood that she was out of money, but actually she had been told there were "insufficient funds" to complete the last full year of study. She now had a mind-boggling $320,000 that had grown over the years from less than $20,000 she had left in the fund by mistake. The account had been invested in an aggressive portfolio of stocks and had averaged more than 10 percent annually. Grace had worked her way through the last year of her education thinking she was out of money. Grace remembered the struggle, the poverty, and the hard work she had endured to finish that last year. She was furious. She said to John, "I was miserable, scared to death, but I went to work every day and struggled at night to keep up. What a stupid mistake! I can't believe that happened."

John couldn't believe her reaction. He lightly smacked her on her head, saying, "Grace, will you forget that misery now and look at these numbers? You managed to save yourself a small fortune. It's over three hundred thousand! Are you kidding? You misunderstood for a good cause. You wouldn't have saved a nickel if you had known. Get real. Let's celebrate this and think about what it means. You got some extra money, pretty girl."

It took Grace a few minutes to grasp the irony; her emotional monkeys were at it again. She began to cry as she realized the blessing involved. Between crying and laughing, she said, "John, thank you. Sometimes I fall into total insanity, don't I? God has probably been keeping this for me until I could receive it with gratitude. I don't remember ever feeling gratitude for that trust. I was mostly mad because it had to be spent on education, and you're right, I would have spent every penny. Let me think about God's purpose, and I'll figure this out."

A few days later, Grace had pulled herself together; she had a plan. She told John, "This educational trust will be held in place for Al and Ronnie to attend college. The boys make good grades, but they will never be able to afford college on their own. I'm going to give them a chance to benefit, just like I've been able to do. My mother would approve of that."

When she went to talk with John and his boys, the whole family was speechless. The boys started jumping around, asking their dad, "Can we do this, Dad? Can we do this? Man, oh, man, off to college, like rich kids—what a trip! Can we do it, Dad?"

John cautioned his boys, saying, "I'm pretty sure Ms. Grace will have some conditions, like grades at a certain level, and none of that drinking-and-partying stuff." He gave Grace a sly glance, and she caught it.

"Indeed," she said, "your Dad has that right. You're grade point averages will be at an acceptable level, and I won't contend with careless behavior. That includes making careless mistakes with the girls. No baby-making. You understand what I mean?"

Al asked, "How about a car? We'll need a ride. We have to come home and help out. What can we do about that?"

Grace responded, "There's a ton of work needed around here. You can work at something part-time and use a bicycle on campus. This summer you can both work for me clearing and cleaning around the old farm. It's dirty work, but it pays. It's doable, if you don't waste your money. Otherwise, we drop you off with your rusty old bicycles at the campus and pick you up at the end of the semester."

The boys weren't attracted to the rusty bicycle idea; they'd "earn themselves a car, thank you." Grace smiled at their determination and winked at their dad.

THE ROAD TO HELL IS PAVED WITH... WHAT?

Before Grace left the discussion, John rolled his wheelchair over beside Grace and gave her a warm hug. He said, "My boys can't depend on me, Grace. You can't imagine what his means. You'll be blessed."

"I already am, John," she said. "I told Granny Lucy that I would help your family, and this is it, where it matters for the young people. That's what she said. I'm glad to do it."

Helen was crying when she came to hug Grace. The boys smacked high fives all around and said to Grace, "You call and we'll be there. We know how to work."

*****

True to their word, the young men worked most of the summer, chopping, clearing, sawing, and mowing. The old farm began to take on a whole new look. Grace kept the ice cream, food, and drinks coming. Professor John supervised and kept an eye on the road crew that was building a bridge across the creek. Grace dubbed the whole thing Lawson's Hideaway. It was an expensive endeavor, but Grace did not doubt that God was behind it.

Greg brought his family to visit, and they insisted on staying at the old farmhouse, turning it into a camping experience for the girls. The girls learned the game of horseshoes, and they hiked, fished, and enjoyed swimming in the creek. Nights were spent at a campfire, roasting hot dogs on the fire and eating Grammy Grace's homemade ice cream.

While Greg was in town for a few days, he and Grace checked with the attorneys who handled Bob Henderson's estate. "So far, so good," the attorney said. "No outstanding debts have come up against the estate just yet. The final distribution of assets ought to be soon. We'll be in touch as soon as we know."

Greg and Grace took time to check the Henderson home, making sure vandals hadn't ruined it. Greg made a close inspection. There were over three thousand square feet of living space overlooking a pond and the horse pastures. Greg said, "If this falls to us, I would like to buy your share. I can make this place beautiful, and the girls love horses. What do you think?"

Grace wanted to shout and dance, but she didn't. She simply said, "Greg, you do what is good for your family. What's good for them will be all right with me. You make them your focus. We'll work the money out if we need to. You ask your wife and kids what they think."

A day or so later, Greg and Grace brought the family to look at the "horse farm." After the girls had a look at the horses, they were all about moving to a place with horses.

After touring the Henderson home, Grace decided to take the family to visit Aunt Lucy at the nursing home. Aunt Lucy would surprise them with some happy news of her own.

Dear Aunt Lucy was delighted to introduce them to her new friend, Arnold. Arnie, as Aunt Lucy called him, was her new partner; they played music together, and he escorted her around the facility, even taking her on walks outside when the weather permitted. They were totally taken with each other. Arnie was a very handsome older fellow with very good eyesight—a blessing, indeed.

Grace didn't know if she should laugh or cry. Later, on the way out, Greg's wife whispered to Grace, "What harm can they do? I hope I can get a man to look at me when I'm her age."

Grace whispered, "What harm indeed. She's happy. I'm happy for her."

Grace knew Aunt Lucy would wring happiness out of every day she had left, a lesson that didn't need to be wasted. With her wedding coming up, Grace set her intention to thoroughly enjoy the whole experience. Good life lessons are learned, she thought, if one's brain is not hijacked with alcohol. Grace decided to revel in God's plan and purpose; that old craving for alcohol could be ignored. She made a promise to herself to stay in the moment, like dear old Aunt Lucy, and make every day count.

Wedding Gifts from Beyond

John and Grace would say their wedding vows at the old Bethel Baptist Church that, in recent days, Grace had come to love. Grace had worked out all the arrangements with her God Squad friends. Pastor would come and perform the ceremony. Stella would be her bridesmaid, and Spotter, with three other members of the recovery group, would stay at the old farm for a week's free vacation. Greg would be walking his mother down the aisle, while Aunt Lucy played the wedding march. The girls, Jill and Jodie, would be flower girls, much to their delight. Al and Ronnie would serve as best men for their Papa John, to his delight.

Grace had no idea that Spotter and his band of friends would team up with Greg to come up with a brilliant vision for the old farm. She'd be delighted later to find that her generosity with the old farm had produced some excellent benefits.

*****

Greg popped in early in the week prior to the wedding day to inform his mother that the Henderson estate was ready for settlement. Grace donned her business clothes, thinking, *Of all things right now, when I don't need any more stress, but this has been too long in coming. We need to get it over with.*

She and Greg were leaving for the attorney's office, and Grace could sense the stress Greg was feeling; he was much too quiet. She tried to ease the stress by saying, "You know, Greg, we might encounter a nice mess right here, but I'm getting accustomed to cleaning up messes. We can handle this, whatever happens. If we come away with nothing, what have we lost? We simply learn a lot and move on. Henderson tried to make up for his mistakes—that's something to remember, you know."

Greg agreed, saying, "Yeah, I'm just concerned about entanglements with Henderson's associates, if he left enemies who will cause trouble at the last minute. Some people are paying a heavy price for their association with him. The law says we're not responsible, but it still concerns me. I don't want to put anybody at risk, certainly not this family."

At the law office later, while waiting for her attorney, Grace brought Greg's concerns to the attention of the counsel. She was told, "Nobody is in a position to throw blame at anyone but themselves. Some may never be prosecuted—they've left the country. The others will serve their time and find another place to conduct their trade. I doubt if we'll be seeing them again. Just use caution and make sure you know whom you are dealing with before you trust them."

Greg seemed to relax after their comments, and Grace welcomed her attorney when he appeared.

A summation of the decedent's remaining assets was passed around for everyone to follow as the discussion proceeded.

"As you can see," the lead attorney said, "there is almost six hundred thousand dollars of assets to be divided after all legal fees are paid. I'm assuming that you, Ms. Lawson, and your son won't leave everything in both names. In case you can't agree at some point, it might be advisable to divide the assets now. We can start with the largest value, which is the old Henderson home. Anyone interested in owning that?"

Grace was quick to speak, saying, "Greg can have that. I'm already in possession of more real estate than I can handle."

The attorney asked, "Okay, Greg, do you agree?"

Greg was quick to say, "Yes, we agree on that."

Surprisingly, Henderson had two tracts of land, free of liens, plus his old law office and plot. All the land together was valued at more than a quarter of a million dollars.

The lawyer asked Grace, "Can you handle all the tracts of land, or do you want to negotiate with your son around the remaining assets? There is a car worth around twenty thousand and a certificate of deposit of fifty thousand. The remaining bank account holds enough money to cover the legal fees and settlement costs."

Grace's attorney spoke up. He said, "Ms. Lawson, you can keep the cash from the CD and let your son have the law office and its plot if he is interested. That comes out to about even. You'll be left with two tracts to sell. That leaves you two about even when the real estate fees are paid on the sale. That seems fair to me."

The parties quickly agreed, and the lead attorney proceeded. He said, "Okay, that leaves us with a car valued around twenty thousand. That's what we have left to scrap over. Who wants to go first?"

Greg didn't say anything. Grace spoke up. "If Greg will allow me to have the car, I'll pay him for his half. I've got some young people who need a car for college this fall."

"That sounds like a good plan," the attorney said. "Now, if there are no more questions, we can get the paperwork completed, and you can expect verification of ownership in the next few days."

With paperwork properly signed and notarized, Greg and Grace left to inspect the old law office and the tracts of land Grace had inherited. Grace said to Greg, "Bless Henderson. He had to give up everything. He just surrendered everything he worked for, right here. But, Greg, we are going to make the most of his gift. It won't be wasted. It's going back into the properties."

As they were trying to locate the remaining properties, Grace asked, "Greg, I feel awful that Margie didn't claim a thing. Why do you think she did that?"

Greg responded, "Because she didn't want to bother with it. She told me, last time we talked, that her mother and dad had a paid-up life insurance policy on their son, which she would inherit. She said it would be worth over half a million dollars about now. She simply didn't want anything else. She was afraid of the debt load. That concerned me too. But actually, we came out very well. She may have intended to dump the whole mess on us, but we can make it work to our advantage. I'm pleased with the outcome. Aren't you?"

Grace responded, saying, "Yes, I'm pleased. You can make something lovely out of that old Henderson place. I can recover some of what Henderson made using the old farm for illegal profits. The boys, Al and Ronnie, can work and earn the car. I think we'll all come out well. Your father was not a bad man, Greg. He was a sick man, and he was trying to atone right here."

"I agree with that," Greg said. "If alcohol hadn't destroyed him, he would have been a great man to know. I'm sorry he isn't with us today."

They made an inspection of the inherited properties, and on the way home, Greg asked, "Could I stay in your place while you're away next week? I need to be here, and Gayle and the girls will come on the weekend. We need to work on plans together, and Gayle needs to check out where she might get a job. She's a nurse, and she wants to look at her options."

"Sure," Grace said. "We won't be back until the weekend, anyway. Help yourself. We'll stay in the motorhome while you have the house. The girls can enjoy my little theater."

*****

On Saturday, the little Baptist church was beautifully decorated, and Aunt Lucy was at the piano when Greg walked his mother down the aisle. Pastor, the first black man to ever conduct services in the old church, held the witnesses in awe as he conducted the ceremony with praise and good humor. He was promptly loved and accepted. He and Stella would later be married at his home church and become regular visitors to the community of Lawson Creek. They became part of the Lawson family.

Grace and John held their reception at the old Lawson farm. The wedding party drove over fresh gravel and a newly constructed bridge to enjoy the old farm and its emerging potential. They all donned casual clothes and enjoyed a tour of the old place, praising Grace for her courage.

After the wedding party circled the newlyweds and had a prayer of praise, Grace and John were sent on their way, the lovely motorhome covered in graffiti. At the first car wash, John promptly took care of that festive annoyance and then set out across the country with his beautiful bride by his side. Never in all her life had Grace felt such pure joy and happiness. The occasion would be etched in her memory as one of the happiest days of her life.

*****

Back at the farm, every evening after work, Greg took burgers and fries, pizza, or fried chicken to the four men left on the farm. Together they examined the old house, inspected the barn, and appraised the land. They tossed around ideas on how to put the farm back into function as a profitable enterprise. Five bright and imaginative minds worked at repurposing the property as a rustic hideaway, with some of the acreage in the lower pastures turned into grape vineyards as a profit-making endeavor. The old Lawson Hideaway could become a retreat for recovery groups, church groups, children's groups, and other people looking for a rustic wilderness experience. Money could be made without resorting to illegal activities, as some had already done. The grape vineyards could be leased to grape farmers and bring in some good profits.

Greg and his newly found friends made a trip to the Henderson horse farm to share opinions about Greg's new challenge. The men all agreed that with hard work and some imagination, the property could double in value. However, they were not impressed with the old law office. Their advice came to sell that to the medical complex and rent an updated office in a more prominent area. "You're an engineer, after all." Greg didn't argue with that; they had a legitimate point.

Greg's wife, Gayle, and the girls arrived for the long weekend and spent all day at the Henderson home, making plans for their new residency. They talked about improvements and horses, horses, horses. The girls were so excited; Greg was almost in tears. He said to Gayle, "I'm turning into Grammy Grace, crying about everything these days."

*****

The following Saturday night, when all was quiet on Lawson Creek, Grace and John returned from their weeklong trip across the country and slipped the motorhome into its space down on the creek. They didn't stir again until noon on Sunday, when they walked hand in hand across the pasture to Aunt Lucy's cottage. Greg and his family were missing, but Greg had left the refrigerator plastered with sketches of the old farmhouse and barn, depicting how it might look when restored. Grace was fascinated; the man had talent and was very visual with his details. She said to John, "If only my budget would cover all this, we could do it."

John spoke up, saying, "Well, you know, I have recently become a permanent fixture around here. I might be able to stretch the budgetary restraints for you, you know."

Grace replied, "John, I don't expect you to spend your money on my projects. You need to think of your heirs."

"That's the problem, Grace," he said. "There aren't any heirs, so your family, particularly Al and Ronnie, will be my heirs. I'm their Papa John, you know. I'm part of their family now, and I want to do what I can for you and these boys. We can agree on that, I'm sure. You're all about the young people, and so am I."

"John," Grace said, "let's get our legal paperwork done to reflect our intentions. We both want the same thing, and I want to leave the Lawson property to Greg and his girls. You leave your estate to the boys, if that is what you want to do. I will be quite happy with that."

Soon Greg and his family came bouncing in. The girls were all excited to show their pictures of the old valley. They had been up to the scenic overlook on the west ridge, and their pictures showed Papa John's metal garage, housing his motorhome, glistening in the sun. The girls were so sad because they would have to be back in school on Tuesday. Their hearts were already attached to Grammy Grace and Papa John and, of course, the idea of horses, horses, horses. Their parents hoped to get them relocated during the Christmas holidays.

While the girls made themselves busy with Grammy Grace's theater, the adults had a lengthy discussion about the plans and possibilities that had emerged. Everyone seemed excited.

THE ROAD TO HELL IS PAVED WITH... WHAT?

John and Grace grabbed a flashlight and took a romantic stroll through the pasture and up the creek to their motorhome. At the temporary quarters, Grace said to John, "I've never felt such joy and happiness in my entire life. I wonder if my addiction has been broken."

John grabbed his bride, gave her an enthusiastic hug, and said, "No, your addiction has found me. I'm your craving now, and I'm taking advantage of it. Yes, I am."

After a good, exhausting pillow fight over that statement, they sat laughing and enjoying the bliss. Grace said, "It's almost like a dream—it's unbelievable. I'm married to the only man I've ever respected and trusted. I've been given my adorable son and two beautiful granddaughters, an instant family. Aunt Lucy is happy, and her family is so relieved. I'm teaching and educating people all over the county. The old farm is being resurrected and restored to a profitable purpose. It was only a few months ago, not even a year ago, that God sent His personal rescue squad to pry open my spiritual eyes. How can I comprehend it all? It's a miracle. My bonds have been broken. I have been set free."

John responded, "And you are feeling overwhelmed with gratitude and joy. What would your aunt Lucy say about this?"

Grace simply said, "Hallelujah! Praise His name! Thank You, Lord."

A Hard Reality Check

Fall came, and the leaves changed; the mountains put on a display of brilliant colors. While the tourists and what was referred to as leaf peepers were plentiful, Grace was able to sell the Henderson properties she had inherited. She immediately put the money on reserve for the old farm; she wanted water in the house, bathrooms, and modern heat and air-conditioning. She wanted the place upgraded while maintaining its rustic appeal. The project would be challenging, but Grace was determined to spend every penny restoring the old home and barn.

During the day, she worked on the projects but kept a busy schedule on weekends. She had become a popular speaker for the twelve-step movement and the churches that sponsored it. She rarely declined an invitation to speak or teach. Grace was determined to "pass it on," as her old recovery friends had taught her.

Grace made it her habit to check in with the nursing home to keep up with Aunt Lucy. Dear Aunt Lucy and her friend Arnie were making music together and simply enjoying life. On one of her visits, Aunt Lucy had snickered and whispered to Grace, "Arnie still doesn't know how old I am. He's only eighty-six. I don't have to tell everything I know."

Grace had so enjoyed the humor she adopted that remark at home. Every time her beloved John would ask, "Where are you going?" Grace simply said, "I don't have to tell everything I know." She and John would have a good chuckle and cherish the memory of

Aunt Lucy's secret. After all, when a lady is ninety-eight years old, she is allowed a few secrets, they said.

*****

Thanksgiving was approaching, and Grace noticed Aunt Lucy's enthusiasm was waning; she spent more and more time in bed. When Grace asked, Aunt Lucy said, "I'm just feeling a bit droopy, maybe because winter is coming. I'm cold all the time. Arnie comes to help me and keeps me company."

One morning, when the roommate couldn't wake Aunt Lucy, the staff was called and they found she had passed away. She had a big smile on her face, as if she had passed while in a dream. But that didn't comfort Grace; she went completely numb and speechless.

*****

The funeral was held at the old Bethel Baptist Church, and Grace walked through hundreds of people in a robotic state of function. She managed to greet all the visitors, thank everyone for coming, and get through the funeral service. Her old aunt was buried between her "boys," the beloved husband and son, right where she had said she belonged. Grace's feelings were frozen; she couldn't cry.

John wouldn't let Grace out of his sight. The God Squad had warned him, "She's only been sober for about a year. She's not out of the woods, especially when grief hits like this. Keep her busy and let her scream and cry when she needs to. She'll eventually get through it."

When, finally, Grace could manage to express herself, the issue was not the reasonable loss of her beloved aunt; it was pure guilt and rage at herself. Grace was mad at herself for having missed so many years when she could have been involved; she could have been there supporting Aunt Lucy. When she voiced her guilt and rage at herself to John, he asked, "And you would have come back and brought your dysfunction with you? How would that have helped anybody? Maybe God's timing is perfect. You might have made a mess of the whole thing and followed your grandpa, or Henderson. Don't forget that, Grace."

To be sure, Grace talked her rage out with her beloved God Squad; they all agreed with John. She calmed down long enough to realize she'd been hijacked by the emotional demons again. She knelt and surrendered her feelings to God, asking for strength to move on.

Grace said to John, "I feel like Rip Van Winkle. I've been asleep for forty years. I'm realizing how much time I've missed with family, how much I've lost in my relationship with life in general, and how much of God's abundance I simply missed. I sat in alcohol abuse until it turned into a disease. I had no awareness. That shut me out of joy and happiness. I'm mad because I can't undo any of it now."

John listened with patience and understanding to the exasperation and anger, then he suggested, "Why don't you make yourself a promise? Be mindful of the present time, make sure you enjoy the abundance of each and every day. Aunt Lucy has taught you that. Follow her example. Just ask yourself every day, 'What would Aunt Lucy do?' I think that will help."

Grace smiled through her tears as she responded, "Yes, and enjoy a handsome old fellow who likes me, for as long as I can. I can do that. I got you, babe."

*****

With Christmas coming and Greg's family moving to the area, Grace turned her attention to the upcoming festivities. She reminded herself, "I've missed enough already." She kept her attention on the Word, especially Proverbs 24:6, "By wise guidance you can wage your war and in abundance of counselors there is victory."

Grace had God's Word, her beloved John, and her recovery friends to turn to for help. She made up her mind to simply march on, one step at a time, one day at a time, praising God for His love and His abundance.

Old Case Closed

Sheriff Cosby and his assistant, Drake, were in the grocery store one morning when Grace stopped in for her pastries. They expressed their sympathy about Aunt Lucy's death and reminded Grace of a promise she had made weeks ago. Drake said, "You remember when you told us you would be willing to help with the old cold case when someone with information passed away? We thought you might have meant your aunt. Is that the case, or did you mean someone else?"

"Oh, mercy, I had forgotten that! I've been so busy," Grace said. "But no, it wasn't Aunt Lucy. She had always believed my grandma Lawson committed that crime. To be truthful, I got my information from the old veteran Brandon O'Neil, who, I'm sure, passed away shortly after I talked with him. I don't want to hurt his reputation now. Could we just keep quiet about what he told me? I'll show you where he said we could find evidence to prove that my grandma Lawson didn't do that awful thing."

Sheriff Cosby spoke up. "Ms. Grace, if you are willing to help us close that old cold case, I promise we won't talk to the press about it. I would hope that we could share the news with old Sheriff Tate. That's the only case he couldn't close. He's in the nursing facility, and he'll be glad to hear about this. I can assure you; he won't say a word."

"Okay, Sheriff," Grace said. "I'll hold you to that. You guys come up to the Lawson Hideaway and bring your metal detectors and long-range cameras. I know where we need to look. Mr. O'Neil said my granny helped him with food and water, but he said, emphatically, that she did nothing to harm anybody. She never committed any crime. I'd really like to know if the evidence is still where he said he left it. It's well hidden, if it is still there."

*****

It was Monday before Thanksgiving when the sheriff and his team arrived at Lawson's Hideaway, and Grace escorted them to the old spring where the waterfall poured out of the cliffs. Grace relayed to them the exact words the old veteran, Mr. O'Neil, had said to her.

The sheriff's team hacked vines and tangled growth from the top of the stacked-stone facade Grandpa Lawson had built in front of the waterfall. Soon a gap appeared between the stone facade and the rock cliffs behind it. They pulled and piled brush away from the gap until they could shine their flashlights into the narrow space. They fished their metal detector down through the gap and toward the western end of the wall. The metal detector started to beep. Their remote-controlled camera was carefully slipped into the gap and maneuvered into place. Grace held her breath. The men were intense in their efforts; something was about to show up.

A rusty-looking metal pipe appeared to be stuck between the rock wall and the cliffs. A careful maneuvering of the camera showed a metal buckle dangling from what looked to be a shoulder strap found on some long guns. An adjustment of the camera brought the whole thing into view. The metal rod was the rifle barrel, jammed into the rock wall, and the butt of the rifle was resting in a crevice in the old mountain cliffs behind. Mr. O'Neil had told the truth; his rifle was hidden there at the spring, and he never came back to retrieve it.

The sheriff's team was jubilant, but how to retrieve it without damage to the evidence became a challenge. Over time the old weapon had rusted and weathered, taking on a fragile look. The space between the rock wall and the cliffs behind was narrow and almost impossible for a full-grown man to access.

Grace was watching the activities with great interest when she remembered something. "Guys," she said, "I remember as a child I helped my granny put jars of milk back behind that wall to keep cool. If you step sideways past the waterfall, you can inch toward that end of the wall, and you might reach that crevice, push the rifle back into the crevice, and you might release the whole thing. You can turn it straight up, and someone from the top can reach it. I was really young and small back then, but I know it can be done."

One of the smaller men volunteered to give that a try. Grace rounded up some waders and a thin raincoat for the volunteer. He squeezed himself past the waterfall and inched sideways toward his goal. He braced his back on the stacked-stone wall and planted his feet on the solid rock in front of him. He carefully inched his way up the wall until he was directly underneath the rifle. With help from lights above his head, he carefully moved the old rifle from its hiding place to a vertical position, lifting it to eager hands above his head. He quickly scanned the rest of the area with a flashlight and made his way out of that tiny space. The team cheered when he emerged, a big smile on his relieved face. He was wet and a bit cold but otherwise unharmed.

*****

Later, the sheriff's office determined the weapon to be a military-issued assault rifle. Grace gave her deposition, and the case was closed. Sheriff Cosby and Grace delivered the news to Sheriff Tate at the nursing home. The old fellow was delighted. He said to Grace, "I made one mistake: I didn't ask your Granny Lawson if she had seen anybody else around that morning. She never lied. I just didn't ask the right question. She kept that soldier's secret by keeping the focus on herself. That took character. She made the best choice she could at that time."

*****

Grace made a special visit to her Granny Lawson's grave. She brought some fresh flowers and had a chat with her granny to celebrate. The inscription on the tomb, "He Hideth My Soul," finally made sense. That tiny little Cherokee lady could have clearly seen the evidence hanging over her head when she stowed her milk to cool. She chose, however, to keep the focus on herself and leave a message on her tomb.

The old hymn came to life as Grace began to sing. "He hideth my soul in the cleft of the rock, that shadows a dry, thirsty land. He hideth my soul in the depths of his love and covers me there with His hand, and covers me there with His hand."

Afterword

Grace Lawson "set her face" to answer God's call on her life, and she marched right on, with faith and determination, in that role for another eighteen years before her health began to fail. Over fifty years of alcohol use and abuse had weakened her body; the high blood pressure had taken its toll, and she suffered with heart disease, pancreatitis, and kidney problems. Despite her discomfort, she continued sharing her story of recovery to everyone who would listen. Her beloved husband, Papa John, found her early one morning slumped at her desk with her head on her arm, as if sleeping. The rescue people simply shook their heads. She was seventy-five years old, and her remarkable journey had ended. Her influence, however, had affected the entire community of Lawson Creek and beyond.

Papa John, her devoted husband, was heartbroken. He had been by her side through all the tough episodes of her recovery. He lived another two years, supported by his "rascals," his adopted grandsons, Al and Ronnie. He had tutored and encouraged them through an extended education and into professional careers. He had helped establish grape orchards on their family property, which turned the family fortunes in a much more prosperous direction. During a cold winter, he succumbed to a bout of pneumonia; he was eighty-two years old. His role and his influence would live on in that community forever.

During their years on Lawson Creek, Grammy Grace and Papa John educated, tutored, counseled, and encouraged everyone they could help. They were credited with changing the Lawson heritage from one of hardship and disadvantage to one of healing and hope.

Many recovery groups sprang up around the area, and the direction of many lives was changed as a result of their presence.

Today, Lawson Hideaway serves as a retreat for Christian recovery groups and an educational center for underprivileged youth groups. Some of the local churches still conduct their baptismal services in the old creek. When the fall season comes, the old farm serves as a tourist attraction. It has become a great source of pride for the community.

Those of us who were privileged to walk with Grace Lawson would be forever grateful for her presence in our lives. When she first started her journey, she laughingly referred to us as the God Squad. Later, she apologized for her contemptuous attitude and praised God for providing a "personal rescue squad" to help save her life. We became her closest friends, and ultimately her family. We miss our dear friend, but our recovery work goes on. An anonymous poet describes the work we hope to do.

>There are those who live within the sound
>Of the church or chapel bell.
>And some who work in the rescue tents
>Just a few steps out of hell.

Appendix 1

Alcoholics Anonymous

The Twelve Steps of Alcoholics Anonymous

- Step 1: We admitted we were powerless over alcohol, that our lives had become unmanageable.
- Step 2: Came to believe that a power greater than ourselves could restore us to sanity.
- Step 3: Made a decision to turn our will and our lives over to the care of God, as we understood Him.
- Step 4: Made a searching and fearless moral inventory of ourselves.
- Step 5: Admitted to God, to ourselves, and to another human being the exact nature of our wrongs.
- Step 6: Were entirely ready to have God remove all these defects of character.
- Step 7: Humbly asked Him to remove our shortcomings.
- Step 8: Made a list of all persons we had harmed and became willing to make amends to them all.
- Step 9: Made direct amends to such people wherever possible, except when to do so would injure them or others.
- Step 10: Continued to take personal inventory and, when we were wrong, promptly admitted it.
- Step 11: Sought through prayer and meditation to improve our conscious contact with God as we understood Him,

praying only for knowledge of His will for us and the power to carry that out.
- Step 12: Having had a spiritual awakening as the result of these steps, we tried to carry this message to alcoholics and to practice these principles in all our affairs.

The Twelve Traditions of Alcoholics Anonymous

- Tradition 1: Our common welfare should come first; personal recovery depends upon AA unity.
- Tradition 2: For our group purpose, there is but one ultimate authority, a loving God as He may express Himself in our group conscience. Our leaders are but trusted servants; they do not govern.
- Tradition 3: The only requirement for membership is a desire to stop drinking.
- Tradition 4: Each group should be autonomous except in matters affecting other groups or AA as a whole.
- Tradition 5: Each group has but one primary purpose—to carry its message to the alcoholic who still suffers.
- Tradition 6: An AA group ought to never endorse, finance, or lend the AA name to any related facility or outside enterprise, lest problems of money, property, and prestige divert us from our primary purpose.
- Tradition 7: Every AA group ought to be fully self-supporting, declining outside contributions.
- Tradition 8: Alcoholics Anonymous should remain forever nonprofessional, but our service centers may employ special workers.
- Tradition 9: AA, as such, ought to never be organized, but we may create service boards or committees directly responsible to those they serve.
- Tradition 10: Alcoholics Anonymous has no opinion on outside issues; hence, the AA name ought to never be drawn into public controversy.

- Tradition 11: Our public relations policy is based on attraction rather than promotion; we need always maintain personal anonymity at the level of press, radio, and films.
- Tradition 12: Anonymity is the spiritual foundation of all traditions, ever reminding us to place principles before personalities.

Appendix 2

Questions Asked About Alcoholism and Addiction

Nonprofessional Answers

In compliance with Tradition Eight of Alcoholics Anonymous, twelve-step recovery groups are conducted by nonprofessionals. The following outline of major questions asked about alcoholism and addiction might be helpful to other nonprofessionals who need help. More professional and scientific explanations are readily available with research outside the groups.

What Does the Bible Say?

The earliest definition of *alcoholism* is found in Proverbs 23:29–35. Other related verses are Proverbs 2:1–11, 3:5–8, 4:19–23, 23:19–21, 20:1; 2 Corinthians 3:16–18; and Ephesians 5:14–20.

What Is Alcohol?

Alcohol is produced by a simple fungus with a ravenous appetite to eat away the protective covering around the seeds (the fruit/pulp) of fruits, grains, etc. It is a natural process of nature designed, we believe, to eat the fruit/pulp away from the seeds so the hard-shelled little seeds can fall to the ground in a process of perpetuation. (Think moldy, rotting apple.)

The excrement of the fungus is a very concentrated form of simple energy called alcohol plus carbon dioxide. (Think poop and gas that accompanies the digestive process.)

This simple molecular structure of concentrated energy is empty of food nutrients; however, it is highly toxic to some human bodies and penetrates/diffuses all the cell membranes in the brain and body. All major organs can become swamped with this highly toxic poison. The liver has the responsibility of filtering the toxicity from the human system and becomes compromised in its function as it tries to "burn" away the intruding "high-energy" substance. Therefore, most abusers of alcohol eventually become malnourished. They develop a disease process that eventually kills them if they do not stop ingesting alcohol and its poison.

The liver of a normal human can only metabolize about one-half ounce of alcohol per hour. Those humans predisposed to alcoholism do not have the liver enzymes that break down the alcohol, so the body cannot move the toxic substance from the body. It settles in all the major organs, the circulatory system, the brain cells, permeating all the cell membranes and changing the molecular structure of the chemistry required to allow the normal function of the brain.

Alcohol in small amounts has a stimulating effect, but as the blood alcohol level (BAL) rises, the stimulating effect turns to a sedative effect, not unlike morphine might do. The liver struggles to break down the alcohol to acetaldehyde (highly poisonous), and then to acetate (poisonous and caustic), and then to a derivative that can be eliminated. This process fails in some people because of their particular biological makeup. These highly toxic chemicals bind to and distort the natural chemicals in the body. The whole function of the natural body is compromised, and the disease process has overpowered the brain's ability to do its job of keeping the body healthy and sane. Insanity is often the result, if the major organs do not fail first.

The alcohol itself hides its poisonous effects by the stimulating kick, and that feeling of euphoria and relaxation, that it produces.

Adaptation begins to take place in the body as the body tries to adjust to the changed chemistry. The rate of adaptation depends on the individual, with some adapting faster than others.

This adaptation is the first sign that the individual is gradually becoming "tolerant." (Think, who can drink others "under the table"?) The phenomenon of tolerance identifies an "abuser" or "alcoholic." This one cannot drink without doing harm to the body.

Why Does the Alcoholic Drink?

It is legal, and it is culturally/socially promoted and sold everywhere.

Ignorance—does not have an adequate knowledge about the drug, thinks it is a beverage, and has no knowledge of susceptibility.

Economic power players of "big business" do not have any interest in properly warning the public; after all, they're in the business of making money.

Enchantment with the role alcohol plays in our entertainment industry, sports, and social functions.

Emotional pressures, job stresses, financial stresses, deep psychological hang-ups, buzzing with friends, golfing, fishing, and a million or more other reasons.

What Happens When the Alcoholic Drinks?

Cells of the brain/body begin to prefer the high-energy form of the alcohol over food nutrients. The body becomes dependent on a constant supply, rejecting the slower process of metabolizing food.

The mitochondria within the cells, whose job it is to produce the energy for the body to function, become altered and misshapen; normal function cannot occur, and brain cells are continually dying.

Neurotransmitters produced in the brain cells are being held hostage by the simple molecular structure of the poisonous substance, and the biochemistry of the brain goes haywire. The cells struggle to function, but they are toxic. The electrical system of the brain/body function is overpowered, and the nerve cells are agitated.

The craving for the simple concentrated form of energy becomes the norm. All kinds of misery break loose if the BAL drops.

The poor, unsuspecting addict is now impaired throughout the brain and body. The craving becomes a driving force in the mind of the addict, similar to the need for water and food in the nonaddict.

The alcoholic *must* drink; the medicine that seems to soothe what ails the body becomes the body's poison.

What Keeps the Alcoholic Drinking?

Denial—the first and foremost defense that anything is wrong; after all, it feels right, and it feels good.

Alcohol hides its effects, much like mental illness, AD, dementia, etc. The poor addict has no awareness that anything is wrong until some consequences of behavior start happening.

Even then, the addict blames outside forces (job pressures, family, financial problems, etc.), the only thing that makes any sense to the logic/mind that is impaired.

Why Not Just Quit?

At every stage, the disease prevents the realization that anything is wrong.

The addict doesn't know his cellular structure has been altered.

Advancing disease governs the behavior.

There is no capacity of "self-will"; it is now biological.

Strategies to control the drinking do not work well.

Hiding of the alcohol is common and necessary in an alcoholic's mind.

The addict may be scared, paranoid, guilty, shamed, etc. Nevertheless, he feels he must drink; there is now a total loss of control.

Skid row becomes a space between the ears, not necessarily a geographical location. Only a small percentage of alcoholics live on what is generally accepted as "the street." (Think 5 percent or less.)

Stages of Advancing Alcoholism

Early symptoms: Denial, blaming, mood swings, depression, distancing, irritability, being argumentative, anger, rage, lashing out, bouts of poor judgment, suffering job performance, etc.

Advancing stage: Adamant denial, hiding bottles, personality deterioration, isolation, "shot" nerves, DUI charges, job loss, etc.

Late stage: Nerve damage and nervous system disorders, advanced aging, major organs affected, physiological damage, logic and reason impaired, intellect/talents wasted, self-esteem and self-respect eroded, depression and suicide threats common.

Advanced disease stage: Argues with medical experts, drinks all day every day, hospitalizations, hallucinations, paranoia, dementia, brain atrophy, major organ failure, death. Pneumonia, cancers, diabetes, other diseases are common.

Advanced late stage: Commonly institutionalized as CID (chemically induced damage), dementia, disease. The death is ordinarily accredited to the prevailing "symptom": liver failure, heart disease, kidney failure, etc.

How Do Genetics Play a Role in Addiction?

The dysfunction of addiction may be God's way of pointing us to our own spiritual responsibility. This must not be confused with religious behavior. It is a personal journey into our own hearts, being good stewards of our own God-given purpose.

A great portion of the out-of-control behaviors we witness has its origin in generational learning, like a giant snowball rolling downhill, picking up speed, right through the next generation, teaching the children to follow the same road. Children copy what they see, not what we say.

Genetics, just pure old brain wiring, has a lot to do with the abusive temperament and the poor life choices that follow. None of us can control that, nor did we cause it. Boundaries, however, must be put in place to protect ourselves from it.

If we are to stop the generational snowball from rolling its poison right through the children, if we wish for them better lives than we have had to endure, then the process of recovery must begin with each one of us. Personal responsibility for change is a necessity.

The road to recovery is not easy; change is scary. People may have to be offended. Our knees will knock, and we may have to pray without ceasing. We may cry through many a dark night. However, we are being called out of personal misery into the light of truth.

It's a personal choice. Yes, there's a financial, emotional, and sometimes life-threatening risk we have to take. Truth is, we're taking risks every day. God's guidance will put the odds in our favor.

Where genetics are involved, we must face the challenge and find the spiritual strength to effect change before the next generation is lost in the same self-destructive darkness.

It's a spiritual journey. We can make a difference if we devote ourselves to truth, and each one, reach one, and teach one.

How Do We Who Live with the Alcoholic Handle It?

If the story of our lives has been an assault on our minds/bodies by alcoholism, we must return to our spiritual nature. Otherwise, we lose our God-given potential, our sanity, our health, and we will die from the same process we are witnessing in the alcoholic.

Twelve-step programs teach us to return to the heart, where the higher power speaks. Listen for that guidance, stay close to our spiritual community, and "guard the heart, from it comes the wellspring of life" (Prov. 4:19–23).

The higher power brings us through our own personal struggles to empowerment, peace, love, compassion, joy, gratitude, etc. Serenity empowers our health and sanity.

We begin to understand a higher purpose for our lives. We may have a God-given role we never dreamed of, and we work in the context of that purpose with a glad heart.

We learn to live from Spirit, one day at a time.

About the Author

The author was raised in a remote valley deep in the hills of Appalachia. Despite poverty, disadvantage, and hardship, the author was able to obtain a BA from the University of Florida and worked at an MDiv in Christian counseling at a well-known school of theology.

After a devastating start into early adulthood, the author began a much-needed recovery program in the 1980s, which led to a different direction in life and subsequent devotion to twelve-step recovery groups of all kinds. She committed herself to understanding addiction and its destructive impact on the surrounding community. For well over thirty-five years, she has attended group meetings, educated, encouraged, and sponsored others in recovery groups.

Now retired, the author spends her senior years writing some of the miraculous recovery stories she has witnessed. In keeping with the tradition of anonymity respected by all twelve-step groups, the stories are fictionalized, all names and locations changed. The basic stories, however, are true. The stories, hopefully, provide hope and inspiration to those lost in addiction.

The author lives in a small town in Appalachia and writes under a pen name.

CPSIA information can be obtained
at www.ICGtesting.com
Printed in the USA
LVHW032024110121
676219LV00003B/404

9 781647 737887